THE DARK AGES

THE DARK AGES

by

W. P. KER

Fellow of All Souls College Oxford
Professor of English Literature
in University College London

With a Foreword by

B. IFOR EVANS

Provost of University College London

GREENWOOD PRESS, PUBLISHERS
WESTPORT, CONNECTICUT

Library of Congress Cataloging in Publication Data

Ker, William Paton, 1855-1923.
  The Dark Ages.

    Reprint of the 1955 ed. published by T. Nelson,
London.
    Includes bibliographical references and index.
    1. Literature, Medieval--History and criticism.
I. Title.
PN671.K4 1979b   809'.02   78-27533
ISBN 0-313-20933-2

First published by William Blackwood and Sons in their
series "Periods of European Literature" 1904

Republished by Thomas Nelson and Sons Ltd on the
centenary of the author's birth 1955

Reprinted in 1979 by Greenwood Press, Inc.
51 Riverside Avenue, Westport, CT 06880

Printed in the United States of America

10 9 8 7 6 5 4 3 2 1

FOREWORD

by B. IFOR EVANS

WILLIAM PATON KER was born in Glasgow on 30th August 1855, so the re-publication of *The Dark Ages* will mark the centenary of his birth. It is also appropriate that this centenary edition should be produced by the collaboration of the University of Glasgow and a Scottish publishing house. For Ker received his first academic training in the University of Glasgow in the years 1870-74, and his own loyalty to Glasgow and to his native West of Scotland remained warm and permanent throughout his life.

He was of the same generation as George Saints-bury, though Saintsbury was ten years older. They belonged to a wide-ranging tradition in scholarship and criticism, the last Renaissance scholars in the great European tradition, who following the example of Francis Bacon took all knowledge, or in their case, all literary knowledge to be their province. In the exercise of that devotion Saintsbury became the Editor of a series entitled " Periods of European Literature " with the bold explanatory title " A Complete and Continuous History of the Subject." *The Dark Ages* was the first volume in the series and was published in 1904, when Ker was forty-nine years old.

It is typical of both men that Ker wrote one

volume in the series and Saintsbury three. Saintsbury had a greater facility, acquired in his years as
a journalist, but Ker was more profound. Saintsbury
walked into a new subject as if he were on an endless
ramble, while Ker with his synthetic power of
uniting, often across the centuries, apparently dis-
parate ideas, gave a strange and fresh illumination
to the themes he explored. Nowhere is that quality
illustrated more clearly than in *The Dark Ages*.[1]

In his own day Ker's reputation stood very high,
and some would claim that his was the most considerable mind to engage on academic studies in
English Literature in Great Britain. Since his death
his name has been less often heard, and I find some
younger scholars unaware of either his work or his
reputation. I assign the reason to the changes in
academic criticism which, beginning in the early
years of the present century, have gained in
emphasis, particularly since Ker's death in 1923.
In the last thirty years bibliography and the science
of editorial scholarship have developed in a manner
of which Ker was scarcely aware. W. W. Greg's
List of English Plays was published as early as 1900,
but no one could then have anticipated the more
esoteric refinements of bibliographical science as
illustrated, for instance, in Greg's *Calculus of
Variants* of 1927. Similarly the Record Office had
not in Ker's time received its full dedication as an

---

[1] I have here and elsewhere used some phrases which I
employed in the W. P. Ker lecture which I delivered at
the University of Glasgow in 1954 on *W. P. Ker as a
Critic of Literature.*

avenue to literary research. Leslie Hotson's *The Death of Marlowe*, which revealed what new and exciting discoveries might suddenly emerge from the search amid the endless ranges of seemingly unpromising documents, was published two years after Ker's death. Even if the choice had been squarely before him he would, I think, have preferred to the door of the Record Office the door of the British Museum Reading Room, or of the Bodleian, or of his own endless and unordered library, with its two " departments," one in Gower Street and the other at All Souls. Ker's two-volume edition of Dryden's *Essays* was published in 1900, and while it still remains valuable, it would probably be found wanting if subjected to the severe tests on minutiæ which modern scientific editing would exact.

Ker would not have disdained these new disciplines, nor minimised the remarkable successes they have gained in the last quarter of a century. Probably he would have left it to others to suggest what had been lost by the narrow specialisation they exacted. For Ker the training of the scholar in English Literature, though he would not have used that heavy language, began in the mastery of the classical and the " gothic " tongues and of the main languages of modern Europe with a particular affection for Icelandic, and for all that concerned the Scandinavian literatures. It was such interests, which might be summarised as an attachment to philology in the broadest interpretation, that made a volume such as *The Dark Ages* possible.

He would not have conceived his studies as part

of the solemnity of literary research but rather as a pleasure based on a discipline. He would sometimes speak of literature as an idle study, and he was very aware of the world of action, of the practice of law, of medicine, and the sciences. He would sometimes almost admit their strength as secular occupations for the human mind as if they had an ampler justification than literature. Yet the magic of the idle studies appealed to him overwhelmingly, and they were pursued with a rigorous attention to accuracy and with unrelenting energy. One felt that he might be imagined like some Cervantes adventuring in a world different from the real world where the romances might be pursued as strenuously as a campaign in battle but with a due attention to grammar and philology, and to the forms in which they were composed. He remained unmarried and the whole background of his life, the house in Gower Street and the rooms at All Souls, were settings for this consistent and consuming pleasure. He lived in his own endless library in both places, books on shelves, books stacked on the floor, in every room, in the corridors, and the hall. He seemed to know where everything was, and what was in them all, and from his reading there emerged the notes and lectures, and the books. J. H. P. Pafford's bibliography [1] shows how extensive were these writings: he records, as volumes, articles, reviews and other pieces, over two hundred and thirty items. In addition, at University College, London, there is a large collection of unpublished papers, from which

[1] *W. P. Ker,* 1855-1923, *A Bibliography,* London, 1950

Professor James Sutherland is preparing a selection for publication.

Ker's publications were the accompaniment of a long career of academic teaching. At the age of twenty-four he had become assistant to W. Y. Sellar, Professor of Humanity, Edinburgh, and in 1883 he moved to be Professor of English Literature and History in the new University College of South Wales, Cardiff, where he remained until 1889. In that year he came to University College, London, as Quain Professor of English Language and Literature, and there he remained until his retirement in 1922. It is not too much to claim that it is with the tenure of the Chair at University College that the great years of his work and career are associated. But his loyalty to Oxford remained permanent and profound. From 1874 to 1878 he was at Balliol, and in the next year, when he went as Sellar's assistant at Edinburgh, he was elected to an All Souls Fellowship, and All Souls remained the society he most frequented outside London until his death. From 1920 he was also Professor of Poetry at Oxford. He died in Italy while climbing at Macugnaga on 17th July 1923. Unfortunately he had no period of leisure, after retirement from his Chair, for the organisation of his unpublished work.

Apart from the liberal vacations which were a normal feature of life before the First World War he divided his life between Oxford and Gower Street: from Monday to Friday in London and the weekends at All Souls. A professor in those days would lecture eight or nine hours a week, and Ker would do this and more and cover everything from the translations of the Scriptures into Gothic by Ulfilas to contemporary literature where the narrative would have references to " Mr Meredith " and " Mr Swinburne." Each lecture was delivered without notes, but the text was taken down by members of the department, by Dr Hitchcock and Miss Husbands, and so a record was kept. He would speak in a slow emphatic voice, at dictation speed, pausing at times while he stood, his hand outstretched even as if in pain. His eyes would sparkle and the whole face lighten in anticipation of a stroke of wit, and the voice would grow even thinner and quieter than in the main discourse ; he would read and quote frequently while the sounds would rise and fall through a wide range of tones. He was conscious that the academic study of English Literature was new and untried, watched with a critical disdain by the entrenched representatives of the older disciplines. His own scholarship permitted him to challenge any of his contemporaries in the classics or in the historical fields and by exactness in detail and width of approach to establish the student of English Literature, as neither one who existed within " some little allotment assigned to him, some block of fifty years " nor as " a vagrant on the confines of things in general."

Of all his books *The Dark Ages*, published some years after his *Epic and Romance*, illustrates the strength of his mind, his loyalties, and the principles of his approach to literary studies. Further, it is a book that only Ker could have written. He was impressed by the sudden emergence of modern literature in the twelfth century, and affirmed that the centuries from the Fall of the Roman Empire onwards were " really and not merely conventionally separate from what came after in literature." With the twelfth century or the thirteenth, in French or German, with Chrestien de Troyes, Walther von der Vogelweide, a modern literature had begun. However difficult the language, the tunes and the devices would be heard again and continuously to the eighteenth century and the nineteenth. He would recall this when he came to speak of Burns, whose favourite metre, he wrote, " was invented by the first of the Provençal poets, William Count of Poitiers. After nearly 700 years the Provençal tune sounds again in Ayrshire—the tune that amused Count William the Crusader with his courteous tongue that was not to be trusted by any lady and his capabilities also of devotion—he went to the Holy Land, and forsook the sable fur . . . this tune was used, under a different sky, for *Holy Willie's Prayer* and helped to lead off the new music of the nineteenth century." [1]

The Dark Ages, as has been suggested, illustrates the method and quality of his criticism. His distinguishing gift was his power of bringing a wide range of reference to the illustration of a single idea, or the concentration in a few lucid phrases of a complex and extended tradition of composition. Examples in this volume abound, but one appears in

[1] This passage, which I think is unpublished, has been taken in an abbreviated form from one of Ker's manuscripts at University College, London.

the Introduction in his treatment of Latin literature
in the Dark Ages. The reading behind those few
pages is formidable, and yet the resulting conclusions
are exposed with a seemingly effortless clarity. In
defining his theme his mind looks forward to the
ambitious writing of the Renaissance, and to the
spirit of emulation created later by court and patron.
Armed with these thoughts he returns to discuss
Latin literature in the Dark Ages : and concludes
that " the Latin author has no contemporaries.
He is a fellow-worker along with Cicero and St
Augustine, and ought to be satisfied with that."

His method was only possible because of the
strength and accuracy of his memory, which canalised
his vast reading and so held it at the service of his
critical intelligence. Apart from social activities, his
whole life, as has already been suggested, was devoted
to reading and writing. Nor was there ever any
economic pressure to flog him towards composition
unless he had something he wished to say. Yet
whatever his opportunities his power of retention
and synthesis were formidable, and the talent for
comparison remained the most telling element in his
criticism. Nowhere did it serve him better than
where he illuminates unfamiliar matter by allusion
to themes more generally available to the reader.

Finally this volume represents his loyalties in
literature. It seemed sometimes as if he found all
periods equally interesting. He would wander
everywhere, knowing, as he once said,[1] that " the
earliest beginning we can make is already late and

[1] In a manuscript at University College, London

old : not so early but that we can find in it something of our own." But the Middle Ages and the Dark Ages preceding them were his own choicest field ; there where the classical ages and the new literatures met and where the exploration had to be carried on through the Latin authors into the Teutonic tongues, and the Romance languages where epic still existed and where the romances and the modern lyric began.

It may be that this centenary year, and the publication of this volume, and Professor Sutherland's anthology from the unpublished criticism will arouse an interest in Ker in a younger generation who seem to have neglected him. His ideal of criticism would be a corrective to much that is happening today both in the University departments and outside. He had, of course, his own limitations, no statement of absolute principles, no direct encouragement to the contemporary writer. In compensation he indulged in no phrenetic excitements, certainly not in *enthusiasm* in the eighteenth-century sense of the word. His understanding of literature was rather such enjoyment as comes from a world of good taste, the ideal of the world of the eighteenth-century gentleman with leisure to read, and intelligence to maintain discernment among the things that he had read. Added to this, and unlike many eighteenth-century gentlemen, the curse of Babel and the diversity of tongues seemed to cause him no problem whatsoever.

B. I. E.

AUTHOR'S PREFACE

THE scope of this book is described in the Introduction (chapter i) and in the Editor's account of the whole series, in the next volume, so that there is the less need for a formal Preface. It may be explained, however, that some freedom has been used in the selection and arrangement of matter. Old English literature has been treated, for example, with less detail than Icelandic, because it is more familiar ground in this country, and has been well described in many recent works. In Icelandic, the poems of the Elder Edda have been taken as more important than anything else, but very little is said of the problems of their date and origin. The notes on Irish and Welsh literature are intended merely as illustrations of certain general topics; a fuller account was hardly possible: as it is, this chapter trespasses too far in regions where the author has no special credentials. At the end of the book it was found unnecessary to make any recapitulation, because things are summed up already, to the best of the writer's power, in chapter ii. (The Elements), and also because the way is easy and unimpeded from Roncesvalles at the close of this volume to the French heroic poetry in the next period. I regret that the newly discovered *Chancun de Willame* should have appeared too late to be recorded in its proper place. I take this opportunity of referring to the article on the subject by M. Paul Meyer in *Romania*, and of thanking the unknown benefactor who has printed this epic of William of Orange—older, it would seem, than the poem of *Aliscans*.

The following works, among others, have been of very great service : Ebert, *Allgemeine Geschichte der Literatur des Mittelalters in Abendlande*, 1874-87 ; Gröber's account of mediæval Latin literature in his *Grundriss der romanischen Philologie ;* Mone, *Lateinische Hymnen des Mittelalters*, 1853-55 ; Edélestand du Méril, *Poésies populaires latines antérieuses au douzième Siècle*, 1843 (in which will be found the specimens of Latin popular poetry quoted in chapter iii, pp. 208-217) ; Poole, *Illustrations of the History of Medieval Thought*, 1884 ; Paul, *Grundriss der germanischen Philologie ; Corpus Poeticum Boreale*, edited by Gudbrand Vigfusson and F. York Powell, Oxford, 1883 ; *Eddica Minora*, by Ranisch and Heusler, 1903, containing the old-fashioned Northern poems that are not included in the great Copenhagen manuscript ; Finnur Jónsson's history of old Norwegian and Icelandic literature (*Den oldnorske og oldislandske Litteraturs Historie*, 1894) ; Kelle, *Geschichte der deutschen Litteratur*, 1892-96 ; Krumbacher, *Geschichte der byzantinischen Litteratur*, second edition, 1897.

Mr Stevenson's welcome edition of Asser, with strong arguments in favour of the *Life of Alfred* as an authentic work, has only been published within the last few days.

I am greatly indebted to Mr H. W. C. Davis of Balliol for many suggestions in chapter iii ; to Dr Kuno Meyer for advice about Celtic literature ; and to Mr Saintsbury for his editorial care throughout.

W. P. K.

LONDON, *25th January* 1904

CONTENTS

CHAPTER I

CHAPTER II

THE ELEMENTS

CHAPTER III

LATIN AUTHORS

CHAPTER IV

THE TEUTONIC LANGUAGES

CHAPTER V

IRELAND AND WALES ; GREECE ; THE ROMANCE TONGUE

THE DARK AGES.

CHAPTER I.

INTRODUCTION.

THE Dark Ages and the Middle Ages—or the Middle
Age—used to be the same; two names for the same
period. But they have come to be distinguished,
and the Dark Ages are now no more than the first
part of the Middle Age, while the term mediæval is
often restricted to the later centuries, about 1100 to
1500, the age of chivalry, the time between the first
Crusade and the Renaissance. This was not the old
view, and it does not agree with the proper meaning
of the name. The Middle Age, however lax the interpretation might be, distinctly meant at first the
time between ancient and modern civilisation. It
was a large comprehensive name that covered everything between Romulus Augustulus and the taking
of Constantinople by the Turks, or between Claudian
and the revival of Learning; it might include any-

thing in past history that was too late to be classical
and not yet modern. "The Monks finished what
the Goths begun" is Pope's summary of the matter:
and again in the Prologue to Thomson's tragedy of
Sophonisba (1730)—

> "When Learning, after the long *Gothic* night,
> Fair o'er the Western world renew'd his light,
> With arts arising *Sophonisba* rose."

Or, in other words, the darkness of the Dark Ages
comes to an end about the time when Italian scholars
reproduce the forms of classical poetry in their
modern tongue. Trissino's *Sophonisba*, the first Italian
tragedy in regular form, was an historical beacon marking the limit. Over the Gothic centuries the historian travels quickly till he comes to "at length
Erasmus." It is all dark, and it is all "middle."
The biographer of Dryden's friend, Mr Walter Moyle,
expresses the common opinion: "From Ann. Dom.
440 to 1440 was a long but dark Period of Time, and
he aimed only to preserve a Thread of the History
of that Middle Age."

Goldsmith was heretical and original in his *Inquiry
into the Present State of Polite Learning* (1759) when
he ended his chapter on the Obscure Ages much
earlier, and began the new world of polite learning
with Dante, "who first followed Nature, and was
persecuted by the critics as long as he lived." Goldsmith also tried to correct the ordinary opinions
about the want of learning in the Obscure Ages.
"The most barbarous times had men of learning, if

commentators, compilers, polemic divines, and intricate metaphysicians deserve the title." But Goldsmith does not recognise what has now come to be
the commonplace arrangement among most historians,
separating the Dark Ages from the "Mediæval Period
properly so called," which is really improperly so
called, by a rather violent wresting of the term
"mediæval." The old division was much more logical,
a consistent and definite refusal to see anything
worth the attention of a scholar in the period between
the fifth and the fifteenth century. All was "Gothic,"
all was "Dark"; "dans la cloaque des siècles cal-
igineux et dans la sentine des nations apedeftes,"
as it is expressed with unusual levity by the poet
Chapelain, in his most honourable defence of Lancelot
and the old romances.

This old reckoning of "the long night of the
Middle Ages," which Goldsmith had begun to criticise, is preserved in full force by one modern historian,
in terms that express a very distinct opinion, not
merely a traditional commonplace: "The Græco-
Roman world had descended into the great hollow
which is roughly called the Middle Ages, extending
from the fifth to the fifteenth century, a hollow in
which many great, beautiful, and heroic things were
done and created, but in which knowledge, as we
understand it, and as Aristotle understood it, had no
place. The revival of learning and the Renaissance
are memorable as the first sturdy breasting by
humanity of the hither slope of the great hollow
which lies between us and the ancient world. The

modern man, reformed and regenerated by knowledge,
looks across it and recognises on the opposite ridge,
in the far-shining cities and stately porticoes, in the
art, politics, and science of antiquity, many more
ties of kinship and sympathy than in the mighty
concave between, wherein dwell his Christian ancestry,
in the dim light of scholasticism and theology." [1]

But the Renaissance does not often nowadays speak
with such conviction, and "mediæval" has generally
lost its meaning of "dark." The change was really
brought about by those very books of chivalry for
which Chapelain, the correct epic poet, made so un-
expected and so pleasant an apology. When Lancelot
came back with Gawain "out of Faerie," when
"Gothic" — that is, mediæval — art and literature
revived in credit, and "the fictions of the Gothic
romances" were more or less restored to honour, then
followed naturally a new division of history, throwing
back the darkness, and redeeming the proper centuries
of romance from the disrepute that had befallen them.
The Crusades, cathedrals, tournaments, old coloured
glass and other splendid things, coming to be popu-
larly known and appreciated, naturally determined
the meaning of "Middle Ages" and "mediæval" so
as to denote especially the centuries to which these
matters belonged—that is to say, roughly, from 1100
to 1500. "Dark" ceased to be a popular term for
times so interesting as those of *Ivanhoe*, of *Notre Dame
de Paris*, of *Tannhäuser:* the change in the meaning
of "Gothic" corresponds with this general change of

[1] *The Service of Man*, by James Cotter Morison, 1887, p. 177.

the popular historical conception: "Gothic," with all its offence withdrawn, was restricted to a type of architecture not older than the twelfth century: it used to be a common term of contempt for everything in art, manners, and literature before the return of Greek grammar to the West.

The change of view may be defended as a sound and reasonable one. The date 1100 is an epoch, if there is anything to be called an epoch in the whole course of history, though "mediæval" may be a doubtful word for what began then. The Middle Age, regarded as an interval of confusion between two periods of more or less rational order, really ended at the close of the eleventh century. It was then that the wandering of the German nations was completed; out of the Teutonic anarchy came the unity of Christendom, consciously realised in the enterprise of the first Crusade. The establishment of the Normans in England meant the end of the old roving business, however it might be kept up in remoter places here and there. Magnus of Norway, the last king of the old fashion, died in 1103: his son was Sigurd the Crusader. The Northern world before 1100 was still in great part the world of the *Germania*, with its indomitable liberty, its protestant self-will; after 1100 *Germania* is harmonised in the new conception of Christendom. Tacitus gives the key to the earlier period; now, the interpreter is Dante in the *De Monarchia*. Or it might be said, using the words of Polybius when he foresaw the majesty of the Roman Empire, that in 1100 history became "all of one piece." If this be illusory in some ways, if the apparent unity of Christendom cover no less misrule and unreason in the twelfth century than went naked in earlier times, still it is hardly possible to mistake the growth of a new spirit, in virtue of which the different nations are related more closely than they had ever been before.

One chief agent in this change is not religious doctrine nor politics, but the new languages. The great historical fact belonging to the close of the eleventh century, besides the Crusade, is the appearance of French and Provençal poetry, which is the beginning of modern literature. With hardly a warning came the rhymes of William, Count of Poitou, the first of a school that includes every modern poet. Everything that is commonly called poetry in the modern tongues may in some way or other trace its pedigree back to William of Poitiers singing—

"Farai chansoneta nova,
Ans que vent ni gel ni plova;
Ma domna m' assaj' em prova
Consi de qual guiza l'am."

The thrill of rhymes like these is the first awakening of the world for that long progress of literature in which the Renaissance and other momentous changes are merely incidental and ordinary things, compared with the miracle of their first beginning. About the same time also the poetry of France declares itself, and the French authors begin their work of providing ideas, subjects, stories, useful information, and instruction in manners for Spaniards, Dutch, Welsh, Danes, English, and other nations; whereby the nations altered their character generally, and became, some more and some less, but all in an appreciable measure, French in their literary fashions: as the Editor of these histories has explained in the volume that follows this.

Everything that we can think of in modern poetry (except always the survivals and revivals of Teutonic alliterative verse, and some few other antiquities) is related to the French and Provençal literature of the year 1100 as it is not related to anything in the Dark Ages—the earlier Middle Age. There is nothing abrupt, no shock of sudden transition in turning from the verse of Goethe, Hugo, or Tennyson, to the rhymes of Provence. These are modern poems:—

> "Quan la douss' aura venta
> Deves vostre païs
> M'es vejaire qu'eu senta
> Odor de paradis."

Or again:—

> "Quan vi la laudeta mover
> De joi las alas contral rai,
> Que s'oblid' es laissa cazer,
> Per la doussor qual cor li vai."

Only the language is difficult to a modern reader: there is nothing old-fashioned in the manner of the verse.

This definite new beginning of French and Provençal, —which is also the beginning of Spanish and Italian, and a fresh opening for English and German poetry, —while it is a term from which to reckon the life of a new world, is no less decisively the end of an old

one, in literary history, at any rate. The Dark Ages
in the history of literature are distinctly a period:
they have a definite end, whatever their beginning
may have been. Their end is marked by the appearance of the new Romance languages and their poetry,
which take captive the Teutonic countries, and destroy
the chances of the old Teutonic manner of composing
verse. The Teutonic fashions are displaced, on their
own ground. No Teutonic verse is so near to modern
English poetry as the Provençal measures are. When
Wordsworth imitates the stanza of Burns he is really
imitating William of Poitou, who used it seven
hundred years earlier: the melody of Bernard de
Ventadour—

"Quan la douss' aura venta"—

may be heard in any number of modern poets. Without any archaism or any difficult research, Victor Hugo
can repeat the patterns of verse that were in vogue in
the days of St Lewis. It is a different thing with
verse of the old Teutonic school. It is possible to
understand it, but in spite of blood-relationship its
character is strange. The beginning of *Volospá*, for
example, the old Northern hymn of the Doom, is something unfamiliar, as an Arabic verse might be. It is
not of our own life, in the same intimate way as the
Provençal measures :—

"Before the years, when Naught was ; was neither sand nor
sea nor cold billows ; earth was seen not, nor high heaven ; there
was the gap gaping, and grass nowhere."

"Ar vas alda, þat es ekki vas ;
Vasa sandr né sær né svalar unnir."

It belongs to the humanities, but it is not modern. The form is not that of the modern world. But the relations of the Provençal school are everywhere, and they can be proved by historical evidence without any hazardous speculation on poetical affinities They include all sorts and degrees of poets. By contrast with what precedes 1100, the whole of modern poetry since then appears like one community. Dr Watts is related not distantly to Ariosto, if one looks at the connections of literary schools from a point at the close of the Dark Ages. The chief rules of their art were fixed for them when the Dark Ages came to an end: not in any definite manner earlier than that, but long before the Renaissance.

The Dark Ages in their more limited meaning, and for the editorial purposes of this Series, are the centuries of the barbarian migration, before the establishment of the Romance literatures, or of the kind of civilisation that is implied in them. Of literature in the Romance tongues there is little more than the rudiments to be considered before the eleventh century. The richest vernacular literature of the Dark Ages is found in other regions. The chief part of it, for students in this country, in spite of the fascinations of the Celtic genius, must be the body of the older Teutonic poetry in the Teutonic alliterative verse. This belongs properly to the Dark Ages; and it comes to an end with almost as certain a date in history as that from which the succeeding schools of Romance begin. It comes to an end before the Crusades, except in Iceland, the dissident and long-resisting country

where the old forms of language and poetic diction are
better protected than elsewhere against innovation,
especially against the innovations of the Romance
tongues and their poetry.   Everywhere else the old
forms of Teutonic literature disappear and are replaced
by novelties; also the language changes.   At the same
time as the new literatures of France and Provence
make their appearance, the older German tongues are
greatly altered.   There is a new English and a new
German in the twelfth century : in the profession of
Philology they are called Middle English and Middle
German, so that the authority of Grammar is added to
that of Politics and Rhetoric in marking a date about
1100 as a division between an older and a younger
system of things.

In Latin, which is the principal language of the
Dark Ages, there is no such decisive limit,—indeed
there is no limit at all to the Latin of these times.
The old Teutonic literature does not begin till the
darkness has set in; it belongs to the nations who,
according to the usual reckoning, were the causes of
the darkness,—the "Goths" of Pope's summary,—and
it ends, or at any rate it changes from "Old" to
"Middle" with the beginning of the next period.
But the Latin literature descends without a break
from classical times, and it lasts for centuries after
the old German tongues have been forgotten.

The Teutonic nations brought new languages and
new subject-matters into the system of European
literature ; they also brought originality.   The Latin
authors had a different kind of work to do ; they

carried on the traditions of classical education; they taught the liberal arts; they collected material for natural and civil history, and expounded it; they preserved the classical forms of verse and prose, with modifications according to their taste; they served the Church in the teaching of Divinity. In one kind of composition only are they innovators; the rhyming hymns are the original Latin poetry of the Dark Ages; apart from these the universal language is employed for purposes of education—to convey knowledge, or to illustrate in rhetoric the precepts of the schools. So it had been before the Dark Ages began, and so it continued afterwards. The Latin literature of the Dark Ages has not a definite character of its own, in the same way as the old Teutonic poetry. That body of poetry belongs properly to the centuries from the sixth to the eleventh. The Latin literature of the Dark Ages is not their exclusive property; it begins before them and is continued after them; its period is a much longer one, a period which at the lowest reckoning includes the whole of the Middle Age in the old wide sense of the term, down to the Revival of Learning. Even this is too narrow, for the Latin literature of the Middle Ages is in many things conservative, and it is difficult to stop in tracing it back to its sources: many of its favourite ideas and principles are those of Cicero, and many of them were in his time far from new; and at the other end of the history there may be found a similar difficulty when things supposed to be peculiarly mediæval show themselves proof against the Renaissance, surviving quite

happily in the minds and writings of humanist reformers. The German literature of the Dark Ages
makes one group of writings with a life and character
of its own ; the Latin literature is merely a section,
with an arbitrary date to mark the dividing-line.

In the vernacular literatures there is, of course, a
great deal which, as far as ideas and matters are concerned, really belongs to Latin. Not all the vernacular literature is fresh, barbarous, and original;
much of it is translation, much is adaptation and
exposition of Latin knowledge. The significant distinction for the Dark Ages is not between Latin and
vernacular utterance, but between Latin and barbarian
ideas. For instance, the works of Ælfric or of Notker
Labeo belong to the Latin world, the common educational tradition. They are Teutonic in speech, and
they come into the history of English and German
culture. But they are not English and German literature in the same way as the heroic poems about
Sigemund or Hildebrand.

In all sorts of ways the two influences cross and
mingle, to pass into the blended stream of the later
mediæval literature. One of the great attractions of
the Dark Ages is that they exhibit, sometimes, more
clearly than was possible later, a different kind of
literary tradition from the classical ; the pure elements
contributed by the barbarians to the literary art of
Europe. The value of this may have been exaggerated
or wrongly judged by enthusiasts. But no exagger-
ation, and no reaction against it, can destroy the
importance for literary history of the remains of that

Teutonic poetry which was least affected by Rome. Whatever its intrinsic value, it gives the starting ground, the background, the relief, in relation to which the new schools of the twelfth century are to be estimated.

The Latin literature and the Teutonic literature of the Dark Ages make up a considerable body of writings, but there are others besides, other languages and authors belonging to the history of the world and entering more or less into the common traffic of ideas. Greek, Celtic, and Arabian authors have a claim to be noticed in any full account of the literary productions of those centuries.

Greek in the Dark Ages has influence upon the West for the most part indirectly: either through its old-established partnership in Latin culture, or in ways not literary at all, by means of travellers, pilots, and traders; so that what comes through is generally either ancient, if there is any scholarship in it, or unscholarly, if it is new. The part of Greece, however, as an intermediary between the East and the West, and a channel of information, is of very great importance for the history of literary intercourse and the distribution of popular stories and popular science of all kinds. After Greek had ceased to exercise any distinctly literary influence on the West other than that which had long been known, if not exhausted, in the rhetorical schools, it continued to provide new matters for amusement and edification; saints' lives and fables, romances like that of Alexander, like Apollonius of Tyre: while doubtless in many easy ways, without writing or literary form, it helped to carry westward the themes of Eastern stories for the future profit of minstrels. It gave the *Physiologus* to all the modern tongues; it translated the Buddha into the legend of *Barlaam and Josaphat.*

Arabian literature affects the West in a somewhat similar way. Arabian learning, itself derived from Greek, passes into Western Christendom through the Schools, which bring it into conformity with the accepted educational usages. Arabian fancy makes its way by the contraband methods of popular story-telling. *Aucassin and Nicolette, Flores and Blanche-floure,* may well be Moorish stories. But their descent is not recorded, except in their character, their manner, some facts of custom that they imply (the *serraglio* in *Flores*), and the etymology of a name (*Aucassin*). They have no literary ancestry that can be traced in books. The Arabic literature that was produced in the Dark Ages is not related to the West in any literary manner. The Arabians give scientific matter, and they give the subjects of stories, but their own literature is something apart. It was "not destined to be ours," though the student of heroic poetry may turn for a moment from the themes of Attila or Sigfred to admire the temper of the Arabian Dark Ages—"the Ignorance"—before the chivalrous imagination of their earlier poets was transformed by the False Prophet and his polygamous methodism. As critics of life, the old Arabian poets may compare with the most heroic authors in the North, or even with Odin himself.

" But as for my people, though their number be not small,
   they are good for naught against evil, however light it be.
They requite with forgiveness the wrong of those that do them
   wrong,
   and the evil deeds of the evil they meet with kindness and
   love ;
As though thy Lord had created among the tribes of men
   themselves alone to fear him and never one man more.
Would that I had in their stead a folk who, when they ride
   forth,
   strike swiftly and hard, on horse or on camel borne ! " [1]

The case of the Celtic literatures, Welsh and Gaelic,
might seem at first to be quite analogous to that of
Greek or Arabic. Here again are masters and
teachers who have a large share in making the system
of education for the whole of the West ; missionaries
and scholars who give the spirit of their lives to
animate the brutish mass and turn it into Christendom. Here again the work of the teachers is made
by their pupils to conform to the general type, and the
national and local character, when it gets away from
home, is for the most part obliterated and merged
in the common tradition. Though there may be
"sentimental traces" of the Celtic ancestor at Jarrow,
or at St Gall, never wholly lost either in the Teutonic
or in the common Latin features, still the Celtic
character is never other than subordinate in the
schools of the Scot abroad ; just as the Greek and
the Arabian character have to be assimilated to
the common Latin temper. The Celtic imagination

---

[1] From the first poem in Sir Charles Lyall's *Translations of Ancient
Arabian Poetry*, 1885.

again may be found in the romances of the Middle
Ages in the same way as Greek or Arabian fictions
there ; unmistakable, but without an authentic history
to explain its presence.   The prose and poetry of
the Celtic tongues are as unfamiliar to most people
as the poetry of Arabia in the Ignorance, and far
less available for modern students than the later
literature of Greece.   They belong in date to the
Dark Ages, but are they a proper part of the subject
for an historical sketch which is bound to keep to the
principal lines of progress, and to avoid the temptations of Bypath Meadow ?   Celtic literature is part
of the subject by something other than the mere
obligation of dates, and for another reason than the
indebtedness of Western Europe to its Irish teachers,
great as that is.   Celtic is the counterpart of Teutonic,
closely related in its origin, as is proved in a thousand
ways, and exposed to the same influences.   Early
Irish and Welsh literature, like early English and
Icelandic, is largely that of an heroic age, which has
borrowed its pens and ink from Latin clerks, and
is never wholly exempt from the touch of Latin learning.   The literary problems of the Irish and the early
English were nearly alike : both wanted to find the
best way of story-telling ; both were attached to the
heroic traditions of their own people ; both were
obliged to trim between their natural affection for
mythology and their duties in the schools.   They
followed different methods even in the schools, where
the subjects were common to both ; still more in the
epic stories, where they were less restricted.   But

though it may be possible to understand the one fairly well without the other, a history of Western Christendom in the Dark Ages requires both Teutonic and Celtic literature.

The Dark Ages are really and not merely conventionally separate from what came after, in literature. Poets of the twelfth or thirteenth century in French or German, Chrestien de Troyes, Walther von der Vogelweide, are really part of modern literature: their vocabulary may be difficult, but their poetical forms and devices, if they trouble the beginner at all, surprise him oftener by their familiar look than by their strangeness. To go back to the ninth or the tenth century is to find a different world. Not only are the languages of a more ancient type: the ways of imagination are different, the tunes of poetry are different; and there are still older things than those of the ninth century with which the traveller has to be acquainted. It is not wonderful that the times should have been judged severely by scholarly persons who found themselves astray there. The literary taste of Heorot, the Danish hall where Beowulf listened to poetry, or of the House of the Red Branch, where Conchobar, king of Ulster, was at home, is far more difficult to appreciate than that of the later Middle Ages, and almost as remote from the prevailing fashions of the twelfth, or the fourteenth, as from the eighteenth century. Dr Johnson is hardly farther from *Beowulf* than Chaucer is.

The earlier literature, it is true, had some share in the great romantic movement. Gray, though he ad-

B

mired Froissart and Gawain Douglas, went farther back in his researches, and his contributions to the cause of the romantic schools came from old Icelandic and Welsh, not from the more familiar and generally more profitable times of chivalry. Some time before him Dr Hickes had broken new ground : his translations from Anglo-Saxon and Icelandic were not left to their learned dignity in the great philological *Thesaurus.* By some happy fortune he had chosen for translation one of the Icelandic poems about the value of which there is least chance of disagreement : the story of Hervor was noticed, and read, and copied out of the folio volume of Hickes to be included in a popular anthology. Percy's " Runic Poetry," about the same time as Gray's *Descent of Odin,* helped in the same way to revive some interest in an order of poetry more ancient than his *Reliques.* The success of Macpherson proved that the Dark Ages were not in themselves enough to alarm the reader. Balclutha really had some of the work of the Dark Ages in it, besides the eighteenth-century restorations and plasterings.

But it is not necessary to apologise for the things touched upon in this essay, however much the writer may find himself at fault in his treatment of them. They need interpretation, as all literature does when its own day is over. Many of them are difficult and strange. Literature is in some respects the most conventional of all the arts ; Poetry, for all that it may boast of a universal dominion, changes its character with every province and dialect, one thing in

Warwickshire, another in Glamorgan : it is not wonderful that the poetry of a thousand years ago in
a number of old languages should be unfamiliar and
repellent at the first sight of it. The essential thing
is to find out whether and in what sense it has any
present value. As a preliminary, with regard to the
common learned prejudice against the barbarians,
there is nothing better nor more auspicious than
Daniel's memorable protest and noble defence :—

" Me thinks we should not so soon yield our con-
sents captive to the authority of Antiquity, unless
we saw more reason ; all our understandings are not
to be built by the square of Greece and Italy. We
are the children of nature as well as they ; we are
not so placed out of the way of judgement, but that
the same sun of discretion shineth upon us. . . .
Time and the turn of things bring about these
faculties according to the present estimation ; and
Res temporibus non tempora rebus servire oportet. . . .
It is not books but only that great book of the world
and the all-overspreading grace of heaven that makes
men truly judicial. Nor can it but touch of arrogant
ignorance to hold this or that nation barbarous, these
or those times gross, considering how this manifold
creature man, wheresoever he stand in the world, hath
always some disposition of worth, entertains the order
of society, affects that which is most in use, and is
eminent in some one thing or other, that fits his
humour and the times. . . . The Goths, Vandals,
and Longobards, whose coming down like an inun-
dation overwhelmed, as they say, all the glory of learn-

ing in Europe, have yet left us still their laws and customs, as the originals of most of the provincial constitutions of Christendom, which being well considered with their other courses of government, may seem to clear them from this imputation of ignorance. And though the vanquished never speak well of the conqueror, yet even through the unsound coverings of maledictions appear those monuments of truth as argue well their worth, and proves them not without judgment, though without Greek and Latin."[1]

To subdivide the literature of the Dark Ages, historically, is not easy, for in the vernacular tongues the dates of authorship are seldom certain, often not to be fixed within a century or two: while in Latin, where some of the ordinary classification is possible, it is not remarkably useful.   The great fact in Latin of these days is the decline and revival between the time of Gregory the Great and Charlemagne, after which there is a fairly continuous succession of learned men and, with many eccentricities, no such general decay as happened in the sixth and seventh centuries.   The history of Latin is the history of education, and follows the great schools.   There is a line from Ireland and Iona to Jarrow and York, and from there to the Court of Charles.   Alcuin's school at Tours is the parent of the school at Fulda where Hraban carried on the same work.   Different lines of descent are united at Reichenau and St Gall, which are in relation with the newer school at Fulda on the one hand, and with the Irish on the other.   Bede

[1] Daniel, *A Defence of Ryme*, 1607.

(Jarrow) taught Egbert (York), who taught Alcuin
(Tours), who taught Hraban (Fulda), who taught
Walafrid Strabo (Reichenau): that pedigree roughly
indicates one of the chief lines along which literary
studies were carried. But the stages do not mean
the same thing as the literary generations in later
history, where definite fashions change through all
sorts of ambitious experiments and new inventions,
Ben Jonson giving place to Dryden, Ronsard to Mal-
herbe, and so on. Here the life is of a different sort.
In Latin there was no opportunity for such triumphs
and glories as came later in the new languages. Here
success meant obedience to the old models; or if
rebellion took its chance and tried to make something
new, it was always something exceptional, and often
turned out to be exceptional in a hackneyed way
after all. Even in the Latin hymns, the greatest
achievement of the language in those times, there is
an uncertainty and intermittent character about their
production, unlike the energy with which new types
of poetry are taken up, and exhausted, where the
conditions are more favourable. There was no
"town," in the pleasant literary sense of the word,
to make an audience for literary adventurers, to give
them the illusion of fame which counts for so much
towards the reality of literary success. Even where
there was something like a court and an Augustan
patronage, under Charles the Great, it brought out
nothing new—only repetitions of the sort of thing
that had been done better two hundred years before
by Venantius Fortunatus. Latin, it is true, is capable

of life; but its life comes from the individual temperament of the man using it, and not from any such tide of inspiration as carried the Elizabethans even beyond their natural powers. The Latin author, if he is a strong man like Bede, or a lover of adventure like Paul Warnefrid, or a lively person like Liutprand of Cremona, will make the language do what he pleases, and will not fail to express his own character in so doing. But he cannot have, in the Dark Ages at any rate, the lift and impetus of contemporary ambitions all moving the same way, with a vague certainty that something new will come of it somehow. The Latin author has no contemporaries. He is a fellow-worker along with Cicero or St Augustine, and ought to be satisfied with that.

There are some general subjects, in which the literature of these ages can be grouped, better perhaps than under distinctions of time. The characteristic teaching of the Middle Ages is much the same in Cassiodorus, in Isidore, in Alcuin and Hrabanus Maurus. *The Liberal Arts,* or perhaps even better, the whole of didactic literature, may be taken as one department of the history. Among the barbarous nations and their poetry and stories, apart from those vernacular books where the common educational work was carried on, there are certain chief interests easily discernible—that of *Mythology* and that of the *Heroic Poem*—according as the nations are affected by the marvels of their old traditions, or by the dramatic attraction of more recent great exploits. In connection with these latter it will be found that there are many ideas and motives not restricted to the barbarian lands — Greek mythology, for example, finding its way in among Irish and Anglo-Saxons. The following chapter takes up these generalities; and first of the Liberal Arts.

CHAPTER II.

THE ELEMENTS.

<small>THE LIBERAL ARTS—HISTORY—MYTHOLOGY AND LEGEND—THE HEROIC POEM—COMMONPLACES AND COMMON FORMS.</small>

I.

THE darkest time in the Dark Ages was from the end of the sixth century to the revival of learning *The Liberal Arts.* under Charles the Great. Bad grammar was openly circulated, and sometimes commended. St Gregory the Great quoted the Bible in depreciation of the Humanities, "Quoniam non cognovi litteraturam introibo in potentias Domini" (Ps. lxx. 15, 16). The study of heathen authors was discouraged more and more. "Will the Latin grammar save an immortal soul?" "What profit is there in the record of pagan gods or pagan sages, the labours of Hercules or of Socrates?"[1] Books

---

[1] "Quid posteritas emolumenti tulit legendo Hectorem pugnantem aut Socratem philosophantem?" This is a quotation from Sulpicius Severus (A.D. 400), but the same sort of argument is used in the time of Gregory the Great, and later.

came to be scarce; the industry of copying was not applied to the poets or orators of the ancient world, except a very few. But the decline of education was not universal. If studies failed in Gaul or Italy, they flourished in Ireland, and later in Britain, and returned later from these outer borders to the old central lands of the Empire. Further, in spite of depression and discouragement, there was a continuity of learning even in the darkest ages and countries. Certain school-books hold their ground with little fluctuation of popularity, keeping an honourable position as representatives of classical culture. Martianus Capella *On the Nuptials of Mercury and Philology;* Fulgentius, *Mythologiarum* Libri iii.; Orosius, *Historiarum adversum Paganos* Libri vii.; Boethius *De Consolatione Philosophiæ;* Cassiodorus, *Institutiones;* and later Isidorus of Seville, with a number of other authors, are found in the ages of distress and anarchy more or less calmly giving their lectures and preserving the standards of a liberal education. Much of this work was humble enough, but it was of great importance for the times that came after. For these later times it did not matter that many great authors had been unread and unvalued by the contemporaries of Gregory of Tours and Gregory the Great; but if Martianus Capella had been forgotten, with the school-traditions exemplified in his book, there would have been no chance of a revival of learning. As it was, the elementary and often pedantic matter of the favourite school-books was enough to foster the taste for literature; it had the seeds of literature in it. The darkest ages, with all their negligence, kept alive the life of the ancient world. What is more, their elementary text-books gave a character to the literature of Europe that it never lost. Their work was poor and low compared with what followed it, but it was never undone. They preserve out of classical times the things that were best available for the largest number of scholars, for the multitude of preachers. The learning is popular, not difficult or recondite, except perhaps in such displays as the ornamental rhetoric of Martianus Capella. Generally the text-books of the Dark Ages make things easy, and simplify the results of ancient learning for simple audiences. There were many temptations to be over-subtle, whether in orthodoxy or heresy, and some praise must be allowed to the educational writers who were content to explain the elements.

The paradox of the Dark Ages is that this period, which at first seems to be so distinctly marked as a gap and interval between the ancient and modern worlds, is in its educational work and general culture both ancient and modern. Most of the intellectual things on which it set most store are derived, on the one hand, from ancient Greece, and on the other are found surviving as respectable commonplaces, scarcely damaged, in the Augustan Ages of Louis XIV. and Queen Anne.

Great part of the educational furniture of the Middle Ages, the favourite views, opinions, and classifications, may be found already in the *Republic* of

Plato. The four Cardinal Virtues of popular doctrine in the Middle Ages, familiar in preaching and
allegory, are according to the division and arrangement adopted by Plato. The persons of Prudence,
Fortitude, Temperance, and Justice [1] represent a very
old tradition. It might be fanciful to derive the
three Estates—*oratores, bellatores, laboratores*—from the
Republic, though nowhere in history are the functions
of the three Platonic orders of the Sages, the Warriors,
and the Commons more clearly understood than in
the mediæval theory of the Estates as it is expounded,
for example, in the book of *Piers Plowman.* There
is, however, no doubt about the origin of the mediæval
classification of the Liberal Arts. The *Quadrivium*
is drawn out in the *Republic* in the description of
the studies of Arithmetic, Geometry, Astronomy, and
Music, though Plato does not allow the mediæval
classification of Dialectic as a Trivial Art along with
Grammar and Rhetoric. Furthermore, the vision of
Er the Pamphylian is ancestor, through Cicero's Dream
of Scipio, to the mediæval records of Hell, Purgatory,
and Paradise; the mediæval reverence for the heavenly
spheres and their intelligences and their song is anticipated in the same passage, as again in the *Somnium
Scipionis.*

It is in allegory that mediæval literature sometimes
appears to be most distinguished and to
Allegory. differ most from the clear humanities of
classical art. It is not wonderful that many English

---

[1] See, *e.g.,* the English thirteenth-century allegory of *Sawles Warde,*
translated from a Latin original of the school of St Victor.

students of history find their notion of the Renaissance summed up conveniently and pictorially in a contrast between the drowsy allegorical Rose-garden of Chaucer's youthful worship and the wakefulness of his Canterbury prologue. There, in the *Romaunt of the Rose*, are the Middle Ages and their fantasies and dreams; here, in the Kentish April, is daylight, clearness, the old humanities restored without superstition. So also the beginning of the Reformation is often illustrated, as it was by the Reformers themselves, with a contrast between the absurd allegorical commentaries of the old school and the rational single-minded interpretation of the text. But while all this may be convenient and satisfactory, and while it may be admitted that the allegorical methods are in a special sense the property of the Middle Ages, there is also something else to be said before the Gothic period is closed, and the allegorical spirit dismissed to its shadowy dwelling-place. Mediæval allegory is derived from a very luxuriant stock in classical literature. As a mode of imagination, making pictures and stories, it is almost wholly drawn from classical precedents as old as Homer. Rumour painted full of tongues, in the *Æneid*, is responsible for many things in mediæval literature—a figure whose portentous and prodigious attributes might have strained the most courageous "Gothic" artist to depict. As a mode of interpretation, to get hidden values out of documents that mean something different on the face of them, Allegory is equally the product of classical times. The mediæval expositors applied it largely and freely to

new subjects, but they discovered no new principle
that had not been known to old interpreters of Homer.
Plato in his treatment of Homer, as in his allegorical
fables, shows himself familiar with the "Gothic"
commonplaces, and he is surpassed by his mediæval
followers only in the extent and variety of their
enterprise, and not by any fresh discovery of methods.
Nor is it the case, at the end of the Middle Ages,
that the allegorical devices are blown at once contemptuously to their limbo with the other trumpery.
Tindal and Rabelais might join in their scorn of
Friar Lubin and his receipts for finding any meaning in any text, but the allegorical method survives
their satirical protests. The "imitation of Nature,"
though generally recommended by the contemporaries of Cervantes, Shakespeare, and Molière when
they discussed the principles of art, was by no means
generally regarded as disqualifying the old and
honoured methods of allegory. The historians of
the Renaissance may contrast the liveliness and
truth of the new order with the tedious conventions
of the Middle Ages; may find in art and literature
an assertion of Reason and Nature against "Gothic"
sophistication and superstition; a preference of
artistic beauty above the edifying moral lesson; a
lively dramatic study of humours and motives in
place of the abstract sentiment of the *Romaunt of the
Rose*. But it will not be found that this change of
platform is generally acknowledged by the writers
themselves or by their attendant critics. On the
contrary, from Petrarch and Boccaccio down to Pope

there is a general submission to the rule of **Allegory.**
"Reason" and "Nature" by common consent are
held to include the allegorical value of the fable,
whatever the fable may be, whether the plot of an
epic or an eclogue. In spite of the mockery of
Rabelais and the *Obscurorum Virorum* — "hæc est
via qua debemus studere in Poetria"—there is no
commonplace more general or more tyrannical in the
sixteenth and seventeenth centuries than the allegorical principle. All the most respectable critics
acknowledge it; it is laboured by Tasso in his care
for the reputation of his *Jerusalem;* it is admitted
by Pope in the preface to the *Iliad.*

Nothing is easier than to make the learning and
thought of the Middle Ages look ridiculous by isolated
quotation of some of the common absurdities, and
the allegorical method more than anything else
gives scope for this sort of treatment. Fulgentius,
the *Moralia* of St Gregory, the old French version
of *Metamorphoseos* with the moral exposition—*Ovide
moralisé,* — any of these will at once provide any
number of examples, "good cheap," to show the
absurdity of mediæval reasoning. Virgil and Ovid
are reckoned along with the Scriptures, and Theodulfus, the poet of the Court of Charlemagne, speaks
for the whole world when he addresses them as
teachers :—

> "Te modo Virgilium, te modo Naso loquax :
> In quorum dictis quanquam sint frivola multa,
> Plurima sub falso tegmine vera latent."

But if it be true that similar methods are found

luxuriantly flourishing in ancient Greece (as may be seen demonstrated in Dr Hatch's *Hibbert Lectures* for example), then they cannot be made distinctively a part of the Middle Ages. Still less when the inaugurators of the new world of Humanism are found in possession of the same antique devices. Petrarch interprets the *Æneid* in the manner of Fulgentius. The winds of the First Book are the Passions, Æolus is Reason who controls them, Venus is Pleasure, the true subject of the poem is the Perfect Man. If it be said that allowance is to be made for Petrarch because he was still on the fringe of the Gothic darkness, and inevitably bound to comply unconsciously and against his better judgment with some of the old fashions in which he had been educated, there are still other, much later, witnesses for the defence, who may show that two or three centuries after Petrarch these commonplaces were still as vigorous as in the time of the moralisation of Ovid. Sir John Harington's treatment of the *Orlando Furioso* is in no way out of keeping with the method of St Gregory on Job.

Chapelain in the Preface to his Heroic Poem, *La Pucelle ou la France délivrée* (1656), writes in the same manner as Petrarch of the allegorical sense :—

"France represents the soul of Man at war with itself, and labouring under the most violent Emotions: King Charles, the Will, mistress absolute, tending to the Good of its own nature, but easily turned to Evil: the English and the Burgundian, the divers transports of irascible Appetite, conflicting with the

4

just empire of the Will: Amaury and Agnes the different movements of concupiscence, which corrupt the innocence of the Will by their inducements and their charms," &c.

So it may be assumed as proven that at any rate in some common matters and manners of education the Dark Ages were not remarkably inferior to these more brilliant periods; not wholly distinct, in their educational tastes, from the age of Plato or the age of Bacon. The Dark Ages did not invent their absurdities. The elementary classical commonplaces, the popular methods of explanation, are preserved and continued during the Dark Ages. If there is anything ludicrous in them, it belongs almost as much to the days of Queen Elizabeth or Louis XIV. as to the early mediæval centuries.

Perhaps the most singular thing in all this part of the subject is the predominance of Rhetoric in education, or, to speak more exactly, of *The Trivium.* Grammar and Rhetoric, in the senses proper to these two parts of the old Trivium. The third art, Dialectic, was generally less important in the scheme of studies.

One is prepared for barbarism in the Middle Ages, for the decline of Latin, the loss of Greek, for a general confusion of tenses and cases; we know what to expect, or rather what not to expect, from Franks or Saxons imitating Cicero or Virgil. But on the other hand it is difficult to appreciate rightly the extraordinary care and affection bestowed on the preparation for literature; Grammar being the proper comprehensive name for that study, with Rhetoric to continue it. The classical tradition of the rudiments of polite learning was embodied in Martianus Capella, and in those works of Cassiodorus and Isidorus which were devoted to this part of their Encyclopedia. It took possession of Ireland; it came back from Ireland to Britain and Germany. It might languish in some places and times, but it was never quenched. At Clonmacnoise or in the palace of Charlemagne, at York or St Gall or Fulda, the old liberal arts were cultivated and kept alive. Instruction in grammar was to be obtained from many masters, with phonetics even as a basis, for Martianus Capella attends to this, like the tutor of M. Jourdain—"*B* labris per spiritus impetum reclusis edicimus," and so forth. The figures of speech were generally a favourite subject, as they were in Elizabethan days and afterwards, when they helped to form the Complete Gentleman. The Venerable Bede's early work in this field is carried on by Puttenham in *The Art of Poetry* and by Richard Blome in *The Gentleman's Recreation* (1686), which begins with Grammar, Poetry, and Rhetorick, and goes on to everything else, through Chronology, Fortification, Opticks, and other things, down to Cock-Fighting.

Bede's handbook of Prosody represents another much cultivated department of literature: the eccentricities of mediæval Latin verse are not to be excused by the want of proper instruction in the rules. The rules were well known and frequently explained, sometimes perhaps, as was also the case in the teach-

ing of Figures, with a rather inordinate relish for
the technical terms : thus Aldhelm, in quoting a
verse, must stop to remark " brachycatalectic," and
plays the terms *penthemimeris* and *hephthemimeris*
apparently for their pure ornamental value as " beautiful words." One most interesting effect of the rhetorical studies of the Dark Ages was the attention
paid to literary decoration of all kinds in original
composition, frequently with great profusion of all
the available resources in different inflammatory ways,
but not always without sobriety. The extravagances
of style in the Dark Ages might in most cases refer
to some ancient if not reputable author for their
precedents. Their florid exercises are derived from
models of the classical period ; ultimately, as has
been shown with great learning in a recent German
treatise,[1] from Gorgias himself. Gorgias is responsible
for a good deal of Aldhelm, as well as for Euphues :
the old joke of Plato's *Symposium*, " turned to stone by
the head of Gorgias," might be taken all but literally
of the whole mass of rhetorical decoration in the
Middle Ages. Chiefly the mediæval taste in Latin
prose was derived from Apuleius and his school,
Martianus Capella having probably more effect in
this way than any other writer. *The Marriage of
Mercury and Philology* was a book that no library
could be without, and it is not wonderful that the
barbarians were attracted by the exorbitant riches of
its language, nor that they should have gone much

---

[1] Norden, *Die antike Kunstprosa vom vi. Jahrhundert v. Chr. bis
in die Zeit der Renaissance*, 1898.

further than their masters in the use of emphasis
and gaudy words. They tried everything. They
"did somewhat affect the letter, for it argueth
facility," and the alliterative amusements of Elizabethan Euphuism, the alliterative passages that so
charmed Don Quixote in his favourite authors, are
of the same school as Aldhelm. The extraordinary
foreign vocabulary used in a certain order of mediæval
Latin prose and verse, in some of the old English
charters, in Abbo's poem on the siege of Paris, was
founded long ago in the experiments of Apuleius.
There was a continuous process of development.
The whole efflorescence of language in the Dark Ages,
even the ineffable *Hisperica Famina*,[1] is the com-

---

[1] The *Hisperica Famina* (ed. Stowasser, Vienna, 1887), as perhaps
the most extreme thing in mediæval Latin, ought to be described
here, if description were possible. A short quotation will probably
suffice to show the nature of the work : "Novello temporei glob-
aminis cyclo hispericum arripere tonui sceptrum ; ob hoc rudem
stemico logum ac exiguus serpit per ora rivus. Quod si amplo
temporalis ævi studio ausonica me alligasset catena sonoreus
faminis per guttura populret haustus ac immensus urbani tenoris
manasset faucibus tollus," &c. It appears to be a student's exercise.
There are extant pieces of three different versions where the same
themes are treated apparently under the same rhetorical rules.
Thus one asks, "Non ausonica me subligat catena?" and another
affirms, "Nam strictus romani tenoris me septricat nexus," both
in this strange way boasting that they have the Latin of Italy,
which is what is meant by *Hesperic* and *Ausonian*. The several
subjects treated are first *the day of a student* (*lex diei*), and then a
number of common themes—*Sea, fire, earth, wind, clothes, tavern,
table*, &c. The rules are, first, always to put a verb between
adjective and noun ; and secondly, to find for every simple idea a
word from the " Hisperic " vocabulary, which is that of Apuleius,
Florus, and Martianus Capella, exaggerated out of all measure. Dr
Zimmer thinks that these essays possibly come from the school at

pletion of what had begun in the first conscious efforts of Greek prose.

It is not wonderful that the vernacular languages, when they began to be used for literature, should have copied in their own way the prestige of the Latin eloquence, especially when, like the Teutonic and the Celtic languages, they were subject in their older native verse to the charm of alliteration. The poetical prose of Ælfric, which is English in its rhythm and founded upon the model of Teutonic verse, is also greatly under the influence of the ornamented and rhythmical Latin prose: without that example it might not have occurred to an Englishman to beautify his sermons in that particular manner.

The over-ornamented styles are of course far from universally prevalent or obligatory in the Middle Ages. Then, as at other times, though certain customs of expression may become traditionary, there are indefinite possibilities of variation, and style remains the character of the man himself, where a character can be discerned.

The educational work of the sixth or the ninth century is (with notable additions and improvements)

Llantwit Major in Glamorgan, where Gildas and St David were educated. The manner of writing was certainly in favour in Britain, as is shown by the Latin of the Anglo-Saxon charters, and to a less degree by that of Gildas in one century and Asser in another. The whole subject is discussed by Dr Zimmer in *Göttingische Nachrichten*, 1895, and in *Nennius Vindicatus*, appendix. See also the Papers of Henry Bradshaw, the *Crawford Collection of Early Charters*, ed. Napier and Stevenson, and *Journal of Philology*, xxviii. 209, an article by Mr Robinson Ellis. A new edition of *Hisperica Famina* is promised by Mr Jenkinson at the Cambridge Press.

largely the same as that of the thirteenth. Nor is it
left in the later period entirely to humble men of
industry; it is pursued with the diligence of a con-
scientious clerk by the men whose original genius
and poetic inspiration might have been held to relieve
them from duties towards philology and the other
sciences. The Dark Ages reveal the prosaic ground
of mediæval romance. The foundations are laid by
Orosius, Boethius, and Isidore, and not only that,
but the builders of the crypts are recognised and
honoured by the masters of the pinnacles; the poets
in their greatest freedom of invention are loyal to
the grammarians and moralists, the historians and
lexicographers, upon whose work they build. They
are also ready to take their turn at mason work in
the lower regions of study, not only without grumb-
ling, but apparently with zest. The classical encyclopedias of Boccaccio (*De Genealogia Deorum, De Casibus
Virorum Illustrium,* and the rest), the moral and
scientific essays of Chaucer, are conducted with as
light a heart as any of their poetical vanities. They
are composed with the same motives and in the same
spirit as the treatises which gave instruction to the
Dark Ages, and those treatises must be understood
if these later authors are to be rightly estimated
The honour of Boethius and the other doctors is that
they were not found antiquated at the Revival of
Learning.

II.

The historical work of the Dark Ages was hindered by
the difficulties of language, and scarcely found in any
History.   writer a proper and convenient style.   The
classical tradition, while it kept before the
minds of historians a lofty pattern of eloquence, also
tended to restrict their liveliness by the requirements
of good grammar: while those who, like Gregory of
Tours and others, were indifferent to grammar had
no vernacular idiom to fall back upon.   In England
and in the English Chronicle a valiant attempt was
made to use the native language for historical prose;
but, noble as it is in many respects, the English
Chronicle wants the magnitude and fulness required
for efficient history.   One great difference between
the earlier and the later Middle Ages is that the
earlier time has nothing like the free idiomatic
narrative of Snorri or Sturla, of Villani or Froissart.
The historical genius is muffled in Latin prose.

Even so, however, the historical genius asserts
itself.   History more than anything else in the Latin
literature of the Dark Ages reveals the character of
the individual writers: more distinctly than the
literature of theology or philosophy, more than the
poetical works of the time.   In history, dealing as
it largely does with contemporary subjects, the author
is left to express his own opinion about his matter
and to choose his own form: he is tested in a different
way from the author who has to expound more abstract themes.   The homilist, the moralist, was

allowed and expected to repeat what the elders had said before him : the master of the liberal arts incurred no blame for drawing upon Isidorus or any other encyclopedia. The historians also availed themselves, wherever they could, of previous histories, but the nature of their subject forced them to be original. The Latin chroniclers of the Middle Ages, though their language interferes with them, are as various in character as the authors of any other period : the commonplaces of their style, the conventions of respectable grammar, the tedious inherited phrases, are not able to smother up the differences of vision and sentiment. It is possible to take this historical literature and make it a store of specimens to illustrate faults of composition and errors of judgment : it is more cheerful and profitable to see in it a diversity of talent expressing itself vigorously in spite of adverse conditions. There are two opposite points of view, and both are justifiable. Regarded in one way, the historians represent the Dark Ages and all the darkness of them ; in another aspect they come out distinct from one another as original minds. There is as great a difference between Gregory of Tours and Bede, or Paulus Diaconus and Einhard, as between Froissart and Commines. Their qualities are felt to be mainly independent of the conditions of their time. Paulus Diaconus was a born storyteller, who only wanted a better language to make him one of the masters of narrative prose. The versatile humour of Liutprand might have worn in another age something different from his Greek-Latin-

Lombard motley, but as he is, he is unmistakable and distinct. The genius of Bede is perhaps the clearest demonstration in the whole world of the independence of genius: the sanity and dignity of his mind are his own, and transcend the limitations of his time: he has the historical gift, and he finds its proper application. If the first impression of early mediæval Latin history is one of monotony, and if monotony never wholly disappears from the Latin page and its conventional formulas, nevertheless, the true, the ultimate judgment in respect of these authors will see them each for himself, each with characteristics of his own. There is no want of variety among them.

In history there was no commanding authoritative model to interfere with the freedom of individual taste. It is true that Orosius has a place at the beginning of mediæval history to some extent resembling that of Boethius in philosophy: his short history of the world is a prologue to the work of the following centuries which is not allowed to fall out of reputation at the close of the period. But while the two, Boethius and Orosius, are regarded in a similar way as authorities by King Alfred and by Dante, the value of the historian is inferior to that of the philosopher: Boethius not only introduces the course of mediæval speculation but transcends it: he is not refuted: his doctrine is as fresh in the fourteenth century as in the sixth, a perennial source of moral wisdom. Orosius is much less important. Although his exposition of the meaning of history, his justification of the ways of Providence, is held in respect, he does not, like Boethius, command the whole field of operations. His religious view of history and his pathetic sermonisings are followed in spirit and style by many mediæval authors, but the interest of history was too great and varied to be ruled by the formulas of Orosius: the chroniclers generally find their own points of view for themselves, and these in very many cases, fortunately, are not those of the preacher. Orosius could not teach anything to writers who, like Einhard, knew the character and business of a great statesman, or, like Paulus Diaconus, had stories to tell.

III.

Classical literature perished from a number of contributory ailments, but of these none was more *Mythology* desperate than the want of romance in *and Legend.* the Roman Empire, and especially in the Latin language. It may have been the original prose of the city of Rome, the disastrous influence of the abstract gods, male and female, whom St Augustine describes satirically—Volupia, Cluacina, Vaticanus, Murcia, and the rest, *turba deorum*. It may have been the long-engrained habit of rhetoric, an absorption in the formal machinery of literature, that blighted the fancy of the poets, and turned the old mythology into a mere affair of diction. It is true that there were exceptions. Apuleius, with all his rhetorical tastes, was at home in a fanciful world utterly remote from the "hypocritical and hackneyed course of literature" as practised in the schools. He

leaves modern authors of Romance very little to invent in addition to his discoveries. He gives up the
accepted Olympian tradition, the deities of the professional epic, and goes to look for new fancies in
local superstitions, in old wives' tales, in a strange
country, full of terror and laughter, the Thessaly of
the Classical *Walpurgisnacht.*

Lucian also, in emancipation from the traditional
literary forms, allows his fancy to play mischievously
about the subjects of mythology, and converts them
to new uses; he extracts a kind of volatile essence,
a new wonder, from their ashes. The incidents of
his *True History* have been found by modern readers
to contain another element besides the burlesque—
a strain of romantic freedom. At the very lowest
estimate of his work, he showed that for modern
literary purposes the myth is what the author makes
it; it is a theme, a suggestion, from which new fancies
may rise. But Apuleius and Lucian had no followers,
and the promise of a romantic revival died away.

"The Gothic mythology of fairies," as Dr Johnson
calls it, was no less the property of Italy than of
the North. In any mountain village the poets might
have found the great-grandmothers of those story-
tellers for whom Boccaccio in his *Genealogy of the
Gods* offers a courteous defence. The elves and fays
of Italy, *Lamiæ,* as Boccaccio calls them, might have
refreshed the poets. But the old wives and their fairy
tales are left unnoticed, except by Apuleius. The
poets might praise the country life, but this part
of it, known to Shakespeare, Herrick, and Milton,

was hidden from their view. The kind Italian genius, that had saved so many Latin poets from the curse of pedantry and dull magnificence, was still able to do something for Claudian, as his *Old Man of Verona* is sufficient to show. But while the blessing of light and air and the quiet life was not withheld, there was something that kept the Latin language almost wholly ignorant of fairy tales.

One glory of the Dark Ages and the barbarian tongues is that they made up for this, with results that are not yet exhausted; among other things with rather important results for the reading of Greek and Latin poetry. It is impossible to say how much the modern poetical interpretation of Homer or Virgil is affected by "the Gothic mythology," or by the tone of mediæval romance. Ever since the modern nations began to be educated, their study of Greek and Latin has been influenced, for all but the most precise and accurate, by the associations of Northern legend. Not only the mediæval readers who calmly accepted Æneas or Ulysses in any sort of byrnie or breeches that happened to be the fashion of their own day, but even more scrupulous and scholarly persons find themselves reading a "Gothic" Homer, whose incidents are sometimes like a border raid, sometimes like the adventures of Tristram or Lancelot. There is seldom, in spite of archæology, any thorough revelation of Greek life untouched, in the reader's mind, with "Gothic" colours. He makes his own scenery from what he knows in his own land:

"And Lochnagar with Ida looks o'er Troy."

Nothing in mediæval literature is more important than the revival of imagination through the influence of barbaric myths and legends; and in this the Celtic and Germanic tongues had a chief share between the ninth and the fourteenth century, to take no wider limits than these. But while the genius of each race may claim its due honour, the one for Tristram, the other for Sigfred, they have also a common merit, transcending that of their separate contributions to the life of the world. They brought literature back into relation with something which is neither German nor Celtic in any special sense; the common heritage of fancy, found, as the mythologists have proved, all over the world. The barbarian invasion in literature is in its own way a renaissance —a revival of old common tastes in story-telling, a rediscovery of the world of Homer, or indeed of something more ancient still.

The new sources of terror and wonder revealed in the Celtic and German legends are not their exclusive property. Ulysses had sailed to the West before Maelduin or St Brandan. Those who would give the Celtic genius an especial right to this kind of adventure seem to be unjust to the genius of Babylon, which knew of a hero voyaging to find his friend among the dead and to hear his story. Before the *Hellride of Brynhild*, before the *Death of Balder*, before the chant of Hervor at her father's grave, the same motives of awe had been known to the Babylonian in the *Descent of Ishtar*. But although the mystery of the twilight regions of mythology and the charm of strange adventures are not exclusively Celtic or Teutonic, that does not take away the place of Celtic and Teutonic mythology in the history of the Middle Ages. It merely affects the summing up as to what is to be called especially Celtic or Teutonic in the qualities of mediæval literature. There may be such national or tribal elements to be discriminated; certain differential qualities in the manner in which the commonplaces of myth are presented in Dutch or Welsh, in Norse or Gaelic.

The progress of poetical mythology is on the whole a simple one. It is the victory of imagination over religion in matters where both are concerned; the substitution of imaginative theory for religious belief. Imagination and the pure delight in stories drive out fear.

This process was carried out to the fullest extent in the Teutonic world, partly through the circumstances of Teutonic history, and mainly through the genius of one branch of the race, the Scandinavian. In the Celtic lands the clarifying of myth was interfered with, because the Celtic religion was not left to itself; it had to compete at a disadvantage with the official religions of the Empire, first pagan, then Christian. The Germans were under the same oppression, and in the same way, after conversion, allowed their ancient fancies to be confused and obliterated—all but the more Northern tribes. The families that were last to come under Latin influence retained their mythology longest; the English longer than the Goths or the Lombards; the Danes longer

than the English ; Norway, Iceland, and Sweden longer
than Denmark.   Partly through the flourishing in
Norway and Iceland of an order of poetry that required a conventional sort of mythological ornament,
the myths were preserved in memory, even while the
gods were rejected, and even with an accession of
intellectual freedom on account of the religious rejection of the gods.   The chief memorial of this
remarkable emancipation of literature from religious
prejudices is the *Edda* of Snorri Sturluson, written
about 1222, in prose, with verse quotations from old
heathen poems.

In Ireland and Wales the old mythology was preserved in stories where the ancient gods retained
their marvellous nature to a large extent, though
losing largely in the special characteristics of divinity.
The gods became heroes.   For imagination and for
literature the change did not matter much.   Cuchulinn
is not less interesting because he is possibly less divine
than Hercules, and Odin and Thor are heroes, with
the dignity of gods—a kind of peerage which scarcely
affects their value in a story.

Grimm in his Teutonic Mythology has tracked the
myths in their disguises through the poems, chronicles,
and popular stories of the German countries not
Scandinavian, the regions of *Germania* which had lost
their gods long before the Icelandic scholar wrote
his account of them in the thirteenth century.   Celtic
students have done similar work in the other province,
with this great disadvantage, that there is no Celtic
Edda, no clear statement of the old mythology by

one who had command of pure heathen sources. The ironical and impartial genius of Snorri Sturluson is something exceptional in history; his rationalist clearness and his imaginative sympathy with myths are qualities that will scarcely be found repeated in that degree in any age, except perhaps in some that have no myths of their own to boast of.

But whether in the Teutonic countries, which in one of their corners preserved a record of old mythology, or in the Celtic, which allowed mythology, though never forgotten, to fall into a kind of neglect and to lose its original meaning, the value of mythology is equally recognisable, and it is equally clear that mythology is nothing more nor less than *Romance*.

Everything in the poets that is most enthralling through the mere charm of wonder, from the land of the Golden Fleece to that of the Holy Grail, is more or less nearly related to mythology.

The "natural magic" of which Mr Arnold spoke in his lectures on Celtic literature, he connected no less truly than persuasively with Celtic mythology. The end of mythology is in that way; it passes into poetry, and the barbarous terror of a world not realised becomes the wonder of *La Belle Dame Sans Mercy* or of *Hyperion*.

The Northern mythology as recorded in the *Edda* cannot be taken any longer as it used to be by enthu-
The Edda. siastic antiquaries and made into the common original property of all the Teutonic tribes. The tribes had stories of their own about Woden and Frea, like the Lombard one preserved by Paulus

Diaconus; the Norwegian stories, which may be possibly better, are not exactly the same. Not only may we suppose that the Norwegians, who are our chief authorities, had their own selection of stories about the gods, not the same as the Gothic, Vandal, Saxon, Lombard, or any other group of stories; but the Norwegians had time to find out new things about the gods in the additional centuries of their heathendom, when the other tribes had gone over to the Christian Church. The *Edda* is not a document for the whole of Germany, except in so far as it gives in the finest form the mythology of the purest and the least subdued of the German races. What is Scandinavian is also Teutonic, in one sense, but it is a very special and peculiar development of the original Teutonic type. Yet the mythology of the *Edda*, refined and modern as it is, contains elements that are older than Germany, monstrous fragments of the primeval world, as Carlyle has divined and explained in words that serve for other mythologies as well :—

"All this of the old Norse Belief which is flung out for us at one level of distance in the *Edda*, like a picture painted on the same canvas, does not at all stand so in reality. It stands rather at all manner of distances and depths, of successive generations since the Belief first began. All Scandinavian thinkers, since the first of them, contributed to that Scandinavian system of thought; in ever-new elaboration and addition, it is the combined work of them all."

Perhaps the Northern mythology would be best surveyed in the following way. First come the stories of the cosmogony—barbarous, grotesque, as Carlyle has described them. The world is the body of a giant. His skull is the heaven, his flesh the earth, his brains are the clouds that move across the sky, under the skull of Hymir; his blood made the sea; the dwarfs who live in caves were made out of the maggots that bred in him. The stars came otherwise; they are sparks from the great fiery region of Chaos. There is something national and Northern perhaps, as Carlyle thought, perhaps even more of Snorri himself, in the humorous way this story is given in the *Edda*, but the substance of it comes from a time long before there was any *Germania*.

Next there are myths of the nature powers, such as one finds in other countries, the favourite god being Thunder, that is, Thor, about whom the greatest number of the most entertaining stories are told. In these one can trace the education of the Northmen, the growth of their theory of life. Thor is the typical Northman of the old sort—bluff, homely, reckless, and fearless—not specially intellectual, sometimes outwitted by the cunning of his adversaries, but good at hard work, and instinctively (one may say) on the side of Reason.

Third, there are the myths of Odin. Woden belongs to all the Germans, but eminently to the Northmen, and to them especially at the time when they were beginning to grow discontented at home and to dream of conquests abroad. Odin is the chief of the gods, but he does not sit apart on an Olympian throne, watching the world spin. Odin is a wanderer on the

face of the earth, anxious, a seeker for wisdom, a
benefactor of mankind; Prometheus in the place of
Zeus. He barters one of his eyes for a drink of the
well of wisdom; or, according to another story, ventures
among the giants and steals the draught of wisdom
and poetry, as Prometheus stole the fire of heaven. He
descends into the abyss to find out the hidden things
of the universe. The quickening of mankind out of
brute lumps into reasoning creatures is ascribed by the
Greeks to the wise Titan, by the Northmen to Odin
and his two companions.

Last of all come the myths of the decay of pagan-
ism. It is these that have most impressed the imagination of modern students—the myths of Valhalla
and of the Twilight of the Gods. They are not
original Teutonic beliefs; they grew up in the period
of migration and conquest, when the Northmen first
became acquainted vaguely with the ideas of Christianity in the English, French, or Scottish countries
where they had found a settlement.

Common to all stages of this mythology and to
all the Germans as well, was the conception of the
human world as an enclosure defended against Chaos.
The human world is Midgarth; in Anglo - Saxon
middangeard, the "merry middle - earth" of later
ballads. The *Edda* explains the whole system clearly;
it was more clearly worked out in the North than
elsewhere. In the full Scandinavian philosophy the
human world is contrasted with Asgarth, the citadel
of the Anses, the gods, which rises in the centre of
the circle of Midgarth; and with Utgarth, the outer

circle, the icy barrier of the world, the home of the Giants (Jötunheim), only one remove from Niflheim and the gulfs of Chaos.

The elements are the same as in Greece, but they are differently mixed, and the import is not the same. The Greeks, like the Northmen, thought of the world as encircled by the Ocean stream; they too, as one sees in the *Odyssey*, believed in a strange and desolate country out on the verge; the *Iliad* has knowledge of the ends of the earth not unlike that of the Scandinavian account—the edge, leading down to the depths of Tartarus, a joyless country unblest by wind or sun, the abode of ancient unhappy creatures, Iapetus and Cronus.[1] But what is a passing thought in the Greek mind becomes in the Northern a constant and inevitable belief. Through all his daily life the Northman hears the boom of the surges of Chaos on the dykes of the world. The giants are not disposed of, as in Greece, by a decisive conquest early in history. The Olympians broke the backs of their adversaries in a short campaign; the Æsir, the Northern gods, are like Northern rovers in a fortress surrounded by a hostile country. It is part of the life of the gods to keep watch against their enemies, to catch them asleep if possible; to add to their tale of victories in the unending feud. Thor does most of this work. It

[1] οὐδ' εἴ κε τὰ νείατα πείραθ' ἵκηαι
γαίης καὶ πόντοιο, ἵν' Ἰαπετός τε Κρόνος τε
ἥμενοι οὔτ' αὐγῆς Ὑπερίονος Ἠελίοιο
τέρπουτ' οὔτ' ἀνέμοισι, βαθὺς δέ τε Τάρταρος ἀμφίς.
—*Il.*, viii. 478-481.

is told of him repeatedly in the stories that he was
away from Asgarth, had gone East to thrash
the trolls (*at berja tröll*). It is in this sort
of business that the Thunder-god acquires his character of hero, and his hold upon the affections of the
Northmen. He is a favourite god, a patron, a "friend"
(*vinr*), as the old Northern phrase went.

Thor.

One of the best of the stories of his warfare is
the defeat of the giant Hrungnir, told in the second
part of the *Edda* (*Skáldskaparmál*, c. 17):—

One day when Thor had gone East to thrash the
trolls, Odin mounted Sleipnir and rode into Jötunheim and came to the house of the giant Hrungnir.
Hrungnir asks, "Who is that in the golden helmet who
rides over wind and water? he has a wondrous good
horse." Odin said he would wager his head there
was not a horse so good in all Jötunheim. Hrungnir
was moved by this, and leapt on his horse and rode
after Odin as hard as he could. Odin kept before
him all the way to Asgard, but Hrungnir came burst-
ing in through the gates—and the Æsir had to make
the best of him they could. They brought him plenty
to drink, and the giant drank freely. When he was
well drunk, there was no want of big words: he
said he would take up Valhalla and carry it off to
Jötunheim, and throw down Asgarth, and kill the
gods and carry off Freyja and Sif.

The gods were very angry at all this. Freyja
alone dared to come near him and fill his horn: he
said he would drink up all the ale of the gods.
The gods were weary of his boasting, and called on

Thor. At that instant Thor appeared in the hall. He had his hammer over his shoulder and was very angry. He asked who had allowed rogues of giants to come and sit at drink, or Freyja to pour out drink for him at the feast of the gods? Hrungnir scowled at Thor, and said Odin had brought him in, and was surety for him. "You shall repent this," says Thor. "Little honour to you," says Hrungnir, "to kill an unarmed giant: it will try your metal to come and fight in single combat. It was a foolish work," he says, "when I left my shield and my club at home, but I will call you a coward if you slay me now when I am without my weapons." Thor accepted the challenge, and Hrungnir went home.

When he got to Jötunheim all the other giants came round about him to hear how he had fared, and he told them the whole story.

The giants took it sadly. If Thor killed Hrungnir their champion, they knew what to expect from him afterwards. So they made a mud giant. He was nine miles high and three broad: but they could not get a heart for him till they took a mare's heart and put it into him: it was not steady when Thor came. Hrungnir had a heart of spiky stone. His head was stone also; so was his shield; his weapon was a hone. So he stood waiting for Thor, and Mistcalf, the mud giant, stood beside him; they say that he bewrayed himself for fear when Thor came. Thor came with his henchman Thialfi: Thialfi ran on in front and cried out, "Better guard, giant, for Thor has seen you, and is coming at you under the earth."

So Hrungnir put down his shield and stood on it and took his stone club in two hands. Then he saw lightnings and heard thunder, and Thor's hammer came flying: it caught the hone and broke it, and went into Hrungnir's stone skull and cracked it into little pieces. The hone was broken: half of it went into Thor's head. The mud giant fell to Thialfi, and made a poor end. The healing of Thor's head is another story.

Odin has a different method and a different significance. One of the poems in the *Elder Edda, The Lay of Harbard,* has for its subject the contention *Odin.* of Thor and Odin, of Force and Wit. The spirit of Odin, the scholar-adventurer, was contrasted with the native unsophisticated strength of Thor. So long ago, even before the old faith was discarded, Norway had begun to contribute satirical dialogue to this part of the everlasting comedy, the antithesis of old custom and new reason, in which the latest Norwegian authors still find something to say. And yet earlier and older than *The Lay of Harbard* is the solemn deliverance of the mind of Odin in *The High One's Lesson* (*Hávamál*): "I hung on the gallows-tree nine whole nights, wounded with the spear, offered to Woden, myself to myself; on the tree whose roots no man knoweth. They gave me no loaf, they held no horn to me. I peered down, I caught up the mysteries with a cry, then I fell back. I learned nine songs of might . . . I got the draught of the precious mead . . . then I became fruitful and wise, and waxed great and flourished ; word followed fast on word with me, work followed fast on work with me." [1]

The agony of Odin is a myth of a different sort from the downright methods of Thor with the giants, and the early Northern religious poet knew this and brought it out. As Prometheus takes on an ideal character, with a tragic depth and meaning far beyond the original old conceptions of the philanthropic Titan, so Odin with the Northmen grows more and more in significance, and stands for all the perplexities and questionings of the human race.

The myths of the death of Balder and the Doom of the Gods have been explained and admired too often to need much comment. Perhaps one reason why modern treatment of these subjects is so often found unsatisfactory is that the original documents have left nothing for modern imagination to do. The *Volospá* and *Balder's Dream*, with the prose of the *Edda*, have got out of the myths their whole imaginative essence.

Balder.

The tragedy of the Doom of the Powers, the end of the world, seems to have been the ruling idea of the later Northern mythology, or at any rate that which impressed itself most deeply in poetic meditations on such themes. Perhaps the Teutons had always a suspicion that their gods were mortal. The story of the death of Balder is probably a very old one. Originally perhaps a nature-myth, of the death of summer, or of the day, its ideas of mortality were

[1] *Corpus Poeticum Boreale*, i. 24.

retained after the natural origin of the story was forgotten; it became the symbolic tragedy of all death, the triumph of Time. The idea also that the whole system of the world—Heaven and Earth and the Gods—was fated to disappear, was probably a very old one. Zeus in the *Prometheus Bound* is conscious of danger ahead, though the sympathies of the audience are not attracted to him in the same way. Zeus is in the position of Odin, trying all shifts to get at the mystery of his fate, as Odin goes about asking questions of Vafthrudnir and others, trying to find out all he can of the way things are going " until the wreck of the gods " (*unz riúfask regin*). This situation, which is exceptional in Greek, becomes the ruling motive in Scandinavian legend. The realm of Chaos and old Night is to rise against the gods and overcome them; the Wolf, the old enemy, is unchained; the World-serpent of the ocean raises its head against them. Out of the chaotic fire of Muspellsheim comes a fiendish army led by a king with a flaming sword. The Æsir stand on the ramparts of Asgarth, and with them the heroes who have fallen in battle on earth, and have been chosen by Odin's Valkyries to be the fellows of the gods in the last conflict. Thor slays the Midgarth-worm, but its venom is the death of him. The Wolf attacks Odin; it is written: "Few men can see further than the day when Odin shall meet with the wolf."

The latest prophets of the old faith thought they saw something further: Balder coming again, and a new Heaven and a new Earth. But perhaps this was not the common belief; this part of Northern tradition is full of analogies with the Christian Apocalypse; it belongs, as is clearly explained by the editors of *Corpus Poeticum Boreale*, to the Viking age, when the Northmen in France, Ireland, everywhere, were in close acquaintance with Christian ideas and with repeated pictures of Doomsday. They were not a dull people; besides their economic motives for roving, they had the appetite for seeing the world and learning the ways of foreigners (*at kanna annarra manna siðu*); they could not fail to learn much of the beliefs that provided them with their richest earnings, in churches and convents. What is distinctly Northern in the myth of the Twilight of the Gods [1] is the strength of its theory of life. It is this intensity of courage that distinguishes the Northern mythology (and Icelandic literature generally) from all others. The last word of the Northmen before their entry into the larger world of Southern culture, their last independent guess at the secret of the Universe, is given in the Twilight of the Gods. As far as it goes, and as a working theory, it is absolutely impregnable. It is the assertion of the individual freedom against all the terrors and temptations of the world. It is absolute resistance, perfect because without hope. The Northern gods have an exultant extravagance in their warfare which makes them more

---

[1] The term "Twilight of the Gods" (*ragnarökr*), used regularly by Snorri, is probably to be taken, as Gudbrand Vigfusson explains, for a confusion with "Doom of the Gods" (*ragnarök*) which occurs repeatedly, while the other occurs once only, in the mythological poems.

like Titans than Olympians; only they are on the
right side, though it is not the side that wins. The
winning side is Chaos and Unreason; but the gods,
who are defeated, think that defeat is not refutation.
The latest mythology of the North is an allegory of
the Teutonic self-will, carried to its noblest terms,
deified by the men for whom all religion was coming
to be meaningless except "trust in one's own might
and main"—the creed of Kjartan Olafsson[1] and Sigmund Brestisson[2] before they accepted Christianity.

The Northmen in the Dark Ages had already discovered the imaginative, poetical, romantic value of
myth. They allowed this interest more and more to
absorb what remained of a practical and effective
belief in the gods. The gods became a fable: and
in this way, because the fable, the adventures of Thor
and Odin, the death of Balder, the fall of Asgarth,
was not found inconsistent with new forms of religion, the mythology of the North was preserved,
when the mythology of England and Germany, being
without a poetic mind to translate it into romance,
was driven to its refuges and disguises in common
folk-lore.

The Celtic mythology was not so fortunate as the
Norse; but the same imaginative temper is found in
Ireland and Irish literature, the same refusal to give up
Wales. good stories on account of religious objec-
tions to them. The difference between Ireland and Iceland is that the original heathen traditions had become
much more obscure and corrupt in Ireland before the

---

[1] *Laxdœla Saga.*   [2] *Fœreyinga Saga.*

stage at which the imaginative literary artist began to work on them. Or perhaps it would be truer to say that the imaginative reconstruction of mythology, turning gods into heroes, had already been carried far before even the oldest extant versions of Cymric or Gaelic myth. While the Northmen remembered their gods clearly, and thought of them as gods with a home and a proper life of their own, the Welsh and Irish more and more forgot their divinity, and turned their gods into princes or heroes of Ulster and Connaught, Gwynedd and Dyved.

Like Carlyle with the *Edda*, so with the Celtic mythology a casual observer appears to have summed up the case. Matthew Arnold's remarks in his *Lectures on Celtic Literature* are allowed to stand, by the Celtic scholars who know most about the subject, as a true and satisfactory judgment. " The very first thing that strikes one in reading the *Mabinogion* is how evidently the mediæval story-teller is pillaging an antiquity of which he does not fully possess the secret: he is like a peasant building his hut on the site of Halicarnassus or Ephesus ; he builds, but what he builds is full of materials of which he knows not the history, or knows by a glimmering tradition merely—stones 'not of this building,' but of an older architecture, greater, cunninger, more majestical. In the mediæval stories of no Latin or Teutonic people does this strike one as in those of the Welsh."

The Celtic mythology has been restored and explained by Professor John Rhŷs in his *Lectures on*

Celtic Heathendom and in *The Arthurian Legend.* The first of these books, with its many citations of Welsh and Irish stories, exhibits the confusion and unreason of those ancient monuments of human fancy, which are at first so little attractive to the reasonable and enlightened reader. What can one make of a people whose hero (once a god, it is thought) is called " The Distorted of Ireland," because " when his mind was evil he would draw in one of his eyes so far into his head that a tame crane could not peck it, and shoot out the other one till it grew as big as a cauldron to boil a heifer in," not to speak of twisting round the calves of his legs till they were where the shins ought to be, or absorbing all his hair into his body, with a blood-drop to mark the place of each particular hair, and other variations.[1]

Probably no nation ever surpassed the Celts in enjoyment of this kind of distortion. If other people over the face of the earth can produce extravagant and grotesque beliefs in sufficient variety, none take them in the same way as the Celts. The Northmen have their own humorous stories of the adventures of the gods; the Celts go far beyond them in the revel of fancy supplied from primeval sources, extravagant fables, which are only not monstrous because the reciters see the fun of them. There is an exultant reckless humour in the story of Cuchulinn, a full consciousness of its impossible and outrageous qualities. This is part of the history of Celtic literature, which

[1] Cf. Rhŷs, *Celtic Heathendom,* p. 438 ; *The Sickbed of Cuchulinn, The Feast of Bricriu* (*Irische Texte,* i. 207, 265), &c.

also has another side, as in the Northern mythology likewise there is both comedy and tragedy, on the one hand Thor's adventures, on the other the Dream of Balder. In the literary use of myth among the Celts a graver and more beautiful kind of imagination reveals itself in contrast to the riot of distortion; not always, indeed not often, in contradiction to it; for the Aristophanic blending of beauty with enormous laughter seems to be natural to the Celtic genius, at any rate in their ancient literature; that is their glory. They knew the eternal tragic questions and problems, the strain of hopeless courage and divided duties, as well as the people of the Teutonic race. Cuchulinn's destiny makes him meet his best friend and his son in combat; and the oppositions of loyalty and private affection are tragic motives well understood in the Irish tales. Perhaps the finest mood of the Celtic mythology is chosen in another kind of story. If the imagination of the Northern mythologists was dominated by the thought of the fall of the gods, "the day when Odin meets with the wolf," the Celts have given their hearts to the enchanted ground, to the faery magic, in many stories of adventures in the underworld, and voyages westward to an island paradise.[1]

Where Babylonians, Greeks, and Finns have journeyed, on the seas beyond the earthly coasts, the Irish have no exclusive right. But they have thought

[1] This subject has been illustrated most conveniently and intelligibly by Mr Alfred Nutt in the essays following Dr Kuno Meyer's edition of the *Voyage of Bran.*

more constantly of such things than other people,
Nos manet oceanus. and have made more of them in their songs and stories.   To no people has the sea appealed in the same way, with such a magical attraction.   The Legend of St Brandan, derived from the older Voyage of Maelduin, came to be known everywhere throughout Europe, and quickened the senses of the Mediterranean people with a breath of the Atlantic winds and tides.   St Brandan stirred the thoughts of the less enthusiastic and better balanced Latin minds, and one gift among the many given by Ireland to the Continent of Europe was the spell of the Ocean, the dream of a glory beyond the value of mortal things—

" On that vast shore washed by the furthest sea."

But apart from this influence on the world through St Brandan, which is after all an accidental result, there remain the achievements of Irish imagination in stories and poems that had no influence at all in foreign regions, but are none the less wonderful and honourable: such, for instance, as the prose and verse of the *Voyage of Bran*.   For the Celts in their mytho-logical literature are not merely the channels of primitive tradition; and there is nothing that proves their genius more truly than their imaginative treatment of old barbarous things.   The spirit and suggestion of an old myth works upon their minds and takes new form; myth with them becomes romance.

The importance of the Celtic fairy tales in mediæval literature is proved by a thousand references to "the matter of Britain" in French and English books, and in all the other languages besides—

> " Thise olde gentil Bretons in hir dayes
> Of divers aventures maden layes ; "

and Breton lays are vouched as authorities for many romantic stories besides that of *The Franklin's Tale*. The personages of them are often, as in this one of Chaucer's, unassociated with any mythic or heroic cycle; it is not necessary that the hero should be already well known like Tristram or Gawain. Much of the "matter of Britain" is as vague in its history as the fairy tales that begin anywhere, with no facts at all about the king's son, or the three brothers, or the man's daughter and her step-sister. Some of it, however, is under the dominion of great names. The

Arthur. history of King Arthur, in whatever way interpreted, is a fabric in which all possible strands of myth and heroic tradition have been plaited together: quite unlike the simple stories that begin "Once upon a time," with no historical associations and no solemnity. Arthur becomes many different things in different ages. In Nennius, about the year 800, Arthur is the commander of the British, *dux bellorum*, against the Saxons; he fought the twelve great battles, the last of them at Mount Badon, when nine hundred and sixty men of the heathen host fell before one onset of Arthur, *et nemo prostravit eos nisi ipse solus.* He fell along with Medraut at the battle of Camlan in 537, according to *Annales Cambriæ*.[1] He has this

---

[1] MS. tenth century.

more or less historical character, as a leader in the historical conflict between the Britons and their enemies. But in the tract on the Marvels of Britain, early joined to the history of Nennius, there are vestiges of the mythical Arthur who comes into the story of *Kulhwch and Olwen*, and of the hunting of the mighty boar whose name is Troit: the footprint of Arthur's dog Cabal is found on a stone in a cairn near Builth. In Geoffrey of Monmouth Arthur is a British Charlemagne or Alexander, antagonist of Rome, conqueror of many kingdoms, finding a tragic death through the perfidy of his wife and his nephew. In "the French Book" followed by Sir Thomas Malory, the French *Mort Artus*, the tragedy is deepened, the Nemesis more dreadful. But in many parts of the prose romance, Arthur is as little interesting as Charlemagne in many of the French epics: Arthur and Charlemagne both became, for many story-tellers, mere honourable names to give a centre for the incidents, to preside in hall. Yet for all this degradation neither lost the power derived from their historical and mythical glory; they remained great, for any poet who chose to take them so; Arthur kept his place among the Worthies, in spite of the many feeble things heaped upon him by romancers. He never had, unfortunately, for the English or French the glory that even his own people of Wales too soon forgot, though it is recorded in an old poem which "evidently deals with expeditions conducted by Arthur by sea to the realms of twilight and darkness." His name "gathers round it the legends of heroes and divinities of a past of indefinite extent. In other words, he and his men, especially Kei and Bedwyr, are represented undertaking perilous expeditions to realms of mythic obscurity, bringing home treasures, fighting with hags and witches, despatching giants, and destroying monsters." [1]

This is not his proper work in the French book, though Arthur keeps a little of the dragon-slayer even there. "The horror and the hell" invaded by Arthur in his ship Prydwen did not remain in the imagination of the Arthurian poets: only through antiquarian research is one enabled to look into that strange region. It is a loss for poetry: there might have been yet another mediæval counterpart to the voyage of Ulysses if the ship Prydwen and her fortunes had been better remembered by the Welsh and interpreted to their French or English neighbours.

There were other sources of Romance in the Middle Ages which it is not irrelevant to mention here; the *The Bible.* Bible being one of them. The Bible, which was still printed in the shape of a noble and joyous book by Coverdale and Cranmer, a book to be read, not broken yet into verses for the convenience of Geneva, was the source of some of the best-loved stories. Samson and David took their place freely along with Jason and Lancelot in popular favour, long before the roll of the Nine Worthies was made definite, with its equal allowance of honour to Jews,

---

[1] See Rhŷs, Introduction to Malory (1893), pp. xxxv, xxxvi. The adventures of Arthur belong properly to the second volume of this series ; cf. *The Flourishing of Romance*, c. iii.

Paynim, and Christians. Nor was it only Joshua and Gideon and David's captains that came to reinforce the stories of Ogier or Charlemagne; besides the addition of new histories and adventures to the common stock, the Bible gave to the new languages more than can be estimated of new rhetoric. The diction of the Bible has frequently caused trouble among the classically educated, who have found it sometimes necessary to apologise for the vehement and daring metaphors of the Old Testament. Its influence on styles of composition is a subject which would lead far; but one thing may be said with confidence about its part in the Middle Ages: that it could not fail to attract the vernacular and popular languages to imitate and repeat its sublimities as well as they could. So one finds the mystery of Celtic stories illustrated with citations from the Bible; as where in the Arthurian legend the mysterious delivery of captives in an unearthly place beyond the Bridge of Dread is celebrated as it might be in a chivalrous *Pilgrim's Progress* with the verses of a spiritual song: "Gawain turned and looked back; and behold, across the river, all the streets of the place were filled with men and women, rejoicing and singing in carol-wise: *The people that sat in darkness have beheld a great light.*"

There is another delivery of captives to which the same song belongs more properly, the story of *The Harrowing of Hell* in the Gospel of Nico-demus, which is everywhere known in the Middle Ages, and everywhere the source of poetic in-

The Harrowing of Hell.

spiration and of that wonder which does not belong exclusively to St Brandan and his fellows. No adventure of heroes in the land of the dead is told with more complete imaginative sense of the drama of Light and Darkness than this of *The Harrowing of Hell.* It makes one of the noblest passages in *Piers Plowman;* and it is nothing to the discredit of the author that he has repeated what no length of study could improve, the order of events as they stand in the original Gospel and as they were kept in the drama of the Passion played in various towns in England. As a piece of composition the story has the great advantage over other heroic legends of war against Hell that it begins not from the side of the hero but with the captives in darkness. They see the light far off, they hear the confusion and boastful preparation of the fiends, and the light when it strikes in at the everlasting gates in the name of the King of Glory encounters and defeats a darkness which has held the reader in its tyranny along with the spirits in prison. It is more terrible in that way than if one entered in the company of the triumph. The many later versions of *The Harrowing of Hell* may generally be judged according as they observe this original design or lose the effect of it by beginning the story from the other side, as some of them feebly do.[1]

The romance of Alexander attracted to itself a vast amount of mythology from unknown sources in the East: it is impossible to say how old the stories are

[1] The story is finely given from the *Gospel of Nicodemus* in Mr Raleigh's *Milton.*

that gathered round Alexander, or to trace their influence exactly in the new lands of the West.

Alexander.

The romance as distinct from the sufficiently wonderful true history had its rise in Egypt:
the motive was to find in Alexander the true successor
of the ancient Egyptian line: Alexander is the son
not of Philip but of Nectanebus king of Egypt.[1] The
Greek book ascribed to Callisthenes, really written
about 200 A.D., was translated into Latin and became
popular in the version of Julius Valerius; and besides
that book, the letter of Alexander to Aristotle on
the wonders of India, and the colloquy of Alexander
with Dindimus the Brahmin, circulated independently,
and led to separate works in the different vernaculars.
Probably there is little invention in all the romance:
it drew to itself the fragments of many mythologies.
It may be that Irish or German readers of the
Alexander book found themselves in possession of
something in which they had hereditary right, for
many things in the story resemble passages in Celtic
and Teutonic myth; it may be that the adventures
of Alexander come from the same antique original
as the voyages of Arthur against the uncouth fortresses
named in the old Welsh poem, or the expeditions
of Thor against the trolls.   It is not impossible either
that some of the resemblances may be due to early
Western borrowing from the Alexander legend.   Dr
Zimmer has pointed out that Loeg, the charioteer of
Cuchulinn, is described in the oldest Irish documents
of that cycle as wearing a garment presented by

[1] See *The Flourishing of Romance*, c. iv.

Simon Magus to Darius, King of the Romans. The inference is that a foreign strain may be looked for in very early Irish legend: it is possible that along with reading and writing there may have come the stories of the wonders of India, and other still stranger lands, to increase the Celtic collection of tales; perhaps even the adventures of Alexander may have helped the story of Maelduin. For a large part of the world, at any rate, if not for Ireland, the Alexander romance was an introduction to the Eastern mythology. Some of it appears to be as old as anything in fable. The central and most generally quoted part of the story has three main incidents in it: the ascent of Alexander to Heaven; his inclusion of Gog and Magog in a wall not to be scaled nor broken; his descent into the sea in a glass box. The second of these, Gog and Magog, is connected with the history of Antichrist, for at his coming Gog and Magog, the hideous nations, are to burst from their prison. The ascent of Alexander has a different kind of interest. As generally told, it is an ascent of the same sort as that of Nimrod in Victor Hugo's poem (an Arabian tradition), in a car borne up by eagles. This adventure of Nimrod, which is told of another great king in the poem of Firdausi, seems to come from a Babylonish tale, and may, as Mr Wallis Budge remarks, have been indefinitely old in Babylon. Etanna, for that is the name of the hero, is carried up to heaven by an eagle, who points out to him the diminishing earth and ocean below him—an ancestor, probably, of the eagle in Chaucer's *House of Fame*. The motive is that of the *Somnium Scipionis*, used with a satirical purpose in the *Icaromenippus* of Lucian, and common in many literatures. It seems as if Alexander had taken up, in the East, a number of adventures and attributes which in rather different forms were already known to Greeks, Romans, Celts, and Germans: the romance of Alexander broke into an old treasury of fable which had been partly plundered before. A strange thing about it is that the wildest versions given in Mr Budge's Ethiopic Alexander often contain analogies to Western myth which are not found in the Greek or Latin texts; the Ethiopic Alexander is much more like Maelduin than anything in the Western Alexander books. But that is not for the present occasion; it is enough to recognise the legend of Alexander as a large addition to the literary stock. Alexander became later a chivalrous hero, but before that he was accepted gladly all over Europe as one more of those adventurers who find their way beyond the known limits of the world. The story of his wanderings was valued because it was full of views about far countries. Mandeville continues what the letter to Aristotle began.

Visions of the other world, like those in the Republics of Plato and Cicero, are frequent in the
Visions. Middle Ages, and the source, direct or indirect, of a large amount of literature in verse and prose.[1]

The Vision of St Paul was rejected as fabulous by Ælfric and many others, because of the words of St

[1] Wright, *St Patrick's Purgatory*; D'Ancona, *Precursori di Dante.*

Paul himself—"things that cannot be uttered." But for all that the *Vision* was widely received in all languages. The Visions of Furseus, of Drihthelm, of Salvius,[1] of Wettin, and others, begin in the same way as that of Er in Plato, the man apparently lying dead while his soul is conducted through hell and heaven.

One great beauty in the stories of these visions is that they are indeed explorations of untravelled countries: they are not bound by conventional theories, nor are they mere repetitions of teaching. The places seen by these travellers are not the formal and symmetrical provinces described by Dante; their souls pass out into the waste places of the universe, the regions of a wilder and more primitive belief than that of the *Divine Comedy*.[2]

The vision of Wettin, Monk of Reichenau (+824), is found in his prose life by the Abbot Heito (+836), which is the substance of a Latin poem by Walafrid Strabo: it has the character of a real vision, at least in its independence of the traditional pictures of hell. Wettin travelled through a landscape like that of *The Pilgrim's Progress*, a world like this world in its variety and its surprises. Hell is wide, and much of it is empty. The torments have no allotted place or gradation. Wettin found a former abbot, Waldo, in purgatorial torment on a mountain top, beaten by the

[1] Gregory of Tours, *Hist. Franc.*, vii. 1.

[2] One of the most beautiful stories of this sort is a Maori one, quoted by Dr Tylor in *Primitive Culture*, ii. 50. See also Rhŷs, *Celtic Heathendom*, 265.

winds. The angel, his guide, took and led him by a wondrous pleasant way till they came to high beautiful mountains of marble-stone, as it seemed: round about the foot of the mountain went a fiery river, in which an innumerable multitude of the damned were being punished, many of whom he knew. In one place he saw a hideous castle with smoke rising from it, and was told that it was for the tribulation of certain monks brought together there to be purified; one of them in a leaden ark till the Day of Judgment, because, like Ananias and Sapphira, he had sinned against the order. The place of glory is a city or a castle built with arches of gold and silver, adorned with sculpture (*opere anaglifo*): he comes to it on his way, like Christian; he is not carried up to heaven.

The Bridge of Dread is found in many of these narratives,[1] as in the Irish Vision of Adamnan and the Vision of Tundal—

> "Over that lake thai se lygge
> A wonder longe narowe brygge,
> Two myle of lengtht hit was semande,
> And scarsely the brede of ane hande."

It is known in many romances. Gawain and other knights have to attempt it, for many ways lead from King Arthur's court, some of them in plain daylight, like that followed by Geraint along the ridge from the Usk to Cardiff, others again through valleys of darkness and ominous woods to the river of Death. Be-

[1] Compare also St Gregory's *Dialogues*, iv. 37; St Boniface, *Epistles*.

yond that are walls and towers, and other forests, hills, and plains. There are some knights who have brought back a report of it.

How Buddha came to be a saint of the Church, in the legend of *Barlaam and Josaphat*, has been gradually discovered and explained in the writings of several scholars.[1] Solomon contributed in a less honourable way to the literature of the Middle Ages, through the legend of his unfaithful wife which appears in the romance of *Cliges*, and through the Dialogue tradition, in which his wisdom is met and parodied by the irreverent genius of Marcolf. The same fashion of dialogue led to a different myth about another wise man; Epictetus as well as Buddha becomes a legend, in *Ypotis*, so strangely noted by Chaucer as a specimen of romance.

IV.

"The Heroicall Poetry of the old Bards of Wales and Ireland (and perhaps all other Barberous Nations), who at publique Solemnities were wont to sing the Prayses of their valiant Ancestors, was the Originall of all the more Elegant Greeke and Roman Epique Poems." —Samuel Butler's *Commonplace Book*, fol. 203.

Heroic poetry and the heroic motives in literature were well known in the Dark Ages; indeed they give *The Heroic Poem.* those ages their character more than anything else, apart from the educational Latin influences. It is the age in which the exploits and conflicts of kings and chieftains have transcendent

[1] Gaston Paris, *Poëmes et Légendes ;* Jacobs, *Barlaam and Josaphat.*

importance for the minds of their people, and find
their record in different forms of poetry, to all of
which the name heroic is appropriate.   In the
Teutonic and also in the Romance tongues a kind of
narrative poem is gradually brought to completion, for
which the title of Epic has been found acceptable.
The old Teutonic epic poetry, the old French epic,
Beowulf, and *Roland*,—these are works of the Dark
Ages, which might more honourably be called, and not
less correctly, the Heroic Age of the North.

Beowulf and *Roland* are epic poems, more or less
complete and orderly; but these are not the only
shapes in which heroic themes were represented.
They came at the end of a long process of elaboration, the history of which is not easy to make out.

There are many references in Latin historians to
songs in which Teutonic kings are praised.   The
"Saxon Poet" who turned into Latin verse the life
of Charles the Great says that there were many songs
in the vulgar tongue in honour of the Carlovingian
house, the ancestors of Lewis the Pious :—

> " Est quoque jam notum : vulgaria carmina magnis
>   Laudibus ejus avos et proavos celebrant :
> Pippinos Carolos Hludovicos et Theodricos
>   Et Carlomannos Hlothariosque canunt."

But there are different ways of singing about a king
and hero, and some of these are easily enough distinguished in the history of the Middle Ages.   The
proper epic—the noble and dignified narrative poem—
is too complicated a thing, and requires too much

preparation, to flourish everywhere. There are simpler kinds of verse, ballads sung in country choruses, like the song of Clothair II. referred to in the *Life of St Faro.* Clothair died in 628; the saint's Life was written in the ninth century. There it is told how Clothair's victory over the Saxons passed into popular songs among the common people, and how choruses of women kept time to the song,—

"Ex qua victoria carmen publicum juxta rusticitatem per omnium pene volitabat ora ita canentium, feminæque choros inde plaudendo componebant :

> De Chlothario est canere rege Francorum
> Qui ivit pugnare in gentem Saxonum
> Quam graviter provenisset missis Saxonum
> Si non fuisset inclytus Faro de gente Burgundionum.

Et in fine hujus carminis :—

> Quando veniunt missi Saxonum in terram Francorum
> Faro ubi erat princeps
> Instinctu Dei transeunt per urbem Meldorum
> Ne interficiantur a rege Francorum.

Hoc enim rustico carmine placuit ostendere quantum ab omnibus celeberrimus habebatur (*sc.* Faro)."

In the same sort of words will later historians tell how the heart of the people is touched by momentous heroic or tragic occurrences in their own day, and how they turn their news into ballads. So Barbour of the strife in Eskdale :—

> "I will nocht rehers all the maner
> For quha sa likis thai mai heir
> Young women quhen thai will play
> Syng it emang thame ilke day."

So Mr James Melville of the death of the Earl of
Moray : "the horrour of the deid of Dinnibirsall,
quhilk the unburied corps lyand in the Kirk of Leithe
maid to be nocht onlie unburied amangs the peiple,
but be comoun rymes and sangs keipit in recent
detestation." Common rhymes and songs amongst the
people (*juxta rusticitatem*), ballads sung by girls in a
ring, may have much of the heroic spirit, even much
of the epic manner, but the epic poem does not belong
to those singers or their audiences.   Heroic poetry
requires a court, like that of Alcinous in the *Odyssey*
or that of Hrothgar the Dane in *Beowulf ;* and it is
not in every house, even of great men with a taste for
such things, that the epic narrative is to be found.
Much heroic poetry of the Middle Ages is not narrative
but lyric.   As the girls' dancing song is one of the
oldest, at least one of the commonest, types of popular
poetry in different countries, so the lyric eulogy of a
chieftain (alive or dead) is the established form of
courtly entertainment offered by a literary artist to
his patron, essentially unvarying in motive in different
parts of the world.   The courtly lyric of praise is
specially cultivated by Celtic and Scandinavian poets,
and it may be that their attention to this branch of
the art may have hindered the progress of epic in
Ireland and Norway.   However that may be, the lyric
of praise is something different from the epic of adventure, though the two kinds may have much in
common.   The lyric may have much historical matter
in it.   The Icelandic court poems were used, scientifi-
cally, as sources for the lives of the Kings of Norway,

"There were scalds at the Court of Harald Fairhair, and their poems are known, and likewise poems about all the kings that have been in Norway since. And we have taken evidence chiefly from those poems that were recited before the great lords themselves or their sons: we hold it all for truth that is found in these poems about their expeditions and battles. It is indeed the custom of poets to praise him most before whom they stand; but no one would dare to tell the king of exploits which every one who heard, and the king himself, would know to be vanity and lies; that were scorn and no praise." This is Icelandic historical criticism, in the preface to the history commonly called *Heimskringla.* But the historical matter of the Court poems is not expressed in an epic way. The Oxford editors have given a convenient diagram of the regular Court method, which shows the difference clearly.[1] " The type and plan of the Court poem might be represented in six lines :—

Introduction.	The Poet brings the King a poem.	
Body × *n.*	⎧ The King launched his ship. ⎫	Historical
	He met his foes at N. ⎭	fact.
	He battened the wolf, ⎫	Embellish-
	⎩ And quenched the raven's thirst. ⎭	ment.
End.	The King will reward the Poet.	

And every subject and object throughout every poem is put into a more or less dark and rigid dressing of metaphor." Here the adventures themselves are not the main thing: what the poet wishes to bring out is

C. P. B., ii. 449.

their value as proof of the king's excellence in war. Epic matter goes into the lyric of praise, as in the song of Deborah or in Pindar, but the narrative interest is not the chief motive, and does not determine the form of the poem.

While it is convenient and necessary to distinguish between popular and courtly poetry, the distinction need not be carried too far. It does not mean that there was no relation between the two. On the contrary, the history of the most polite and artificial of the mediæval forms of verse—*e.g.*, of the lyrics of Provence and Germany—proves a close connection between the wild stock and the cultivated varieties, while the Celtic and the Icelandic types of elaborate poetry are found spreading wide among the common people. To begin with, in the great houses of an heroic age there is no very marked difference between the tastes and occupations of the king and his followers, even the meaner sort. What the earl likes the churl can admire in his own way. The epic that requires the society of a court, and something of pride and warlike honour to inspire it and give it substance, is not retained at court and obliged to be exclusively noble. The epic soon finds its way to the same sort of gatherings as listen to the rustic ballads. The minstrel publishes the epic, and is welcomed in simple houses, drawing children from their play and old men from the chimney-corner, like Bernlef, the blind Frisian harper, " who was loved by his neighbours because he was of an open and free nature, and would repeat the actions of the men of old and the contests of kings, singing to his harp courteously " (*non inurbane*[1]), or like Carolan, the Irish bard, described in much the same tone by Goldsmith.[2] Minstrels less gentle than Bernlef or Carolan, the common jugglers of fairs and market-places, took about with them the heroic lays and made them popular. But it was not in the fairs that the heroic poets learned their manners. Their temper is not that of the common people. The kings and warriors of their poems are not the vague magnificences of fairy tales ; they are personages drawn from the life, by authors who understood their way of living and thinking. Heroic poetry, which has no scruples about the truth of historical events, is never far from truth in regard to fashions, behaviour, and sentiment. The manners that it represents are courteous and noble.

It is disputed whether the epic verse of *Beowulf* was meant for singing. But the question rather *Narrative* loses its point when the modern distinc-*verse.* tion between singing and recitation is discovered to have been marvellously uncertain in the Middle Ages, and later. The epic of Tasso is known to have been a song in Venice ; and a Spanish writer

---

[1] *Vita Liudgeri*, Mon. Germ., Scr. ii. p. 402.

[2] " Of all the bards this country ever produced, the last and the greatest was Carolan the Blind. He was at once a poet, a musician, a composer, and sung his own verses to his harp. The original natives never mention his name without rapture ; both his poetry and music they have by heart ; and even some of the English them-selves who have been transplanted there, find his music extremely pleasing " (Goldsmith, *Essay* xx).

on music in the sixteenth century gives the tune belonging to a favourite didactic poem of Juan de Mena, which in print looks tame enough and scarcely chantable. Though *Beowulf* were sung, it would be none the less a narrative poem, and the verse of it is not lyrical. The verse is continuous, not in stanzas; it is recitative verse, fit for narrative. The invention of narrative verse, such as will carry on a long story, is one of the great distinctions that mark the appearance of true epic, and that give to epic its proper nature, unlike the lyrical ballad or the choral hymn, though these of course may have much in common with epic, much history and adventure mingled in their argument. The creation of epic verse was one of the achievements of the Dark Ages, in Teutonic and in French poetry.

Besides the fairly well established types of *Beowulf* and *Roland*, forms in which epic poetry may be said to have culminated in England and France, there are other early kinds of literature with much of the character of epic, narrative literature with much of the epic spirit in it, the presentation of life in an heroic age, yet without the complete poetic form, without the epic verse. Epic in prose is authorised by Sidney, Tasso, Cervantes, and M. de Scudéry (not to speak of Fielding), and the ideal which is described with so much enthusiasm and eloquence by the Canon in *Don Quixote* was already realised in the Middle Ages in the Icelandic prose histories of Grettir, Gisli, and Njal. These come later than our time and are described in the next volume of this series, but the Dark Ages in our restricted sense may claim another order of heroic prose in Ireland; the old Irish tales, mythical and fantastic as many of them are, include also the more human motives of epic; the meeting of Cuchulinn and his son Conlaoch corresponds to the German story of Hildebrand; and the stand made by the sons of Usnech against the treachery of Conchobar is told with the same sort of epic interest, the same tragic heroism, as the death of Roland or of Grettir the Strong.[1]

It is not perhaps of much importance for the history of epic, yet it can hardly be ignored, that *Homeric manners.* there are certain commonplaces of actual life which reappear in the heroic litera-ture of different countries and make a kind of prosaic stuff for the poetic imagination to work upon. Epic requires a particular kind of warfare, not too highly organised, and the manner of the Homeric battle is found again in Germany, Ireland, and old France. The fighters are bound by loyalty to their chieftains; their lords are their patrons and entertainers who have given them gifts. When the time comes they may have to be reminded of their obligations, and one of the constantly recurring pass-ages in epic is the appeal to memory of benefits received. The captain reminds his host, or one of the elder men reminds his associates, of the bygone feasting in hall when the horn went round and the

---

[1] For analogies between the Irish and the Greek heroic ages, see D'Arbois de Jubainville, *La civilisation des Celtes et celle de l'époque homérique* (*Cours de littérature celtique*, Tome vi.)

professions of bravery along with it.   So it is said
at the battle of Maldon, "Remember now our speeches
that we spake at the drinking of mead, when we sat
boasting, heroes in hall, of the stress of conflict; and
now it is come to the proof."

So Wiglaf in *Beowulf* speaks to his companions
when they refuse to follow their king in his last
enterprise :—

"I remember how we promised our lord at the
feast in hall when he gave us rings, that we would
make him requital for the armour he gave us, rings
and good swords, if need should befall, as now it
has fallen."

It is the old Homeric appeal: "Argives, whither
have sped the boastings that ye boasted emptily in
Lemnos, eating the flesh of kine in plenty, and drinking wine in the brim-full cups, when each was a match
for a hundred Trojans " (*Il.*, viii. 228).   The reproach
of Agamemnon to Menestheus and Odysseus—"You
were the first at the call to my feast" (iv. 343)—is
repeated in the king's address to his men in the
Northern poem of *Hlod and Angantyr*.[1]   "We were
many at the mead and now we are few: I see no
man in my company, for all my bidding or the
rings I have given him, that will ride to meet the
Huns." [2]

[1] *Corpus Poeticum Boreale*, i. 351.

[2] "Fulfil now the big words that ye have uttered in the drinking-
houses" (*Battle of Ventry*, tr. Kuno Meyer, p. 15).   Compare also
the Spanish ballad—

> " Aqui, aqui, los mis doscientos,
>   los que comedes mi pan."

The moral of it is given in Saxo Grammaticus in his Latin poem on the death of Rolf:—

"Omnia quæ poti temulento prompsimus ore
Fortibus edamus animis."

Which may be reckoned along with the war-song of Dinas Vawr, as giving, if not the quintessence of epic poetry, at least half the substance of the life on which it draws.

There is reality behind the epic representation, as might be proved in countless ways. The sudden murderous anger in which Patroclus killed the son of Amphidamas at a game of knucklebones, "witless not willing it,"—νήπιος οὐκ ἐθέλων ἀμφ' ἀστραγάλοισι χολωθείς,—is one of the motives in *The Four Sons of Aymon*, and, historically, in the fatal quarrel at chess between Canute and Earl Wolf his brother-in-law. The gibes of combatants in the *Iliad* might be illustrated by many unseemly passages in Icelandic poetry and prose, or from the Latin epic of *Waltharius*, which probably represents a German original. The likenesses between the entertainment of Ulysses in Phæacia and Beowulf in the house of the Danish king have often been remarked and commented on, and still remain wonderful.

These things belong to the matter of epic, and not properly to the poetry. It is not always easy to keep the two aspects distinct. The point of view *The Audience.* is given to the poet by the traditions of the society in which he lives, by what may be called the heroic convention, so that his heroic facts are treated

in a certain obligatory heroic way; his subject-
matter is not purely material; it has been idealised
more or less before he takes it in hand. Epic poetry,
heroic literature generally, implies not merely certain
favourite themes—combats, battles, killing of monsters,
escapes, and defences—but a diffused sympathy for
the heroic mood among the people for whom the epic
is made. We may suppose that where the epic poem
flourishes there is, among the contemporary people
who are not poetical, something like the epic frame
of mind, a rudimentary heroic imagination which
already gives to mere historical events and situations
a glimmering of their epic magnificence. The "multitude" in an heroic age interprets life heroically; and
it is this common vague sentiment of heroism, not
any bare uncoloured unaccommodated thing in itself,
with which the epic poets make their beginning.
Their real life is heroic, because it seems so, both to
them and to their unpoetic fellows and hearers.

If the battle of Maldon becomes Homeric in the
old English poem, it is partly through a traditional
common mode of sentiment and imagination, in virtue
of which an action such as this of Byrhtnoth's,
courageous and admirable enough in itself from any
point of view, is naturally and instinctively put into
an epic frame, and looked at, not as an incident in
the political confusion of Ethelred the Unready, but
as something individual, distinct, apart from all
political complications, for the time being the most
important thing in the world, all-absorbing. How
different the actual history of the Wandering of the

Nations is from the epic poetry of the Germans, how different Theodoric is in Cassiodorus or Charles in Einhard from the epic Theodoric or Charlemagne, is plain to every one. But it is certain that the actual world, so infinitely more complex than the world of heroic poetry, was nevertheless occupied in the Dark Ages with the heroic ideal. Neither Popes nor Emperors nor educational reformers nor improvements in the art of war were able to obscure the heroic view of life. For the purposes of poetry there was retained a kind of archaic simplicity of politics which did not allow the heroes to become too much involved in affairs, which let them stand out, self-reliant and distinct, as heroes of epic should. Similarly the fashions of war, which in the actual world were not purely Homeric, were by common consent, in poetry and story-telling, allowed to keep their old rules; room is left to see how the several champions demean themselves. Also, as if by a kind of instinctive perception that large warfare was too difficult or too complex and abstract for poetry, the epic turns by preference to adventures where the hero is isolated or left with a small company, where he is surprised and assailed in a house by night, as at Finnesburh, or where he meets his enemies in a journey and has to put his back to a rock, like Walter of Aquitaine. The adventures of Robert the Bruce at the ford of the river, and in the deserted house with the three robbers, and elsewhere, are of the kind which the epic tastes of many different nations found convenient for the heroic poet. It is part of the history of mediæval epic that there was this popular sympathy for the right kind of adventure and the right heroic temper, an expectation and appreciation of certain favourite themes; while it was at the courts of great men like those which the poets described that the definite poetic fashions, the proper poetic style and diction, were elaborated.

V.

There are certain common forms of instruction and literary entertainment which have a large influence on the culture of the Middle Ages and may be shortly described in this place; chiefly the *Dialogue* and the *Riddle*.

Commonplaces and common forms.

The Dialogue is used for two educational purposes: as a convenient mode of breaking up and explaining matters of science, and again as a device for exhibiting rhetoric. Both are combined in some of the most popular dialogues: the dialogue becomes a tradition, generally under certain favourite names (*e.g.*, Adrian and Epictetus), admitting a variety of answers to certain common questions. Sometimes the answer gives a fact for information, more frequently a rhetorical amplification of the topic suggested in the query. Alcuin's dialogue with Pippin[1] affords a good example of the game. It is in two parts. In the first, Alcuin (Albinus) supplies poetical para-

The Dialogue.

---

[1] Disputatio regalis et nobilissimi juvenis Pippini cum Albino scholastico. See Wilmanns in *Zeitschrift für deutsches Alterthum,* xiv. 530 *sqq.*

phrases for certain terms—"quid est lingua? Flagellum aeris: quid est aer? Custodia vitæ," &c. In the second Alcuin propounds certain allegorical riddles and his pupil finds the answer—*e.g., Arrow* is thus disguised: "a woman flying with a face of iron, a body of wood, and a feathery tail; bearing death." To which Pippin answers, indirectly, "She is the companion of soldiers." Another is the villainous Riddle of the Fishermen (" What we caught not, we carry with us "), which did not cause the death of Homer, as his fabling biographer asserts.[1] The dialogue thus supplied two common rhetorical wants. It was a sort of rhetorical catechism, or a dictionary of poetical synonyms and periphrases,—varieties of *kenning,* to use the convenient and intelligible Norse name. It might also be the frame of a collection of riddles, which were a favourite exercise for fancy and rhetorical skill combined. The *kenning* and the riddle were two forms of the same thing; the riddle a more fully developed paraphrase of the simple idea. The dialogue, besides, might easily become a debate— *altercatio Hadriani Augusti et Epicteti philosophi*—a *disputison,* to use the favourite English term, a contention, a *jeu parti,* with a wager depending on the result, as in the Northern dialogue where Odin and the Giant debate on Cosmogony or the creation of the world, with their lives at stake. There are some rather strange varieties of dialogue in the Middle Ages; the personages introduced are not always

---

[1] "I cannot think that Homer pined away upon the Riddle of the Fishermen" (*Religio Medici,* ii. 8).

simply the master and pupil, an abstract pair. Some noble names are employed in this service and undergo changes of reputation: Epictetus in one set, and Solomon in another, are the chief of them. Epictetus becomes Childe Ypotis, in a poem[1] which we have Chaucer's leave to call a romance.

> " A chyld was sent of myghtes most
> Thorow vertu of the Holy Gost
> Unto the emperour of Rome,
> A nobull man and wyse of dome :
> The emperour of Rome than
> Men called hym Syr Adrian."

The dialogue of Ypotis does not vary greatly from the common type: most of it is doctrinal, describing the seven heavens, the nine angelic orders, the thirteen reasons for fasting on Friday; but there are some relics of the other kind of answer which paraphrases poetically and does not give any information about facts. Sir Adrian asks, " What is the sea ? "

Ypotis.

> " The chylde sayde wythout lesyng :
> A wylde way of wendynge,
> For such way thou myghtt take therinne
> That thou shalt never to Gude wynne."

But the matter of dialogue is comparatively unimportant: the person of Ypotis is everything in this new version. By no interpretation at the hands of the great doctors and schoolmen, but through an obscure and gradual change in tradition, Epictetus

---

[1] Ed. Horstmann, *Altenglische Legenden*, neue Folge, 1881.

of the dialogue became transfigured, and when the Emperor at the end asks Childe Ypotis whether he be wicked angel or good, the answer is—

> " I am he that the wroughth
> And on the Rode the dere bowghth."

Solomon, on the other hand, obtains little increase of honour in the process of tradition, except that *Solomon and Marcolf.* he is kept in remembrance. In the Anglo-Saxon dialogues[1] he is still invincible in knowledge, and Saturn the other speaker is a gentle opponent; in one of the two disputations he is even a humble inquirer, coming to Solomon to learn the nature of the Paternoster, which is explained to him in a mythological and figurative way. But later Solomon fell from this dignity, when Marcolf[2] took the place of Saturn. Marcolf is mentioned by Notker of St Gall in the eleventh century as an example of vain fables: he contended with the proverbs of Solomon. This was the part he took in the popular literature of many countries, as a representative of the cynical and irreverent wit which parodies every solemn sentence of the wise man, and finds either an exception or a ludicrous illus-

---

[1] *The Dialogue of Salomon and Saturnus*, edited by Kemble for the Ælfric Society (1848); with an elaborate study of the whole subject, and many specimens of similar dialogues. The fortunes of *Solomon in Europe* have been admirably told by Professor MacCallum, of Sydney, in his *Studies in Low German and High German Literature*, 1884.

[2] *Marculfes eard*, Marculf's land, is mentioned in the older Anglo-Saxon poem as one of the places visited by Saturn, but no further reference is made to the name.

tration for every one of his proverbs. Marcolf has
another function in the romance of *Salman und Morolf,*
where he is the squire and helper of the wise king,
and both of them are foiled by the subtilties of
Solomon's faithless queen. That however does not
belong to the Dialogue, though it is part of the
mythology of the Middle Ages, another of the trans-
formations which seem to have been carried out as
effectively in the later mediæval centuries as in the
times of heathenism.

The form of dialogue was not allowed to go out
of use. Among the most popular books of the fourteenth century are the French *Sidrac* and *Placides et
Timeo,*[1] which went abroad to other nations just as
Adrian and *Epictetus* had done long before them.

The Riddle was much employed in different ways,
besides its appearance in the dialogues. It has a
The Riddle. vogue independent of literary fashions; it
adapts itself to any taste. The essence
of it is that it should be an allegory of some sort.
The answer to it—that is to say, the theme of the
piece—is a simple idea: a cherry, a star, the letter H.
Swift was fond of this game, and so was Hamlet (in
Saxo Grammaticus).

> "I see to me, I see from me,
>   Two miles and ten over the sea,
>   The man of the green coatie,
>   And his shirt sewn with a thread of red."

---

[1] Described by Renan and Gaston Paris in the *Histoire littéraire
de la France,* xxx. and xxxi.

That is the rainbow, in Campbell's *West Highland Tales*, where there are many more of the same sort. This translation of ideas is peculiarly fitted for literary exercises: it requires neatness, point, liveliness; it does not call for the heavier forces of literature. Hence it is not surprising that enigmas of this sort, with nothing altered in their methods of fancy, should adapt themselves to all changes of literary expression. There is nothing to choose between the riddles of Aldhelm and of Swift, as far as the matter goes. The procedure is exactly the same, only the language and the forms of verse are different. The riddles that Odin put to King Heidrek in the old Norse poem have their own poetical quality, a distinct character, but the method is the common one :—

"Who are the brides that walk over the reefs, and drive along the friths? These white-hooded ladies have a hard bed : in calm weather they make no stir." (*The waves.*)[1]

Along with fancies like these go popular jests like the analysis of the cow :—

"Four ganging, four hanging, two showing the way, two keeping the dogs off, one ever dirty lags behind;"[2]—

A piece of the wisdom of Odin which is still remembered in Shetland, in the old language.[3]

Every age and country has its own variety of Riddle

[1] *C. P. B.*, i. p. 90. [2] *Ibid.*, p. 91.
[3] Jakobsen, *Det norröne Sprog paa Shetland*, 1897, p. 17.

poem. Meister Trougemunt in the German ballads[1]
answers the English and Scottish questions—

> "O what is longer than the way?
> *Gar lay the bent to the bonny broom,*
> And what is colder than the clay?"[2]

Poetical riddles were produced in England more
largely than anywhere else in the Dark Ages, both in
Latin and the native tongue. Following the example
of the riddles which pass under the name of Symphosius,[3] a number of English scholars—Aldhelm,
Tatwine, Boniface, Alcuin—diverted themselves with
the composition of short Latin poems of this kind.
Pretty early in the history of English poetry the
vernacular language was applied to the same purpose;
with a surprising difference in literary effect, and no
change at all in the general principles regarding the
matter of the poems. The difference is that the old
English poetical fashions are much more favourable to
this kind of entertainment than anything in Latin.
It is the proper business, one might say, of the old
English poetry to call things out of their right names.
Fanciful disguises of simple ideas may be practised
anywhere, by all the children of the world; but nowhere had this game so much opportunity of develop-

---

[1] Uhland, *Deutsche Volkslieder*, i. 1 ; Müllenhoff and Scherer,
Denkmäler, No. xlviii.

[2] Child, *Ballads*, No. 1, where references are given to similar things
in different languages.

[3] Ed. Riese, *Anthologia Latina ;* Baehrens, *Poetæ Latini Minores,*
v. 364 *sqq.*

ing into showy literature as in England at that time. It was partly, no doubt, the English taste for rhetorical efflorescence that led Aldhelm and Alcuin to their Latin riddles. When English was used for a like purpose, the native verse proved itself infinitely more lively than Latin. Artifice took on a more natural and spontaneous air in the Anglo-Saxon poems of this order: the task was well fitted for the genius of the poetry. In some of the riddles the miracle takes place which is not unknown in literary history elsewhere: what seems at first the most conventional of devices is found to be a fresh channel of poetry. Many of these quaint poems, taking their start from a simple idea, a single term, expatiate, without naming it, over all the life of their theme, and the riddle, instead of an occasion for intricate paraphrase, becomes a subject of imaginative thought. The poets of the riddles are not content with mere brocading work, though they like that well enough: but, besides, they meditate on their subject, they keep their eye on it.[1] The riddle becomes a shifting vision of all the different aspects in which the creature may be found—a quick, clear-sighted, interested poem. Though it is only a game, it carries the poetic mind out over the world: as not unfrequently with the Metaphysical poets, the search for new conceits will land the artist on a coast beyond his clever artifices, where instead

[1] For the imaginative quality of the poetical riddles, especially of English as compared with Latin, see MacCallum, *Anglo-Saxon Jocoseria*, in the volume of *Studies in German Literature*, cited above.

of the vanities of False Wit there are the truths
of imagination :—

"Like golden lamps in a green night."

Among the diversions of mediæval learning few
are more popular than the moral history of birds
and beasts and precious stones.   The chief
The Bestiary. work of this description is known generally
as *Physiologus;* otherwise the Bestiary.   It spread as
far as the stories of Alexander and the jests of Marcolf; its methods, far from outworn in the Middle
Ages, reappeared in the book which expresses, best of
all, the commonplaces of the Renaissance—*Euphues,
the Anatomy of Wit.*   The moral interpretation of
the lion, the eagle, the ant, the spider, &c., which
agreed so well with mediæval tastes, was continued
by *Euphues*, and proved to be almost too attractive
a novelty, though it was as old as the language itself
and had been repeated for centuries unsparingly.
The original *Physiologus* was most probably compiled in Egypt:[1] the animals of the first collection
are Egyptian.   Later versions show, through words
strangely corrupted, how the creatures themselves
have been transformed: thus the whale by its name
Fastitocalon, in the Anglo-Saxon poem, proves its
identity with the original sea-turtle, the *aspidoche-
lone*, whose broad back is mistaken for an island
and turned to a convenient and successful allegory,

---

[1] See *Physiologus* in the *Encyclopedia Britannica*, by Dr Land of
Leyden.

though the whale, later, usurped the turtle's claim. Other treatises in like manner expounded the virtues of precious stones, and in like manner were translated and circulated everywhere.[1] The old Italian poem *L'Intelligenza*, attributed to Dino Compagni, includes an allegorical *Lapidary* along with the adventures of Julius Cæsar and other themes of romance. These tastes and habits of the Dark Ages were as fresh as ever in the time of Dante.

[1] Cf. *Les Lapidaires français du moyen âge*, ed. L. Pannier, 1882.

CHAPTER III.

LATIN AUTHORS.

IT is impossible in this space to give even a bare catalogue of the Latin works written in the Dark Ages. What is attempted here is a review of the more interesting writers, with reference to their value either as representatives of their time, or as models for those who came after, or simply as writers of things worth reading for their own sake. Of these latter there are more than is commonly supposed; but generally it must be allowed there is need for some sense of duty, some unliterary, historical or scientific, motive, to carry the student through.

Taking the prose authors first, it is fairly easy to classify their works as far as their matter is con-
Latin Prose Science. cerned, and as most of them are occupied with instruction, this kind of division is a natural one. One group is formed of the treatises that explain the sciences, from the encyclopedic works of Cassiodorus and Isidore to short essays like that of Bede on the rules of Verse. Along with those technical writings may be included, for the sake of their matter, philosophical authors as different in their method as Boethius and Erigena. The large body of exposition and interpretation, the work of Gregory the Great, Alcuin, Hraban, Walafrid Strabo, and many more, is closely related to the more abstract scientific or philosophical books; though of course the expositors have to follow a different method in their commentaries from that required in dealing with general principles; they have to follow their texts from point to point.

History might conveniently be left separate from the common educational stock, from the books con-
History. cerned with the liberal arts, with philosophy or theology. History, "immersed in matter," gave the writers of the Dark Ages a chance of describing real things, and also of using imagination. The historians who have to do with action and life, in adventures and dialogues, belong to a different class from the purely didactic authors. Of course, there are many who, like Bede, are en-

gaged in all the kinds, history as well as science and divinity.

Romance is not wholly wanting in Latin prose;

Romance. besides the Apollonius of Tyre and Alexander the Great, there are the various legends already spoken of above, and a great quantity besides.

Oratory may be represented by all the homilies. Letter-writing in the Dark Ages belongs to literature,

Oratory and Letters. and there is a large amount of it of different sorts: the show pieces of Cassiodorus in his office of Quæstor, the correspondence of Alcuin and other scholars of the circle of Charles the Great, of Hraban and Lupus of Ferrières, of Rather of Verona, of Gerbert.

Latin verse is less easy to classify, even roughly: division according to subject-matter is reasonable in

Latin Verse. the history of prose, because in prose the matter generally determines the form; but it is less relevant in verse. And in mediæval Latin verse the forms are confused; the old-fashioned classifications fail. The great distinction is that of Bede, between "metrical" and "rhythmical"—*i.e.*, between the verse that intends to follow classical precedent and that which pays no regard to quantity, or rather makes new principles of its own. But although the unclassical Latin verse may form a species by itself with various distinct types included in it, the opposite kind, the verse of the classical tradition, is not classical enough for a comfortable and summary description. There is too much mixture in it; the pedigree is seldom clear.

Many of the poems that profess to observe classical measures are Goths and Vandals in clothes that do not fit them, barbarians trying on things they do not understand, conceited and not sober. But it is possible to select the more reputable examples. These taken by themselves do form a distinct order; the Latin court poetry of which Fortunatus in the sixth century and Theodulfus in the time of Charles the Great are the chief masters. This complimentary rhetorical verse, though it may be heavy stuff compared with the freedom of Latin rhymes or Teutonic lays, is of an honourable descent and has some right to its lofty demeanour. It continues the school of Claudian and Ausonius: it has not all their virtue, though it has most of the defects of its ancestry—the limitation of range which had been the impediment of Latin poetry from the first, the dependent spirit which had accompanied all the poetry of the Empire. Still, it is not to be passed without respect; it had high principles in literature, and more liveliness than might be expected from a creature so full of literary responsibility.

Leaving the division into orders, and turning to the succession of periods, one finds this unsatisfactory *Periods—the seventh century is the Dark Age.* business made easy by the plain fact that there is a vacancy in the seventh century, with little besides the encyclopedias of Isidore and the rhetoric of Aldhelm to fill the gap till the appearance of Bede in a new generation. Thus the sixth century defines itself against the greater darkness of the seventh, throwing into relief the personages of Boethius, Cassiodorus, Gregory of Tours, Fortunatus, Gregory the Great.   At the end of the seventh century Bede comes out to show what traditions of learning had been quietly preserved in Ireland and Britain.   With Alcuin, a century later still, the work of Bede is continued.   The revival of learning under Charles the Great is a means of diffusing widely what Bede had begun.   In the ninth century new schools take up the succession, Fulda especially, then St Gall; new contributions came from the old Irish sources, the scholarship of Sedulius Scottus, the philosophy of Erigena: new forms of verse are invented, the *Sequentiæ* and their kindred.   But there is after that no distinct epoch in Latin literature before the rise of the scholastic philosophy under Anselm and Abelard.

The result of this summary view is that the sixth century is marked off pretty distinctly as a period by itself; and that what follows after Isidore and Bede, though divisible into periods for the sake of convenience, is not broken by any notable revolution, or by any general failure, like that of the seventh century.

The sixth century is well represented by the writers who lived in it.   None of its ideas or moods are left *The sixth century.* unrecorded, except perhaps the barbarian ideas that have come down to us rather scantily clad in the decent raiment of literature.   Even these, however, can be discovered, and putting these aside, there is no want of variety and fulness in the provision of books of different kinds.   Almost everything that is common to the Middle Ages, and much that lasts beyond the Renaissance, is to be found in the authors of the sixth century. Boethius is the interpreter of the ancient world and its wisdom, accepted by all the tribes of Europe from one age to another, and never disqualified in his office of teacher even by the most subtle and elaborate theories of the later schools. His authority is not impaired either by Erigena or by St Thomas Aquinas, and his influence goes beyond the schools to touch the minds of visionary poets; it is felt in the *Romaunt of the Rose* and in the *Vita Nuova.* Cassiodorus is wanting in the graces of Boethius, and he is much sooner forgotten; but his enormous industry, his organisation of literary production, his educational zeal, have all left their effects indelibly in modern civilisation. By his definition of the seven Liberal Arts, and by his examples of method in teaching them, he is the spiritual author of the Universities, the patron of all the available learning in the world. His own remarkable taste in decorated composition is also part of the age, signifi cant not of anything precisely new in style, but of the increasing strength of that kind of rhetoric. The poet Venantius Fortunatus of Poitiers represents the old classical schools in their decline: following Ausonius, Claudian, and Sidonius in complimentary and conventional verse, with a growing tendency to use barbarous and senseless ornament, and also a gift of occasional sincerity, and another of a very different kind in virtue of which he escapes altogether from the routine of the old poetical grammar into a new region of poetry. *Vexilla Regis prodeunt* and *Pange lingua gloriosi* are hymns of Fortunatus, to be honoured among the ancestors of modern verse. His friend Gregory of Tours is one of the first mediæval chroniclers, ill provided with a language, and compelled to use a common kind of Latin, like many other good historians later, for want of a sound vernacular; yet in spite of these hindrances proving himself by his quickness and his love of stories to be of the same spirit with Joinville or Froissart. There are other historians in that century, such as Jordanes among the Goths and Gildas in Britain, but Gregory of Tours has more than they of the interests and the manners that were to prevail in the Middle Ages.

In literary history, the close of the sixth century may be said to belong to St Gregory the Great, in the same way as the beginning of it is ruled by Boethius. It is a different world ; except through the report of Boethius there is no way back into the quiet resting-places of the old Greek philosophy; worldly scholarship is discouraged; in its place there are the lives of hermits, the allegorical method of interpreting Scripture, and the voice of a stern schoolmaster preaching duty, like one who understands what it means and is not concerned to make it easier.   It is a serious change; yet the greatness of St Gregory, even in the fields of literature which he despised, is hardly less certain than the importance of his studies and his teaching for subsequent times.   To command is easy with him, and with all his scorn for rhetoric he makes his language obey his will.   Without philosophy, without science, with no imagination, he leaves in his writings the impression of vast intellectual power—a great engine groaning, thundering, shaking its own framework—and he was accepted by Christendom as a teacher. His spirit was transfused into countless homilies and became part of the common-sense of the world in religious matters: his expositions of Scripture did more than anything to establish the allegorical mode of interpretation for a thousand years.

The *Consolation of Philosophy* has a rank in mediæval literature such as few books in any age have possessed.

Boethius. It belongs to the secondary order, the books that have something less than original genius of invention, the books that are dependent on others, that are reflective, not imaginative nor creative, that are informed by the softer conciliatory graces of the minds for whom obedience, appreciation, interpretation, are the appointed tasks, rather than any original work in poetry or philosophy. It is what Blake might have called an " angelic " work, in the sense the word bears in his *Marriage of Heaven and Hell*. One is naturally led to think of that *Marriage*, that rivalry of the two great forces of Will and of Law, in thinking of the contrast between the Barbarian and the Latin elements in the Dark Ages, and it is hardly possible to mistake the character of Boethius in that part of history, as before and above all other writers the preacher of Obedience in its most ideal form ; the apostle of a worship in which there is nothing local or provincial, the servant of the Universe and of the Light that kindles it, of "the Love that moves the Sun and the other stars." There is no one to be compared with his influence. It runs all through the Middle Ages, distinct from that of all the Doctors of the Church, though acknowledged and honoured by them; a strain of philosophy that would not strive nor cry, a gentle ghost whose presence is recognised in its effect on many minds, persuading them to think wisely about the old commonplaces of Death and Time. It is a spirit of freedom and of courage, unlike the freedom and courage of the Northern fighting temper, and not wholly Christian either, not Christian at all in any confessed or open manner; but as indomitable in its own way as the Northern gods, and as quiet as the first of the Christian martyrs. Boethius in his prison meditations has repeated the lessons and the temper of the *Phœdo* and the *Apology*, and his great work was to give to the Western world a sermon that answered the questions of Christendom in the spirit of Plato. Being admirably clear, and almost as free from technical philosophy as from theological dogma, the *Consolation* was accepted everywhere on its own merits. It was not Christian enough to be heretical, and it had not the pretensions of the philosophical sects; it aroused no jealousies in the Schools.

Boethius was fortunate in the time of his life and death, and in the choice of his theme. No other writer commands so much of the past and future. Between the worlds of ancient Greece and modern

Europe, he understands not merely their points of
The Consola- contact, the immediate and contemporary
tion of turmoil of Germany and Rome; he re-
Philosophy. members the early thoughts of Greece, long
before the Stoic and Epicurean professors whom he
disliked, and he finds the response to his signals not
in the near future only but far off in the distant
centuries: it is commonplace, no doubt, but of a
sort that finds its way into some of the noblest
passages in literature. Boethius is remembered and
his words are quoted by Dante in the meeting with
Francesca, and again in the concluding phrase of
the *Paradiso;* it is a small thing in comparison with
this honour that Dante should have modelled his
Convito, a philosophical treatise, on the *Consolation
of Philosophy.* Boethius has been traced in English
literature from *Beowulf* to *Hamlet* and *Lycidas.* "The
last infirmity of noble mind" is a quotation, and Hamlet is thought to have had in his tablets, somewhere,
Adeo nihil est miserum nisi cum putes. The list of
translators, including King Alfred, Notker the German,
Jean de Meun, Chaucer, and Queen Elizabeth, with
many more, gives no complete account of his influence,
though it proves sufficiently that Boethius was secure
against all changes of taste. Perhaps if one were to
choose any single piece of evidence to show what his
reputation was, it would be a passage quoted from
the letters of Ser Lapo Mazzei, a Florentine notary
of the end of the fourteenth century : Ser Lapo speaks
of the *Consolation* as a work of "highest philosophy,"
though "to-day simple people hold it cheap, because

it is a common book for the youngest pupils in our
schools."[1]   The reason of his popularity and the distinguishing quality of his work is that he saw what
was essential and rejected what was technical and
accidental, in this his latest book.   In his other
writings he had laboured in another way, as his
old biographers tell.[2]

The works of Boethius in Logic, Music, and the other
arts belong to the common educational business of the
time.   The dissertation *De Sancta Trinitate*, not to
speak of the other theological writings attributed to
Boethius, is equally professional.   But the *Consolation
of Philosophy*, written in the prison at Pavia, is free
from all the restrictions of system and school methods.
Its want of Christianity has perplexed the more recent

---

[1] "Oggi da' semplici accetto per vile perchè si legge a corso in ogni
scuola ai più giovani" (A. D'Ancona, *Varietà storiche e letterarie*, serie
seconda, p. 202).   Mazzei read the Gospels, the Epistles of St Paul and
St Jerome, and "el bel libretto di frate Jacopo da Todi."   What use
he made of his Boethius and other moral teachers may be seen in the
following sentence, too good to be left out, against the temptation of
playing at Providence : "Compare, non vogliate voi esser quegli che
voglia racconciare il mondo ; ma lasciate audare il mondo come Dio
l'ordinò, e ciò è che la ruota volgesse sempre; e attendete a governare
voi, e le cose che Dio v'ha prestate.   La cosa va pur così ; andate
colla voga."

[2] Multos libros de græco in latinum transtulit.   Fecit commentum
super ysagogas .i. introductiones Aristotelis.   Edidit et aliud super
Porphyrii periermenias .i. interpretationes quod divisit in duo volu-
mina.   Quorum alterum analitica .i. resolutoria appellavit ubi omnes
syllogismi rethoricæ artis resolvuntur.   Composuit musicam quam
transtulit de Pithagora et Ptolomeo græcis nec non etiam arithmeti-
cam cujus partes sumpsit de Nicomacho.   Fecit et alios libros
perplures.

commentators, but not those who called Boethius their master. The whole plan of the book excluded everything that was formal, and the disuse of Christian terms is hardly more surprising than the omission of Aristotle. The great Aristotelian interpreter was not here engaged in strict philosophical discussion.

Boethius in the *Consolation* writes as if he had foreseen the distress that was to come from technicalities

The Platonic and from the " vermiculate questions " of
tradition. the schoolmen, as if he had known in his
own mind the weariness of systematic philosophy and theology which was to be felt so keenly and expressed so strongly by More and Erasmus. He is led instinctively, while waiting for the summons of the executioner, to look for the point of view from which the most important things are made manifest. There was no time for elaborate work in details. His purpose was to explain as well as he could in short space the philosophical ideas that were of greatest moment as a preparation for death. The book is not philosophy but consolation. It is popular, it is meant for the weaker brethren. The beauty of it, which lifts it far above the ordinary run of reflections on mortality, is that it restores a Platonic tradition, or even something older and simpler in Greek philosophy, at a time when simplicity and clearness of thought were about to be overwhelmed in the mediæval confusion. Boethius saved the thought of the Middle Ages. His protection was always to be

had by any one who found the divisions and distinctions of the schools too much for him. In the *Consolation of Philosophy* there was a place of outlook from which the less valuable matters sank back to their proper place, and the real outlines of the world were brought into view.

Boethius went back to Plato because he required more metaphysical aid for his moral theory than he could find in the *Nicomachean Ethics,* and much less of the details of the practical life. He was not concerned with ordinary right conduct; he was a seeker after a vision by which the moral nature should be regenerate, when the goodness of man should be shown to be none other than that which maintains the universe, and preserves the stars from wrong.

The end of man is to see that there is nothing in the world that is not divine—nothing absurd, nothing unintelligible, nothing merely natural. Plato had said in the *Timæus:* "There are two kinds of causes, the Divine and the Necessary, and we must seek for the Divine in all things, and the Necessary for the sake of the Divine." The "necessary" here means what is mechanical or natural—the "second causes" of later popular philosophy. This is the doctrine taken up and expounded in the *Consolation,* and on this everything depends. Faith or vision—it matters little what it is called—is with Boethius the chief end; from that comes all the rest; the man who has that is unassailable. Morality thus depends on intelligence, on contemplation; the deadliest error is to misinterpret the

world by means of second causes, corruptible fragmentary things :—

> "For nature hath nat take hir beginning
> Of no partye ne cantel of a thing
> But of a thing that parfit is and stable
> Descending so til it be corrumpable."[1]

Chaucer has here put into verse the central doctrine of Boethius, which in prose runs thus :—

> "For the nature of thinges ne took nat hir beginninge of
> thinges amenused and inpartit, but it procedeth of thinges that
> ben al hoole and absolut."[2]

The fragmentary life of this world is a fragment of
what is "whole and absolute"; that which is perfect
gives the meaning of that which is fragmentary. The
beginning of wisdom is to be discontented with second
causes, to look for the vantage-ground from which
they shall be seen in their due relations. Man has
not fulfilled his course until he is taken up into the
mind of God, until in his theoretic knowledge he sees
with the clear vision of one to whom nothing is alien,
and in his practical life has blended his separate being
with the movement of the whole world :—

> "In this one thing all the discipline
> Of manners and of manhood is contain'd,
> A man to join himself with the Universe
> In his main sway, and make, in all things fit,
> One with that All, and go on, round as it."[3]

---

[1] *Knight's Tale*, l. 2149 *sqq.*   [2] *Cons. Phil.*, iii. 10.
[3] G. Chapman, *Bussy D'Ambois, his Revenge.*

How little satisfactory this kind of doctrine often is to the professed philosopher may be readily understood ; how easily it may be misapplied by the professional moralist is likewise obvious. But the happy fortune of Boethius was that his teaching was taken up by the poets. The *Divine Comedy* might be considered as an imaginative fugue on a philosophical theme from Boethius. It was also taken by the philosophers themselves in the right way. There can be little question that Boethius, more than any other philosophic author, helped the great Schoolmen to retain a general comprehensive view of the world as a whole, in spite of the distractions of their minute inquiries. Spinoza often looks as if he were following the commonplaces of Boethius, deepening and distinguishing and making complex what seemed easy and plain, yet without detriment to the main ideas of Boethius.

The *Consolation* is reckoned as a specimen of " Varronian Satire " by the authority of Casaubon, and the old biographies hold that Boethius imitated Martianus Capella. These opinions need not be disputed. The composite structure of prose and verse, and the allegorical mode of presentment, were already well established when Boethius wrote. The vision of a divine interpreter or guide, so full of significance for the later history of literature, may be carried back to the *Dream of Scipio ;* the allegory is found in Fulgentius in a form even nearer to the common mediæval device of the May Morning and the Dream. But it is in Boethius above the rest that some most notable later works acknowledge their patron—especially the *Convito* of Dante.

Philosophy appears to Boethius in the prison as a lady of reverend aspect in fine raiment, overshadowed, *Allegory.* like images that have stood in the smoke, with a hue of antiquity—*quarum speciem, veluti fumosas imagines solet, caligo quœdam neglectœ vetustatis obduxerat.* On the lower hem was a Greek Π (for the practical life), from which there were ladders rising up to another letter, Θ (for the theoretic); and it was seen that the vesture had been rent here and there; violent hands had torn tatters from it. In her right hand were books, in her left a sceptre. Philosophy drove away the Muses whom she found with Boethius, calling them Sirens and *scenicas meretriculas.* There are some things in the description that belong to the more grievous kind of allegory, such as Philosophy's varying stature, which at times appeared to rise above the heaven. But allegory was seldom safe from this kind of disregard for the pictorial effect, even in classical authors, —as with the tongues and ears of Rumour in Virgil. Most significant in this opening scene is the interpretation of the rent clothes. The violence came from the herd of Stoics and Epicureans—*epicureum vulgus ac stoicum.* Considering the close resemblance to the Stoics and their morality in much of Boethius, it is significant that he should reject them here. It attaches his theory all the more definitely to that of

9

Plato, who is claimed by Philosophy as *noster* in the preceding sentence. And so in alternate verse and prose the book goes on. It is something of a shock to come in the fourth chapter on names of adversaries like Conigast and Triggvila. They look like anachronisms, those decent Gothic names of unscrupulous courtiers, coming in a text the matter of which is generally so unlike anything Northern. It is one of Boethius and the passages of history in which the moral Theodoric. seems almost too obviously and epigrammatically pointed, when Boethius, who more than any other man represents and sums up the popular philosophy which the Middle Ages derived from Greece, appears as the servant of Theodoric, who is no less eminent on the Northern side as a hero of epic tradition. The *Convito* of Dante belongs in a sense to the one, the *Nibelungen Lied* to the other. The Gothic names in the *Consolation* are a pertinent reminder of the German world and its occupations. That world had a morality of its own quite different from that of Boethius, except that both were noble. The *Hávamál* in the Northern poetry is a complement and opposite to the *Consolation of Philosophy*.

The matter of the *Consolation* belongs to philosophy rather than to literature, but some passages may be referred to more particularly for their intrinsic value or for their associations :—

II. c. 4 : "Nam in omni adversitate fortunæ infelicissimum est genus infortunii fuisse felicem."

II. c. 7 : "Et illa : Atqui hoc unum est quod præstantes quidem natura mentes sed nondum ad extremam manum

virtutum perfectione perductas allicere possit gloriæ et opti-
morum in rempublicam fama meritorum." [1]

II. c. 8 :   "O felix hominum genus
           Si vestros animos amor
           Quo cælum regitur regat.

These are the three famous commonplaces on *Lost
Happiness*, on *Fame*, and on the *Harmony of the
Universe.*

Another, which is an essential part of the whole
demonstration, is that of the *Patria*, the proper home
of the soul, the leading thought of Dante's pilgrimage,
and of so much more in the devotion of saints and
confessors, and of many broken men as well:—

"*Quorum animus etsi caligante memoria tamen bonum suum
repetit, sed veluti ebrius domum quo tramite revertatur ignorat.*"
(III. c. 2.)

     "My soul with too much stay
     Is drunk and staggers in the way."

The most difficult part of the book is concerned
with Providence and Fate, in a manner that brings
out fully the extraordinary skill of Boethius in dealing with the severest problems. He has succeeded, if
not in explaining the main questions, at least in giving
adequate expression to some distinctions by the way,
from which it is possible to get instruction. If he

---

[1] Cf. Massinger, *A Very Woman*, v. 4—

     "Though the desire of fame be the last weakness
     Wise men put off."

Also *Sir John Van Olden Barnevelt*, i. 1—

     "Read but o'er the Stories
     Of men most fam'd for courage or for counsaile,
     And you shall find that the desire of glory
     Was the last frailty wise men ere putt of."

does not solve Fate and Free-will, he at any rate gives help for the reading of Dante, and his description of the relations between Providence and Fate is a fine example of solemn meditation. It is an expansion of the old passage from the *Timæus*, about the Divine and the Necessary; Fate is Providence looked at from below. Just as the understanding of man, creeping from point to point, breaks into a long analytical series the unity of Divine reason, so the timeless Providence when it is translated into Time becomes the succession of events that seem to be bound together by the necessity of Fate, though they are beheld otherwise when looked upon *ex alta providentiæ specula*:—

"Uti est ad intellectum ratiocinatio, ad id quod est id quod gignitur, ad æternitatem tempus, ad punctum medium circulus : ita est fati series mobilis ad providentiæ stabilem securitatem" (IV. c. 6).

Time is the image of Eternity (V. c. 6), and the endless series of events in Time is a reduction of what is Absolute to a lower grade, an attempt to exhaust the infinite riches of a life for which no time is sufficient. With the expression of ideas like these it is possible to find fault. They are made too simple. But the task of Boethius here is philosophical consolation, not pure philosophy.

Naturally the philosophers are unwilling to see these mysteries made over to the uses of the moral preacher. But the other side must always be kept in mind. The disciples of Boethius have justified him. In that age, and for ages after, the most important

and essential thing was to get some simple comprehensive theory of the whole world, whether scientific or merely literary. There was no want of scientific elaboration later. The magnificent generalisations
of Boethius, coming as most of them do from Plato,
have in the confusion of the Middle Ages the effect
of something still older than Plato: a revival of the
great utterances of the early Greek philosophers, those
who looked to the whole heaven, and were possessed
with the Unity of it, and found that enough for a
lifetime. In the decline of Greek speculation, almost
at its last word, Boethius is often nearer to Parmenides
or Empedocles, in his frame of mind if not in his
doctrines, than to any of the later sects.

The verse of the *Consolation* is that of a prosodist—
somewhat too deliberate in the choice and combination
of metres, not always quite successful, it may be
thought. But the Middle Ages approved and imitated them, as they imitated also those of Martianus
Capella; and the poems have excellences such as
make the expulsion of the poetical Muses at the
beginning appear not only cruel but ungrateful. Not
infrequently the movement is like that of a sonnet,
especially an Elizabethan sonnet made up of examples,
and a concluding moral. Such is the poem of the
second book, c. 3, written in a system of alternate
sapphic and glyconean verses.

> " Cum polo Phœbus roseis quadrigis
> Lucem spargere cœperit,
> Pallet albentes hebetata vultus
> Flammis stella prementibus.

Cum nemus flatu zephyri tepentis
  Vernis inrubuit rosis
Spiret insanum nebulosus auster
  Jam spinis abeat decus.
Sæpe tranquillo radiat sereno
  Immotis mare fluctibus
Sæpe ferventes aquilo procellas
  Verso concitat æquore.
Rara si constat sua forma mundo,
  Si tantas variat vices,
Crede fortunis hominum caducis,
  Bonis crede fugacibus.
Constat æterna positumque lege est,
  Ut constet genitum nihil."

The poem on the *Former Age* (II. c. 5) is an example in verse of Boethius's skill in reviving commonplace themes; it is the original of Chaucer's poem on the same subject. Its conceit of *pretiosa pericula* for "gems" comes in with a very modern sort of grace. The famous phrase, *Ubi nunc fidelis ossa Fabricii manent*, turned so happily by King Alfred ("Where are the bones of Weland?"), is the source of many rhymes on the perished valour and vanished beauty, —an old burden.

The solemn prayer of Book III. c. 9 is in hexameter verse, rightly chosen here, and chosen perhaps with a recollection of its use by Parmenides and Empedocles—

"Da pater augustam menti conscendere sedem
  Da fontem lustrare boni da luce reperta
  In te conspicuos animi defigere visus:
  Dissice terrenæ nebulas et pondera molis
  Atque tuo splendore mica : tu namque serenum
  Tu requies tranquilla piis, te cernere finis
  Principium vector dux semita terminus idem."

There is no author in this period, and few in any part of history, with so many advocates, pupils, and imitators; the reason being that he somehow or other felt what was most wanted in the intellectual confusion in which he lived. He is still an auspicious name, not merely on account of the honour that has been paid him, but because of the sincere and quiet light that he gives, with his fidelity to Plato and his observance of an old Greek fashion of thought, in times when clearness and simplicity were more and more difficult every day.

Cassiodorus (*c.* 480—575), who survived Boethius fifty years, is of no less importance as a teacher of *Cassiodorus.* the later ages, though in a wholly different way. Boethius may still be read, as Dante or Chaucer read him, for doctrine and counsel. Cassiodorus is a founder of educational methods, a purveyor of learning, a historian; but his present literary value consists in nothing more than the curiosity of his overladen style, which is equally inexhaustible and monotonous. As Quæstor under Theodoric he wrote official letters in the most pompous language to the king's correspondents; these were published by Cassiodorus under the title *Variæ*[1] some twelve years after Theodoric's death. His method may be exemplified from the letter in which Theodoric desires Boethius to find a harper for Luduin (that is, Clovis) king of the Franks. Page after page is filled with sentences on the music of the spheres, the moral efficacy of the different

[1] Ed. Mommsen, in *Mon. Germ. Hist.*, 1894.

tones (perverted by the corruption of the world to dancing), the nature of *diapason ;* Orpheus, Amphion, Musæus ; rhythm, metre, oratory ; the different functions of heroic and iambic verse; the Sirens; David; the heavenly psaltery ; the music of the blessed in heaven. Concluding with a return from this digression, the letter hopes that the harper when found and despatched to the Frankish king will contrive, like Orpheus, to tame the fierce hearts of the nations.

Shortly before the taking of Ravenna by Belisarius, Cassiodorus retired to Squillace, his birthplace, where he founded a monastery and set an example of learned industry and care for books, the effect of which was incalculable. In his Institutions of Divine and Human Study he included all knowledge : the second part (the Humanities) established the Trivium and Quadrivium for all future schools. And there were many other works of different kinds besides. The Gothic History, abridged by Jordanes, was written before his retirement. He was a man of some character, a fit representative, in the sixth century, of the liberal arts, genuinely fond of knowledge, and of good writing, as he understood it. His historical importance has been well brought out by the historian of *Italy and her Invaders.*[1] A sentence or two from the letter to Boethius will prove what has been said about his style. On the lute and its virtue :—

Nam licet hujus delectationis organa multa fuerint exquisita, nihil tamen efficacius inventum est ad permovendos animos

---

[1] See especially Epistles of Cassiodorus, translated by T. Hodgkin.

quam concavæ citharæ blanda resultatio. Hinc etiam appel-
latam æstimamus chordam, quod facile corda moveat: ubi
tanta vocum collecta est sub diversitate concordia, ut vicina
chorda pulsata alteram faciat sponte contremiscere, quam nullam
contigit attigisse.

The foundation at Squillace was nearly contemporary with St Benedict's at Monte Cassino; the
St Benedict. character was not the same. The great
Benedictine house had not at first the love
of learning which later became inseparable from the
order. St Benedict had small regard for grammar or
rhetoric, and the Latin of the Benedictine *Rule* has
no pretence to beauty, nor even to correctness. St
Gregory, himself a Benedictine monk, does not go
beyond the principles of the Founder in his contempt
for Donatus. Cassiodorus is on the other side, and
though much of his eloquence may be futile, he at
least helped to preserve the tradition of the humanities
in a time when they were threatened.

The poetry of Venantius Fortunatus[1] is contained
Venantius in eleven miscellaneous books (interspersed
Fortunatus. with prose) and in four books of a longer
poem on the life of St Martin.

The dedication of his poems to Pope Gregory the
Great (in a prose epistle) looks as inopportune in
style as it well could be, if its rhetorical blazes are
contrasted with St Gregory's repeated disapproval of
these vanities. It is as unfortunate, one would think,

[1] *Venanti Honori Clementiani Fortunati presbyteri Italici Opera
Poetica*, ed. Leo, *Pedestria*, ed. Krusch, 1881 (*Mon. Germ. Hist.*, iv.)
Cf. W. Meyer, *Der Gelegenheitsdichter Venantius Fortunatus*, 1901.

as Malvolio's cross-garterings. But Fortunatus, though he could write panegyrics on Chilperic and Radegund, not to speak of Brunehild, could not dissemble his sincere affection for fine language, and in his case, as in some others in the Middle Ages, the wonderful words are often the true expression of the man's nature—not merely something learned, but the proper utterance of a lively, showy mind. There is humour in Fortunatus which gives the torrent of epithets sometimes a touch of comedy. This comes out in his prose dedication in his satire on the manners of Germany.

> "Ubi mihi tantundem valebat raucum gemere quod cantare apud quos nihil disparat aut stridor anseris aut canor oloris, sola sæpe bombicans barbaros leudos arpa relidens : ut inter illos egomet non musicus poeta sed muricus deroso flore carminis poema non canerem sed garrirem, quo residentes auditores inter acernea pocula salute bibentes insana Baccho judice debaccharent."

The taste of Fortunatus is unrestrained, but it is redeemed by his *gusto*, to use the sensible old term of criticism that recognises how much life may do, rules or no rules, for a work of art. Artificiality, brazen rhetoric, all the faults of "a swollen and puffy style," are exemplified in Fortunatus, but they lose their offence, or great part of it, because the author's delight is so sincere and innocent—as when he praises another poet for the things he himself admired most in his own writings (III. 18 to Bishop Berte-chramn):—

> "Ardua suscepi missis epigrammata chartis
> atque cothurnato verba rotata sofo.
> Percurrens tumido spumantia carmina versu
> credidi in undoso me dare vela freto :
> Plana procellosos ructavit pagina fluctus,
> et velut Oceanas fonte refudit aquas.
> Vix modo tam nitido pomposa poemata cultu
> audit Traiano Roma verenda foro."

It is impossible to be seriously offended with so simple-minded an enjoyment of declamation, and Fortunatus escapes by the same licence as some of the poets whom Ancient Pistol admired, and some of a later time. It may be remarked that Fortunatus is seldom affected or artificial in thought; his conceits are not of the hyperbolical metaphorical kind, but for the most part "turns upon words," such as were in favour in Greek rhetoric, and afterwards in the style of *Euphues.*

> "Pictavis residens qua sanctus Hilarius olim
> Natus in urbe fuit notus in orbe pater."

He is exceedingly fond of the epithets *coruscant* and *sidereal;* these are characteristic :—

> "Lucida sidereo cœli strepit aula tumultu
> Laudibus et Domini concutit astra fragor."

> "Aurea tecta micant, plebs aurea fulget in aula
> Et cum rege pio turba corusca nitet."

The same favourite words appear together in the prose preface of his Third Book, to Bishop Felix of Nantes :—

> "Igitur cum considerarem dicta singula de more tubarum clangente sermone prolata et sidereo quodammodo splendore

perfusa, velut coruscantium radiorum perspicabili lumine mea
visi estis lumina perstrinxisse, et soporantes oculos quos mihi
aperuistis tonitruo clausistis corusco."

Fortunatus writes on many different subjects. His
pompous epithalamium (in hexameters) on Sigebert
and Brunehild is interesting on account of its poetical
respect for Cupid and Venus, who speak the praises
of the king and queen in a manner more classical, or
more like the fashion of the Renaissance, than was
common in the Dark Ages. Theodulfus, for example,
in the time of Charlemagne, refers to Cupid as the
demon of adultery—

" Est sceleratus enim mœchiæ demon et atrox "—

and uses mythological terms with caution, but Fortunatus can do without the allegorical theory which
was supposed to justify Christian poets in their transactions with Gentile deities. His poem on the Moselle
is much inferior to Ausonius, but not because he is
indifferent to the beauties of nature: his descriptive
passages are not all mere rhetoric. There are some
very pleasant light poems of his addressed to his
friends, gracefully mock-heroic, like that on his friend
Gogo (vii. 4). What is Gogo doing ? Is he watching
the salmon-nets of Rhine, or walking by the Moselle,
or hunting the buffalo in the Forest of Arden?
Clouds and winds be messengers between Gogo and
his Fortunatus. Again to Lupus, Duke of Champagne
(vii. 8), in a rather more serious tone, he tells how
the thought of his noble friend is refreshing to him,
like shade and cool water to a wayfaring man in the

summer heat when he rests, and remembers the poetry that he knows, Homer or Virgil or David. Lupus in another poem is praised more conventionally for his military exploits. One couplet ("coruscant" again) is worth quoting as a sort of analogue in a different style to the phrases of German poetry where the iron mail, the "grey shirt," of the fighting man is alluded to :—

> "Ferratæ tunicæ sudasti pondere victor
> Et sub pulverea nube coruscus eras."

The name that is always associated with Fortunatus and his poetry is that of St Radegund ; the poetical record of their friendship preserved in the verses of Fortunatus is not the largest part of his works, nor perhaps the best, but it always keeps a value of its own, associations of gentleness and grace, not without some reflections of tragedy from the sorrows of the royal house of Radegund's birth, and the cruelties of the time. Generally, there is little in Fortunatus to recall the facts of Frankish history : the treacheries and murders written about by Gregory of Tours do not interfere with his humanities and civilities, his descriptions of castles and basilicas, his compliments and courtly poems. But he wrote the sorrows of Galsuintha, the unhappy Spanish princess, Brunehild's elder sister, the wife of Chilperic, the victim of her husband and Fredegund. Galsuintha, passing through Poitiers on her sad journey, touched the heart of Radegund, herself an exiled princess. The meeting of the two ladies is described by Fortunatus, and though it is not in his best rhetorical manner it is perhaps the central passage of his works. At any rate, it explains the influence of St Radegund, even better than the elegy written by Fortunatus, in her name, on the ruin of the Thuringian power and the sorrows of her line. The tragic or elegiac note, however, is not what is most usual with Fortunatus. The poems addressed to Radegund, or to Radegund and Agnes, for her spiritual daughter is not to be separated from her, are not too solemn. The themes are not far-fetched; anything is enough for an epistle in verse — presents of flowers or fruit, a dinner, a birthday.

He follows an old line of tradition, which regarded Latin verse as the most splendid form of rhetoric, and used it as a kind of ornamental process, to treat any kind of subject, especially these that came within the range of polite religious persons, living in comfort without much anxiety or strong ambition. Venantius Fortunatus is a repetition of Sidonius Apollinaris, with the same temper of conformity, the same elegant piety; a courtier by temperament, with an ideal of good manners, including the religion of a gentleman and the accomplishments of fine language. The type is continued as from Ausonius and Sidonius to Fortunatus, so from him to the Caroline poets. The equipment of Theodulf at the court of Charles the Great is very like that of Fortunatus, two hundred years earlier; and Alcuin, apart from his professional industry as a teacher, is fond of writing verse in the same manner about the same order of themes.

Gregory of Tours (+594) gives much less attention to grammar than his namesake and contemporary the *Gregory of Tours.* Pope. His *History of the Franks*[1] begins with a complaint of the decay of learning; but the failure of studies ought not, he thinks, to bring with it neglect of history. What he desires is to save the memory of things that have happened, especially of things happening in his own time. He is a French author of Memoirs; his interest is not in beauties of language but in persons and events; also he wishes an audience, and an audience is hard to find for the professional and practised wielder of phrases. "Philosophantem rhetorem intellegunt pauci, loquentem rusticum multi." So he uses in his history the ordinary easy Latin, without rhetorical figures. He could have written otherwise, and his rough Latin is not the language of an unscholarly person; but he chose the right form for the people whom he addressed. His copyists could not spell, and Gregory's style was better than they deserved.

The History goes down to the year 591, in ten books, the author's own recollections beginning in the fourth. As Bishop of Tours, the city of St Martin, Gregory was chief representative and advocate of the Church in France, and naturally had to assert its claims against tyrannical usurpation. His Memoirs are those of a man who has played a great part in the state.

---

[1] *Gregorii Turonensis Opera*, in *Monumenta German. Hist.*, ed. Arndt and Krusch. Migne, *Patrol. Lat.*, 81. One of the oldest MSS. of the History has been printed separately by M. H. Omont, Paris, 1886 (the first six books) another (books vii.-x.) by M. Collon, 1893.

At the same time he has the sense for interesting
things, miracles and adventures, which is sometimes
wanting in historians; and he has also, if not imaginative strength, at any rate a zest and liveliness of story-
telling that quickens even the older parts of his work
before he comes to draw on his own experiences.   He
has preserved some memorable phrases,—the " Mitis
depone colla, Sicamber " of St Remy to Clovis ; " Worship what thou hast burnt, burn what thou hast
adored"; and the dying words of Clotaire, surprised
at the ways of heaven in dealing with great persons,
" Wa ! quid putatis qualis est ille rex cælestis qui sic
tam magnos reges interficit ? "   He is one of the
authors who can sketch things easily : the gift is not
uncommon in the Dark Ages.   Luckily it is not
greatly dependent on grammar, and though some
languages are better than Gregory's unpretending
Latin for the work of a chronicler, Gregory succeeds
with his poor implements where many great clerks
have failed.   The story of the strayed reveller in St
Peter's at Rome, waking sober at midnight and finding
himself shut in, alone, and of the solemn vision that
followed, a story of the days of Attila, is enough in
itself to prove the talent of Gregory.

Gregory of Tours was a friend of Venantius Fortunatus, and the same personages often appear in the
history of the one and the complimentary poems of
the other.   Gregory was present at the burial of St
Radegund : he is not less sincere than her friend the
poet in his admiration for her piety.   But he gives
more space to the unhappy dissensions in the con-

vent of the Holy Rood after the death of the king's
daughter who founded it: describing the grievances of
other king's daughters, one of them Basina, daughter
of Chilperic, who found the discipline too hard.   More
than forty of these ladies seceded from their house
and appealed to Bishop Gregory for protection.   They
travelled on foot from Poitiers to Tours, with no help
on the way : it was at the end of December and the
floods were out: "erant enim pluviæ magnæ sed et
viæ dissolutæ erant e nimia immensitate aquarum."
The bishop treated his suppliants with equal judgment and sympathy, but could not prevail upon them
to submit again to the severities of their abbess.   He
naturally has much to say of the rival queens, Fredegund and Brunehild, and does them justice, we may
suppose ; he gives pretty full particulars regarding the
murder of the Bishop of Rouen, Fredegund's work; and
in his account of that lady's attempt to suppress her
undutiful daughter by slamming the lid of a treasure-
chest on her, nothing essential is omitted.   The
matters of his book continually recall the scenes of
later vernacular chronicles: the brawls of the *chansons
de geste*, the gibes and flytings of Beowulf or the
Icelandic tales, the enterprises in Froissart.   Gregory
stands as near as Sturla Thordarson to the passions
and revenges of the turbulent great men.

In Tours, his own city, there were things done that
might go straight into a ballad.   Sicharius and
Chramsind (Ravenswyth), citizens of Tours, were
enemies: Sicharius had killed the father, brother, and
uncle of Chramsind; however, peace was made be-

tween them with the mediation of Gregory, and they
made up a friendship between them and dined with
one another.   One day Sicharius in the other's house
got drunk and insolent, saying: "Great thanks thou
owest me, fair brother, for that I slew thy kin; the
money was paid in recompense, and gold and silver
poured in; thou wert naught but a starving naked
beggar if this had not filled thee." The other took
bitterly the words of Sicharius, writes the Bishop.
Chramsind said in his heart: "Unless I avenge the
death of my kin, I ought to lose the name of man
and be called a craven woman." And forthwith, the
lights put out, he cleft the head of Sicharius with a
hanger.   It is told in prose, none too eloquent nor
imaginative; the actors were churls in grain.   Yet
it is told clearly and not slurred over, and the plot
is that of a strong simple drama.   These prosaic notes
show, like the Icelandic sagas, though without their
glory, how near the problems and situations of the
epic poetry might come to the familiar life.   Throughout the Latin chroniclers generally, one is in turn
annoyed at the neglect of incident and surprised at
the vividness of it; the tedious conventional record
of victories and defeats, in abstract language, being
varied by the pictures of things actually seen or
distinctly reported.   In reading Gregory of Tours one
is often prompted to look at his figures in the light of
the epic poetry and its favourite situations and formulas: sometimes a word in the Latin will recall the
Teutonic phrase, like *circuli loricæ*, the "hringas," the
rings of mail so common in the war poetry.   At other

times the things told of are the same things as Froissart tells, and on the same ground, " the marches of
Burdigaloys," and elsewhere.   The underground passages of the western castles surprised those who had
to deal with them as invaders and assailants.   " ' Have
the castles of this country such ordinaunce ? ' asked
Sir Gautier.   ' Sir,' quoth Sir Hugh, ' there be divers
such castles as of old time pertained to Raynalt of
Mountalban that hath such conveyance ; for when
he and his brethren kept war against King Charle-
main of France they were made all after this manner
by the counsel and advice of Maugis their cousin.' "
But long before the day of the sons of Aymon,
Gregory of Tours was writing of the same " conveyance," and describing the same business as Froissart.

Being a writer of memoirs also, and not a romancer
or an epic poet, he can introduce many humours besides the incidents of warlike adventure.   His chief
personage on the whole is Chilperic, and Chilperic
is not treated unfairly.   " The Nero and Herod of
our time " he is called by Gregory, but he is shown
occasionally in his hours of ease ; interested in spelling
reform, and debating pleasantly about theology with
Priscus the Jew.   " Taking him gently by the hair
he said to me: ' Come, priest of God, and lay thy
hand upon him.' "   Shortly before he had been vexed
by Gregory's opposition in an argument, but he seems
to have borne no malice.   Gregory is severe upon his
contempt of the clergy ; he jested about nothing more
readily than the manners of bishops.   On the other
hand Gregory criticises the king's poetry : he wrote

two books in imitation of Sedulius. "The weak versicles had no feet to stand on, and wanting right intelligence he made short syllables long and long syllables
short"—in all artistic respects inferior to Nero.

Jordanes the Goth (more accurately an Alan by
descent) has preserved in his abridgment the substance of the lost book of Cassiodorus on
Gothic history. He also wrote a History of
the World, but his work on the Goths has made his
name, perhaps with some injustice to Cassiodorus,[1]
yet Jordanes is more than a copier, and has thought
out his narrative for himself. Jordanes has a place
among the contemporary authorities who have recorded in prose the events that shaped themselves
into a different kind of story for the poets of the German heroic age. He himself has a lofty conception of
the destiny and fortunes of the Gothic race, and his
account of the origin of the warlike nations in the
Northern island, Scanzia, *officina gentium*, corresponds
in prose to the epic genealogies of the poets. He
cannot keep the poets out of his book ; he tells the
story of the death of Swanhild and of the vengeance
taken by her brothers, which no doubt was current in
his day, in Gothic verse, and which takes a new form
later in a younger language, in the verses on the death
of Ermanaric at the end of Sæmund's *Edda*.

The chief personage, however, for Jordanes is not
a Gothic hero, but Attila the Hun, whose history,
derived from Priscus, is told more fully than the rest,
and in a more regular style.

[1] *Jordanis Romana et Gotica*, ed. Mommsen, *Mon. Germ.*, 1882.

Gildas, born at Dumbarton (Alcluith), on the day of Mount Badon, the twelfth battle of Arthur, wrote about the year 540 his book of the ruin of Britain,[1] and represents even more emphatically than Orosius the mediæval affection for lamentation, mourning, and woe. By his birth, the theme of his history, and the temper of his style, Gildas is one of the first authors of the Middle Ages. The conflict of Britons and Saxons in his own lifetime is rendered by him with that pathos which has always accompanied the tradition of those conflicts. It took captive the conqueror, and in a later day of tribulation, before other invaders, the Saxon Wulfstan remembers the lament of Gildas: the sorrows of the isle of Britain are repeated, the humiliation, the call to repentance, when the English in their turn have to meet the force of the Danes. It is a prophetic book: the author knows that he is taking upon him the office of Jeremiah. Great part of his work is not history but denunciation; the history is a parenthesis. In style Gildas is one of the masters of the enthusiastic sort of Latin prose, rich in poetical ornament and a strange vocabulary.[2]

Gildas.

Gildas got his learning from the famous teacher of South Wales, Iltut, at Llantwit Major, and the Latin

---

[1] *Gildæ Sapientis de Excidio et Conquestu Britanniæ*, ed. Mommsen (*Mon. Germ.*), 1894 ; ed. Hugh Williams, 1899-1901 (Cymmrodorion Record Series): cf. Zimmer, *Nennius Vindicatus*, 1893, p. 100.

[2] The *Lorica* ascribed to Gildas, a hymn of prayer for protection, contains a number of Hebrew words such as were in favour in a certain rhetorical school, the school of *Hisperica Famina*. But this Hebrew element is wanting in the prose of Gildas, which is inflated but not unintelligible.

of that school was florid on principle. But Gildas
appears to wear his embroidery with a better grace,
because more naturally, than other rhetoricians of
that kind; there is none of the incongruity many
of them show between the trivial matter and the
intemperate language. The eloquence of Gildas has
fervour in it, and his mind goes out sincerely in
the chanting declamation. His oratorical skill is
shown in his use of Biblical language, and perhaps
the highest praise due to his style is that the quoted
passages are not out of keeping with his own
sentences.

St Gregory the Great is known in the history of
literature as one of the enemies; his writings "reveal
Gregory his implacable aversion to the monuments
the Great. of classic genius; and he points his severest
censure against the profane learning of a bishop, who
taught the art of grammar, studied the Latin poets,
and pronounced with the same voice the praises of
Jupiter and those of Christ."[1] But for all that his
writings are part of the educational tradition; they
have a strong literary character of their own, and
their objection to grammar is capable of a milder explanation than is commonly given. In the preface to
the *Moralia* he utters the same contempt for grammar
as in the often cited letter to Bishop Desiderius: one
might expect, from the interpretation commonly put
upon those passages, that he would have written in
despite of grammar with the freedom used by Gregory

[1] Gibbon, ch. xlv.

of Tours, or even with that of the *Epistolæ Obscurorum Virorum*. But it is not so. His Latin is not regardless or unprincipled. The dislike of grammar stops short of heinous crime. It is the protest of a masterful and practical intellect against the vanities of the ornamental schools of composition. Cassiodorus is probably responsible for the intolerant language of Gregory. No doubt Gregory is carried a little too far,—"indignum vehementer existimo ut verba celestis oraculi restringam sub regulis Donati." But he does not break Donatus's head, for all this desperate profession. "Unde et ipsam loquendi artem quam magisteria disciplinæ exterioris insinuant servare despexi." The very sentences in which the proclamation is made show that Gregory has taken as much as suited him, and as much as was convenient for a freeborn orator, from the studies of the *Trivium*. "Non metacismi collisionem fugio," he says. Sequence of a vowel upon *m* was discouraged in rhetoric and branded *metacismus*.[1] Gregory's slighting notice of this prescription is no more remarkable than the impatience of any practical solid writer of the present day with the trifling concerns of style. The books of St Gregory were taken up and studied everywhere in the Middle Ages—the *Moralia*, his commentary on Job; the *Dialogues;* the *Pastoral Care;* the *Homilies*.[2]

The *Moralia* are chiefly notable in literature as confirming the old method of allegorical interpretation.

---

[1] Isidor., *Etym.* i. 32, *metacismus* est quotiens *m* litteram vocalis sequitur, ut *bonum aurum, justum amicum.*

[2] Migne, *Patr. Lat.,* 75-79.

It does not put out of use the previous commentaries,
but it reduces their value by its greater extent, its
greater perseverance and elaboration. It is one of the
reservoirs in the history of literature,—that is to say,
one of the comprehensive books that gather together
the results of older sources and become the main
source, in their turn, for everything beneath them in
order of time. It is pleasant to compare the functions
of the *Moralia* with that of the *Romaunt of the Rose*.
The books hold the same kind of position, through
the way in which they absorb a number of older
currents, and make themselves into the obvious store
of supply for places at a lower level. There is no
offence in the comparison; the method of St Gregory
allows the juxtaposition of all the most incompatible
things for the sake of the moral. No quotation can
give any proper idea of the amount and the intricacy
of allegorical conceits in the *Moralia*, nor of their influence upon later students. It cannot be described.
One quality it has, however, which ought never to
be ignored. The most appalling, the most deliberate
absurdities of false wit, as St Gregory's expositions
must be judged when taken as mere literature, mere
play of figures, they are yet combined with the strongest common-sense and practical judgment. They
appear, speaking generally, the most enormous riot of
untrained fancy; beside these allegories the most un-
tamed things in history seem merely respectable.
But they are still the work of one of the greatest
men of business in the world, and he shows what
his mind is in the plain statement which he gives, of

the limits of allegory. Not everything in Scripture, says St Gregory, is to be put through those variations. There are many things that are falsely understood when they are wrested from their superficial meaning into allegory. The Holy Scripture has something for all minds. "Habet in publico unde parvulos nutriat, servat in secreto unde mentes sublimium in admiratione suspendat. Quasi quidam quippe est fluvius ut ita dixerim planus et altus in quo et agnus ambulet et elephas natet" (Preface to *Moralia*, c. 4). It is like a river with pools and shallows, where in one place the lamb may wade, in another the elephant may swim. This proposition was generally accepted; it is a favourite quotation with Boccaccio, who used and applied it in his theory of the art of poetry, in his *Life of Dante*, and in his Florentine lectures—a sufficient proof of the authority of St Gregory even in the alien provinces of literary criticism, and at a time when grammar was seeking vengeance for the oppressions of the Dark Ages.

The *Pastoral Care*[1] is a better book than the *Moralia* from a literary point of view. Although there is enough in it of the allegorical method, that does not so much overcome the practical genius of the author as in the *Moralia*, and the style brings out the character of the writer in dealing with perhaps his best subject. He understood both the flock and the shepherds. It is something more also than directions to the clergy. It is a criticism of life (not

---

[1] *De Pastorali Cura*, ed. Westhoff, Monasterii Westphalorum, 1860, ed. altera.

being other than prose, at the same time), and it gave a summary of morals which, starting from less metaphysical ground, was well fitted to support the *Consolation of Philosophy* among the books which were almost indispensable in the Middle Ages. The story in the Icelandic *Bishops' Lives* of the deathbed of Thorlak, the third Bishop of Skálholt (+1133), is a testimony, in addition to King Alfred's translation, showing what efficacy the *Pastoral Care* had, and in what honour it was held. He asked to have it read to him as he lay sick, "and men thought that he looked forward to his death with a better courage than before the reading began." That a manual of directions for the practical work of a clergyman among his people should have been available in this way for the comfort of the dying is some proof of a human virtue in it, besides its ecclesiastical merits.

The Dialogues of St Gregory were more popular still. They also were translated into Anglo-Saxon; they were translated into French.[1]

They are a series of stories, intended to correspond, in the West, to the *Vitæ Patrum*, the lives of the saints in the Desert, the widely read collection of miracles whose vogue appeared to Gregory rather unjust to the fame of the holy men of Italy. One whole book is devoted to Saint Benedict; the others

[1] The old French version, *Li Quatre livre des Dialoges Gregoire le Pape del borc de Romme des miracles des peres de Lumbardie*, has been edited by Dr Wendelin Förster, 1876, with the Latin original. The Anglo-Saxon Dialogues, translated by Bishop Wærferth of Worcester have been edited by Dr Hans Hecht, in the fifth volume of Grein's *Bibliothek der angelsächsischen Prosa*, 1900.

are miscellaneous, and all are interesting in one way
or another. Gregory, at the beginning, complains of
the oppression of duties, the secular business that
attends upon the pastoral care. The Dialogues with
Peter the Deacon are a relief to him. His character
shows itself none the less in his choice of a subject
in which to rest from his worldly avocations. It is
not meditation, speculation, or devotion; it is history
or memoirs, the record of occurrences, that unbends
the mind of St Gregory. He repeats his scorn of
literature in the opening of his *Life of St Benedict:*
"Despectis itaque litterarum studiis . . . sanctæ con-
versationis habitum quæsivit. Recessit igitur scienter
nesciens, et sapienter indoctus" (*Dial.* ii. *Pref.*) He
makes up for this by the stores of legend with which
the *Dialogues* are filled—legend that represents, as
no mere history could, the common mind of the sixth
century. It has no limits, no scruples; it tells how
St Benedict in a vision saw the whole world brought
together in one glance; how the anchorite of Samnium
took a stick to the bears who came for his beehives;
how the hermit of Lipari saw Theodoric the Great, on
the day of his death, carried in bonds between Pope
John and Symmachus and thrown into the Volcano.[1]

[1] A story may be quoted in full, from the fourth chapter of
Book I.:—

"Quadam vero die una Dei famula ex eodem monasterio virginum
hortum ingressa est. Quæ lactucam conspiciens concupivit, eamque
signo crucis benedicere oblita, avide momordit; sed arrepta a diabolo
protinus cecidit. Cumque vexaretur eidem patri Equitio sub celeri-
tate nuntiatum est, ut veniret concitus, et orando protegeret.
Moxque portam idem pater ut ingressus est, cœpit ex ejus ore
quasi satisfaciens ipse qui hanc arripuerat diabolus clamare dicens:

The *Homilies* of the fourth great Latin Father were naturally authoritative for later homilists. But the history of this tradition of sermons is too complex for the present essay.

Between Gregory the Great and Bede, the chief name for learning is Isidore of Seville (bishop 600-636). Few educational writers have had more success. Though little except a compiler, he was recognised as an authority along with the Fathers, and quoted by clerks and laymen down to the end of the Middle Ages. His *Etymologies*, especially (or *Origines*, in 20 books[1]), were used as a supply of ideas, facts, and phrases. An alliterative line in the English *Destruction of Troy* (l. 4426) brings together the author and his book—

Isidore.

"And Ysidre in Ethemoleger openly tellis,"

which is as good an instance as could be found of his popularity. In this way he was thought and spoken

Ego quid feci? ego quid feci? Sedebam mihi super lactucam; venit illa et momordit me. Cui cum gravi indignatione vir Dei præcepit ut discederet, et locum in omnipotentis Dei famula non haberet. Qui protinus abscessit, nec eam ultra contingere prævaluit."

("It befell one day that a nun of the same convent went into the garden; there she saw a lettuce, and desired it and greedily ate it, forgetting to make the sign of the cross for a blessing. Suddenly she fell down, possessed by the devil, and sore vexed. Word was brought at once to Father Equitius, to come with all speed to her help. As soon as he came in at the door, the devil who had entered into her spoke by her mouth, as if to defend himself, and cried, 'What have I done? What have I done? I was sitting on a lettuce leaf, and she swallowed me.' Whom the man of God charged angrily to depart out of her, and to leave the handmaid of the most high God. And he departed forthwith, and had no power to hurt her more.")

[1] Migne, *P. L.* 82.

of everywhere. But Isidore was not only a favourite resource of the half-learned; scholars relied upon him. Hraban of Fulda, who did for the ninth century what Isidore had done for the seventh, founded on *Etymologiarum* his own encyclopedic work *De Universo*.

The seventh century till the work of Bede at the end of it has little historical work of importance. Isidore included history along with all other matters of knowledge in his survey; he compiled a chronicle of the whole world, and added to it a history of the Visigothic kings; he wrote also, following the example of St Jerome, a series of lives of illustrious men. This latter work was continued by Hildefonsus, Bishop of Toledo, while Julian, also Bishop of Toledo, wrote the praise of King Wamba.[1] The history which goes by the name of Fredegarius[2] includes a continuation of Gregory of Tours, with even less pretence of style than Gregory. Julian of Toledo is highly rhetorical, and thus Julian and Fredegarius in the seventh century repeat the contrast of styles exemplified in the previous age by Cassiodorus and Gregory of Tours. In Bede at last is found a proper mean of rhetoric between the pomp of the one school and the bareness of the other.

Aldhelm of Malmesbury, pupil and successor of Maildulf, the Celtic founder of that house, helps to *Aldhelm.* take away the reproach of the seventh century as the least learned in all the Dark Ages. But for all his fame there is little left of his

[1] Migne, *P. L.*, 96.   [2] Ed. Krusch, 1888 (*Mon. Germ. Hist.*)

work;[1] his florid style is monotonous, and, as with
Cassiodorus, might be exemplified sufficiently in one or
two quotations. Aldhelm himself has offered alterna-
tive descriptions of his style, whether it should be
termed *verbosa garrulitas* or *garrula verbositas*, and the
problem has not been decided. Yet there is sometimes wit and fancy in his prose as well as an ambitious vocabulary and formal ornaments of rhetoric;
as where in *De Laudibus Virginitatis* he describes the
working of the bees, and their attention to linden,
willow, and broom.

In a preface to his Latin *Ænigmata*—an epistle to
Acircius, *i.e.*, Aldfrith of Northumberland—he discusses prosody and other subjects. The poems themselves, on the model of Symphosius, are not altogether
conventional: Aldhelm at least thought out these
light verses for himself, if he got nothing very novel
from them. His epistle in rhyme on his experiences
in a storm in Cornwall is a singular thing in the
seventh century. He wrote English verse also, not
extant; if among his English poems there was anything like the humours of this Cornish journey, it
must have been a remarkable exception to the common
Anglo-Saxon manner. As it is, the contrast between
this familiar Latin poetry and the Anglo-Saxon
solemnities is striking enough. Things were possible
in Latin verse which not only could not be expressed
but could hardly be thought in English. It was not
till some centuries later that English poetry discovered
the use of the colloquial manner; Anglo-Saxon

---

[1] Migne, *P. L.*, 89; ed. Giles, Oxford, 1844.

authors could play with Latin as they could not with the literary forms of their own language.

It is unfair to the seventh century not to take Bede's works as representing the learning and intelligence of the time.[1] He did not in his reading or writing go beyond the sources or the models that were commonly accessible. For all that, the impression he leaves is that of something different from his age, an exceptional talent escaping from limitations and hindrances. There is no period in the history of Britain or of the English Church in which Bede is antiquated; in every generation he speaks familiarly. The seventeenth century is less intelligible to the eighteenth, the eighteenth century more in opposition to the nineteenth, than Bede to any one of them; his good sense is everywhere at home. No author in the Dark Ages has so little of the "Gothic" qualities that offended the enlightenment of the Renaissance; and although he wants the imaginative gift through which the mediæval literatures recovered favour in the Romantic schools, he speaks authentically for his own time; he is not prematurely modern. Bede has taken his place through simple strength of mind and character; not by any great discovery, nor by anticipations of later theories, nor any brilliance of fancy or of style, but by applying his mind industriously to his subject, with a firm conviction of its value and a resolution not to be deceived about it. The reputation of Bede seems always to have been

Bede.

[1] Ed. Giles, 1843 ; *Opera Historica,* ed. Plummer, Oxford, 1896.

exempt from the common rationalist criticism, and this although his books are full of the things a Voltairian student objects to. The miracles of St Cuthbert, as recorded by Bede, are not more plausible (in the march of intellect) than those of any other saint, the allegorical interpretations in Bede are not better protected than those of St Gregory against the scrutiny of Erasmus or Tindal, yet somehow Bede is left unchallenged. With regard to the questions of Easter and the tonsure, which made so much difficulty between the Celtic church and Rome in Bede's day, Bede is intolerant.[1] But, like Dr Johnson's refusal to countenance a Presbyterian Church in Scotland, the severity of Bede has been taken lightly by the most sensitive, and has failed to make him enemies, even among the fiercest advocates of Christian charity and impartial toleration. It appears to be felt that he is a great man. The volume of his book is too much for carpers and cavillers.

Bede began by mastering the liberal arts. His whole life was spent, with hardly any change, in the monastery at Jarrow; he was a student from the first, and very early a teacher. Among the busy travelling scholars of those days Bede was sedentary, and he saw little of the face of the world. Like Kant at Königsberg he was content with his own study, but perhaps with more of an effort, more renunciation. Adamnan came with his book on the

---

1 "Unde merito movit hæc quæstio sensus et corda multorum, timentium ne forte accepto Christianitatis vocabulo in vacuum currerent aut cucurrissent" (*H. E.*, iii. 25).

Holy Places to dedicate it to King Aldfrid of Northumberland, and Bede took up the subject, quoting from the book in his *History*, and making a book of his own out of its materials. The latest editor of the *History* quotes a passage from one of his commentaries,[1] in which there is some regret for the indirectness of his knowledge; the Eastern world is known to him only through books, and if he writes at length on the natural history of trees, out of what he has learned in books, it is not for ostentation of knowledge but to instruct himself and others who have been on no voyages, but were born and brought up in an island of the ocean sea, cut off from the greater world.

Bede's earliest writings were in the trivial subjects of literature — the grammar and rhetoric of the ordinary school course. He follows the example of Cassiodorus and Isidore, and does his work, so to speak, as a college lecturer in the humanities, before going on to deeper subjects. His treatise *De Arte Metrica*, a school-book, has the stamp of Bede's intellect upon it. Work of this sort was commonplace, but he could not do it in a perfunctory way. There is a collection of examples of verse; and the forms are carefully explained. Many authors are quoted—Lucretius, Virgil, Lucan; but Bede shows already the signs of his withdrawal from profane learning. In his examples of drama he refers to the Eclogues of Virgil, but these are set off against " our " dramas: " with us the Song of Songs is written in

[1] *H. E.* ed. Plummer, ii. 305.

11

this kind, the dialogue of Christ and the Church."
Against the Georgics and Lucretius stand (*apud nos*
again) the Parables of Solomon and Ecclesiastes;
while in the mixed kind, part narrative part dramatic,
the book of Job is compared with the Iliad and
Odyssey and Æneid. The most original and interesting part of the book is the explanation of rhythmical
verse, the verse of the *vulgares poetæ*, in which
quantity is not observed, but the forms of classical
verse are followed without quantity. Bede has no
scholarly scruples about this modern sort of composition.

It is not correct verse, as he explains clearly; but
having explained he proceeds to admire. It is possible
"to kindle or to slake," in the free verse of the
Ambrosian hymns; and Bede praises especially the
hymn which begins with peremptory defiance of
strict number:

> "Rex æterne Domine
> Rerum creator omnium."

His other work in these preliminary things is not of
quite so much interest as this Prosody; but in his
tract on Orthography, and another on the Figures and
Tropes in the Bible, he shows his good sense; if he
has difficulties with the Latin of the Psalter, he
confesses them and deals with them fairly. In his
other scientific or educational work, his chronography
and the rest, there is the same solidity, recognised by
those who have a right to speak of his subjects. In
what may be reckoned popular science Bede is far
ahead of ordinary opinion.

Besides the *Church History* he wrote other historical books; the *Life of St Cuthbert* (both in prose and verse) and *Lives of the Abbots of Wearmouth and Jarrow*. He wrote commentaries on the Bible (using a Greek text in his work on the *Acts*) and homilies, which came to be a source of future homilies along with the authors from whom he himself had drawn— Augustine, Jerome, Gregory the Great. One of the homilies—a fragment, rather—is extant in an old Low German translation, written on the fly-leaf of a copy of the homilies of Gregory.

The *Church History* is wanting in some of the things to be found in less masterly historians. The chronicle
The Church History. of Gregory of Tours, not to speak of Paulus Diaconus or Liutprand, has more adventure in it, the writer of memoirs having less responsibility and more freedom. There are scenes, however, in Bede, besides the well-known ones, which show the power of the narrator; and the dignity of history does not prevent him from bringing in lively notes, like the description of Paulinus by one who had seen him, or of King Edwin riding on progress with his banner borne before him. There are episodes in Bede that might be quoted as stories merely: the vision of Furseus, though that is abridged and not improved by Bede, and the vision of Drihthelm, which is given more fully. Often as it has been repeated, the story of the conversion of Edwin, the Parable of the Sparrow, remains unspoilt, as sincere as the Anglo-Saxon poetry to which it is so closely related, the elegies over the vanity of earthly glory.

The great literary merit of Bede's *History* lies, however, in its historical sense.   Sound history has a different literary value from unsound, because it implies the literary virtues of judgment and arrangement, which will give a character to a book whatever its grammar or rhetoric may be.   Bede, who was trained in the use of authorities and documents, and possessed of all the living knowledge that came naturally to such a centre as Jarrow, had besides the leisure and capacity for surveying his matter before he turned it into a book.

Bede's Latin style is fluent and clear.   He writes in the universal language, without impediment—a different language altogether from the lively ungrammatical huddle of phrases in Gregory of Tours, and equally removed from the absurd pomp of Aldhelm.

Adamnan, ninth abbot of Iona, +704, 23 Sept., the chief biographer of St Columba, visited Jarrow in Bede's time, and accepted the right view *Adamnan.* about Easter.   Both in style and in matter he differs much from his contemporary, except as regards the essential points of lively interest in his subject and a faculty for narration.   Besides the *Life of Columba*,[1] he wrote on the Holy Places, taking notes from the Frankish Bishop Arculf, who had been in Jerusalem.   He is known in Celtic literature through the Irish 'Vision of Adamnan'[2]— a vision like those of Furseus, Drihthelm, and Tundal.   Historically, he represents the liberal spirit among the

[1] Ed. Reeves, 1857 ; ed. Fowler, Oxford, 1894.
[2] *Irische Texte*, i. 165.

Celtic men of learning, to which so much of Western culture is due, but which had suffered in the Easter controversy and seemed likely to give place to a narrower policy, leaving the Saxons to take care of themselves. The enlightenment of Adamnan in his dealings with Northumberland was of the same kind as the original missionary spirit of St Aidan : it would not keep itself merely to Ireland or to Icolmkil. The great renewal of Irish influence long afterwards on the Continent, in the lifetime of Erigena and Sedulius Scottus, was a victory to which Adamnan contributed when he made terms, so to speak, with the abbot of Jarrow. His book is not the less honourable to his own house in the island of Columba, because he yielded something for the sake of union. Nor is it possible to find fault with it for any want of national qualities, or any attempt to comply weakly with foreign manners.

There are Irish documents where the native idiom brings along with it a savour that has gone from Adamnan's Latin story; in the Lismore *Lives*[1] there are many things stranger, more humorous, more beautiful, than are to be found in Adamnan. Yet he has told the tale of Iona rightly and faithfully, with the authority of the living traditions of the place. His style is much more loaded than that of Bede; he uses more of the diction of Aldhelm. Greek words are fairly common—*onomatis, lithus,* &c.,—and still more common are Latin diminutives—*prefatiuncula,*

---

[1] *Lives of Saints from Book of Lismore,* ed. Whitley Stokes, Oxford, 1890 ; see below, p. 341.

tuguriolum, sermusculus. But in this, with Aldhelm before him, there is nothing to wonder at. Adamnan has not the simplicity and lucidity of Bede, but neither is he one of the extreme cases of false rhetoric. His taste and his scholarship are not quite trustworthy with regard to phrasing, but they do not spoil his story. The quaint things in his language, it may be remarked, are not to be put down forthwith to the credit or otherwise of the Celtic genius. Adamnan was an Irishman (from Donegal), and he shared in the common Irish love of rhetoric and ornamental words. He did not, however, go beyond the rules or invent new devices for himself. The Irish love of rhetoric was not much different from the florid fashions of other people at that time; what is native and characteristic in Adamnan must be looked for in his substance and his sentiment more than in his phrasing.

There are many noble saints' lives in the Middle Ages, and there are many legends too where the charm of a holy life is blended with other things less religious, the colours of romance. There is none where the strength of a sober history is harmonised with the more fantastic spirit as it is in Adamnan's *Life of Columba.* It is this that makes its excellence: Adamnan is in agreement with Bede on the one hand, with St Brandan on the other. He is the right man to speak for Iona. The isle belongs to two worlds (at least). Its history is, first of all, that of a great practical genius who founded and put in order an active religious house of much influence and effect in

the world: that is one side of it. The island and its
saint became powers in the world; the relations of
Iona with larger places are practically important, and
can be explained to any reasonable man. There is
something besides piety in the mind of the visitor to
Iona, even from the days when the first settlers, and
Columcille himself among them, were apt to be dis-
turbed by the voices of pilgrims calling for the ferry
across the sound. Iona was a real place, with a
calculable value, much occupied in affairs. On the
other hand, there are certain lights and certain conditions of the mind when Iona becomes again like one
of the isles of Maelduin or St Brandan. The beauty
of Adamnan's work is that it represents truly, one
cannot but feel, both the serious solid life of Iona,
such as makes it important in history, and also the
vaguer atmosphere about the island. It is not a fairy
story, for all the wonders in it. Yet it is not mere
common-sense. The restlessness of the sea is in it,
the sea that drew the Irish saints on toward the desert
refuge it seemed to offer them; such as was Cormac
MacLethan who, from voyages far to the North, to the
Orkneys and even beyond, was twice brought back, and
touched at Iona and was greeted by Columba. And
in a more familiar way, many things are considered by
Adamnan and Columba besides the fame of their
house: they have to think of the harvest, the cows,
salmon, seals. A seal-poacher from Colonsay was
brought up before Columba, who told him not to be
a thief, but to come and ask if he wanted supplies:
and sent him away with some sheep instead. Swine,

fed on the autumn mast, are admired by the saint, as they are by the Irish poets. Nothing in Adamnan is better known than the story of Columba's last days and of the old white horse that came to say good-bye to him—the old horse that used to carry the milk-pails. Not less beautiful is Columba's thoughtfulness for the tired heron blown over from Ireland, a guest on the island for three days, then returning, as Columba foretold, to "the sweet land whence she came." All Adamnan's stories are true to Iona, and her very sands are dear to him.

Between Bede and Alcuin there is an interval of a generation, during which few books were published —a period of study, especially in Italy and *Boniface.* in the Northumbrian school of York, from which the learning of the Carolingian age was drawn. It was a time also of missionary enterprise. St Boniface had a share in both kinds of labour, and his house of Fulda made a new station in the forest of barbarism, from which the ideas and methods of York were dispensed in due time for the proper training of the Old Saxons. In his own writings Boniface followed the English manner: he has the same tastes as Aldhelm and Bede, shown in his Latin riddles, his tale of a vision like that of Drihthelm, and his general encouragement of literature.

In the later part of the eighth century begins the great age of mediæval learning, the educational work *The Carolingian* of Charles the Great, which in spite of *Age.* political troubles is continued through the century following. The variety of Latin books which appeared in those times is proof that their learning was more than spiritless repetition. There was some leisure and freedom, and much literary ambition. The Latin poets of the court of Charlemagne have an enthusiasm and delight in classical poetry, and also that good conceit of their own immortal works which is common in later humanists. In prose there was no less activity. Besides the scientific treatises and the commentaries, the edifying works of Alcuin and others, there were histories written with different motives. Two authors especially stand out, Einhard and Paul the Lombard— the one distinguished for political sense, the other for his gift of narrative, both of them fresh and independent minds. The scholarly spirit of the ninth century, represented in the letters of Lupus of Ferrières, is not limited to the orthodox routine. One of the chief scholars, with more Greek than most others, Erigena, is famous for more than his learning; as a philosopher who, whatever his respect for the Church, acknowledged no authority higher than Reason.

Alcuin is the name that in general history represents the learning and literature of the age of Charlemagne.[1] His own works hardly equal his

Alcuin.

fame as a teacher, though their very faults, their want of orginal substance, their excess of commonplace, may be due to his educational virtues and his faculty for making things clear to an audience of pupils. Alcuin certainly has nothing like the strong independent mind of Bede, and never takes up any

[1] Migne, *P. L.*, 100 ; *Monumenta Alcuiniana*, ed. Jaffé, 1873.

research for its own sake and the scientific pleasure
of the work. His ideas are all diluted; the audience
is always with him. Of his professional writings, the
dialogues on the *Trivial Arts* are more attractive than
his morality or theology. In the *Grammar* a Frank
and a Saxon pupil take the parts of Sandford and
Merton; in *Rhetoric* and *Dialectic* the pupil is Charles
the Emperor himself.

Alcuin's Latin poems, like those of his contemporaries generally, are greatly influenced by Fortunatus;
they have the same artifice, the same courtly good
humour. Some of his poems are historical—the Life
of his kinsman St Willibrord (which Alcuin also described in prose), the history of York, the elegy on
the ruin of Lindisfarne. But, as with Fortunatus,
the historical poems have less interest than the
occasional pieces, epigrams and epistles, in which
is expressed the life of the poet and the familiar
conversation of other accomplished gentlemen, their
various polite diversions, their game of literature,
their ornamental names. These pastoral vanities of
the great Emperor and his household remain in the
memory, an inseparable accident of the heroic story.

Of all the poems of Alcuin the most notable is the
Contention of Winter and Spring, with its affinities
to widely distant families in literary history; recalling
the debates of the classical eclogues, anticipating the
later mediæval "disputisons" in different languages,
and mingling with the classical type of verse and
expression a thoroughly Northern sort of sentiment.
Here, as in Anglo-Saxon poetry, it is the cuckoo that

breaks the silence of winter, a bird of good omen, though Winter in the dialogue does not think so. Winter loves the rest, the good cheer, the fire in hall, and is slow to wake to the business of spring. There is no peace when once the voice of the cuckoo has been heard.[1]

Alcuin's letters are full of the same domestic interest as his occasional verse; but his prose rhetoric, like the prose of Fortunatus, runs into greater extravagance than his not over temperate poems, and the levities are sometimes depressing. He writes to his friend Bishop Arno of Strassburg by his affectionate name of "Aquila" ("Earn")—"venerando volucri et vere amantissimo Aquilæ Albinus salutem"—and the Emperor is treated with the same kind of florid style as Cassiodorus had used in the service of Theodoric.

Theodulfus,[2] Bishop of Orleans (+821), a Goth by birth, was the principal poet of the court of Charles the Great. Perhaps his value as a repre-

Theodulfus.

sentative person and (in a sense) official poet is gained at the expense of his poetry. He has already been spoken of along with Fortunatus, but he does not come up to the measure of the earlier poet. He has not the same life, the same glorious use of adjectives and sense of the value of syllables; he is more respectable and correct. Theodulfus was a great personage. One of his longer poems, his admonition to judges, contains a long and amusing account of his journey in the South as Missus Dominicus in 798, and

---

[1] Dümmler, *Poetæ Latini Ævi Carolini*, i. 270 (*Mon. Germ. Hist.*)
[2] *Theodulfi Carmina*, ed. Dümmler, *P. Lat. Carol.*, i. pp. 437-581.

of the various kinds of bribes offered to him—Moorish gold, Cordovan leather, a cup embossed with the labours of Hercules. At the close of his life he was suspected of treason by Lewis the Pious, and kept in confinement at Angers. In this trouble he remembered Ovid, and sent an elegiac poem to Bishop Modoin of Autun, in which his Muse acts as his advocate and makes supplication for help—the Muse in her own person. Theodulfus represents in his poetry all the literary ideals of the time, under different aspects. One piece has been often quoted by the historians of learning, because it is good evidence " of the books which I was wont to read and how the fables of the poets are to be philosophically interpreted in a mystical sense." He draws an allegorical picture of the Seven Arts. He touches off the character of his associates and manners of the court. The learned men were fond of exchanging compliments, under their adopted names, Homerus, Flaccus, Naso. Theodulfus varies this with criticism, especially with regard to "the Scot"—probably Clement the Grammarian—whom he did not like.

Flaccus, of course, is Alcuin. Naso was probably an Englishman: he wrote one verse which sums up the glory of the Empire of Charles:—

" Aurea Roma iterum renovata renascitur orbi.'

Homerus is Angilbert, the father of Nithard: a fragment of a poem in honour of the Emperor is ascribed to him.[1] "The Irish exile" (*Hibernicus*

[1] *P. Lat. Carol.*, i. 355.

Exul), whose name may have been Dungal, had written before him in the epic way about the exploits of Charles.[1]

In the next generation an author with less scholarship than Naso or Flaccus wrote a much more entertaining poem than anything of theirs. It may seem unjust that a poet who begins a verse

"Sed quid agam jam jam ?"

should have more space here than the courtly poets. But the epic of Ermoldus Nigellus on the reign of Lewis the Pious—it is written in elegiac couplets, but that does not matter—has more life in it than any of them. If his verse is frequently odd, it is seldom dull. Their verse is not so brilliant, or even so correct, that they need complain of being slighted.

Ermoldus Nigellus.

Ermoldus belonged to the court of Pippin of Aquitaine, and fell under the displeasure of Pippin's father, the Emperor Lewis. The poem *De gestis Ludovici Cæsaris,*[2] written about 827, was intended to make his peace. It touches on the same subjects as afterwards fell to one of the most famous of the *chansons de geste :* the *Coronemens Loois* in the cycle of William of Orange. William himself appears in Ermoldus, and with his epic character, as a champion against the Infidels. The siege of Barcelona (a Moorish city) in the First Book of Ermoldus conforms in all respects to the sound rules of epic. It sometimes uses language that might almost pass for a translation from old

---

[1] *P. Lat. Carol.,* i. 392.   [2] Ibid., ii. 1.

French verse or prose; the commonplace of the sweet
Spring season, when trees burgeon and flowers breathe
odour, and kings go out to defend their marches:—

> "Tempore vernali cum rus tepefacta virescit,
>   Brumaque sidereo rore fugante fugit,
> Pristinus ablatos remeans fert annus odores,
>   Atque humore novo fluctuat herba recens,
> Regni jura movent renovantque solentia reges :
>   Quisque suos fines ut tueantur adit."[1]

The style is a strange combination of the usual
awkwardness and quaintness of mediæval Latin with
a very successful daring in the employment of
classical diction.   The author in his prelude, like
Milton, disclaims the heathen deities:—

> "Nec rogo Pierides nec Phœbi tramite limen
> Ingrediar capturus opem nec Apollinis almi,
> Talia cum facerent quos vana peritia lusit
> Horridus et teter depressit corda Vehemoth."

The influence of the Muses, whatever may be the
case with "Vehemoth," is probably absent from such
a line as

> "Namque unum fateor cogor tibi dicere Vilhelm;"

or

> "Nempe sonat *Hluto* præclarum, *Wicgch* quoque Mars est"

—an interpretation of the Teutonic words that com-
pound the name of Ludowick. But for all that,
Ermoldus was a quick-witted student of Latin poetry,
and his epic similes, beginning with "ac veluti,"
are such as no vernacular poetry could rival before

---

[1] I. 105 *sqq.*

the time of Dante. Many of them are taken from
the birds, and are of the genuine Homeric kind:
thrushes settling on the vintage in autumn, and re-
fusing to be scared by the cymbal of the vexed
husbandman (Ermoldus belonged to Aquitaine); birds
shrieking after the hawk which has carried one of
their party away; ducks hiding from an eagle in the
water-weeds and the mud. Quite as much as in the
similes, Ermoldus shows his power in the way he
tells his stories. The siege of Barcelona is not a
conventional heroic piece, like the battle passages
made to order in the regular epics. The motive is
not literary ambition, but a more simple pleasure;
Ermoldus is the chronicler of things not yet written
down but current orally:—

> "Sed quæ fama recens stupidas pervexit ad aures
> Incipiam canere, cætera linquo catis."

The adventures of Barcelona make a story distinct
from others of the same kind: as where William
cows the Moors by his domineering language, telling
them that he means to stick to the work even if he
has to eat his horse for want of supplies; or where
the Moor, uttering insults in "bombic" language, is
answered with a properly aimed arrow from the silent
Frank whom he is assailing—

> "Never a word of leir had he."

The best part of it perhaps is the story of the
Moorish leader trying to make his way through the
French lines to bring help from Cordova. He is
taken prisoner, and brought up to the walls and

ordered to tell the besieged to open their gates. Before he left, however, he had charged them not to surrender whatever happened to him : so now, though he calls out "open," he holds up his hand with the fist closed as a signal not to obey his words. William saw through this, and admired the Saracen's ingenuity, though he bore him a grudge for it.

There is nothing in the later books quite as good as the siege of Barcelona, but they are full of matter —the crowning of Lewis in the second book, a Breton war in the third, and a wager of battle fought on horseback at Aix, in a manner unusual among the Franks. The fourth book tells of the conversion of Harald the Dane, and his visit to Lewis on the Rhine. The church at Ingelheim leads the poet to indulge, like Dante and Chaucer, in descriptions of pictures. There are fewer similes than in the first book, but one in the second is vivid enough: the good impression made by the French envoy on the Breton king Murman is spoilt by the Breton's insidious wife, as a shepherd's fire in the forest in winter is quenched by a thunderstorm with hail and rain.

Ermoldus wrote besides a suppliant poem from his exile in Strassburg, imitating that of Theodulfus to Modoin ;[1] his Thalia, his Muse, petitions for him, and there is a pleasant contention of the Vosges and the Rhine, which of them does most good to the land lying between them.

Two historical poets belonging to the end of the ninth century may here be named along with

[1] See p. 154 above.

Ermoldus Nigellus—the "Saxon Poet" (Poeta Saxo) who wrote about Charlemagne,[1] and Abbo, the his-

Abbo. torian of the siege of Paris.[2] Abbo's verse is funnier than Ermoldus, with some of the same practices, but with a larger share of the "Hisperic" vocabulary, and much more complacency in his own work. His tastes are those of Aldhelm, degraded; among the things he most admires are the terms of prosody—*episinaliffa* he writes on the margin, to call attention to an artful thing in his verse. Friends of the Renaissance, Protestant orators, and others who wish to show up the Middle Ages, will find the poem of Abbo sufficient for their purpose. It is thoroughly enjoyable.

The more scholarly Latin verse is used by a number of authors in the ninth century after the flourishing days (*c.* 809 - 849) of Alcuin and his friends. Walafrid Strabo at Reichenau, who carries on the educational work of Alcuin, resembles him *Walafrid* also in his historical and his occasional *Strabo.* poems.[3] Among the first is a rendering of the *Vision of Wettin,*[4] and a *Life of St Blathmac* of Iona. The ruin of Iona in a Viking invasion (825) had sent many Scots to take refuge under the Alps, and the Holy Island was celebrated there:—

> "Insula Pictorum quædam monstratur in oris
> Fluctivago suspensa salo cognominis Eo."

The best of the lighter poems is *Hortulus,* a series of short hexameter pieces, describing the plants of his

---

[1] *P. Lat. Carol.,* iv. 1, ed. P. von Winterfeld.
[2] Ibid., iv. 72.   [3] Ibid., ii. 259.   [4] Already mentioned, p. 71.

garden, dedicated to Grimald of St Gall. Elsewhere Walafrid uses a more pompous diction in honour of great personages, such as the Empress Judith and her son Charles.

The chief Latin poet in the middle of the ninth century was Sedulius Scottus, a wandering Irish scholar, named, like many of his country-

Sedulius Scottus. men, after the Christian poet whose *Carmen Paschale* was in the hands of every schoolboy. Sedulius the Irishman has left traces of his work in many quarters, including a Greek Psalter written by his hand. His poems,[1] of the familiar occasional sort, are distinguished by something personal and characteristic. He does not forget his own land; victories of the Irish over the Northmen are recorded; he knows something of Wales, also.

The ninth century is full of learning, and also of theological controversy, but the authors concerned are not to be treated at large in this place.

Hraban. Hrabanus Maurus is the great teacher, following Alcuin, and doing for his generation the old work of Isidore in encyclopedias (*De Universo*, 22 books) and Bible Commentaries. His pupils at Fulda —Walafrid, Lupus, Otfrid, Gottscalc—in different ways have proved the influence and efficiency of his teaching. Walafrid at Reichenau carried on the tradition of Hraban, especially as a commentator. He had many aptitudes, however, and thought for himself while he compiled his authorities. He was freshly interested in German philology; he described the

---

[1] Ed. Traube, *Poet. Carol.*, iii. 1.

Gothic Bible of Ulfilas, and has a curious chapter on German names. Like Ascham and Bacon, he is rather inclined to apologise for his vernacular language : but let us remember, he says, that apes as well as peacocks were brought to Solomon ; what seems absurd to Latin ears may yet be justified; the Lord feeds the ravens as well as the doves.

The controversies of the time, and their partisans, are only to be mentioned here. Agobard of Lyons (+840), in his writings against superstition, has included many lively passages, like the story of the land Magonia and the ship of the air.[1] The debates of Hincmar and Gottscalc, of Paschasius Radbert and Ratramnus, are not thus enlivened, though Gottscalc is to be found again, far from controversy, singing his own song in banishment.[2] But among the theological authors there is one, not any less technical indeed, but technical in a new way, a great speculative genius, whose style is something different from the conventional phrase of the schools, because his ways of thinking are different. Erigena, like other philosophers, causes trouble in literary history. It is hard *Erigena.* to describe his literary qualities apart from their philosophical substance, which is out of our range. In the general history of culture he is noted for his command of Greek, though this was not singular in an Irish scholar. His translation of Dionysius on *The Celestial Hierarchy*, besides its importance for theology, had a large imaginative influence, culminating long afterwards in Dante's *Paradiso*. His great

[1] Poole, *Mediæval Thought*, p. 39, *sq.*   [2] See below, p. 217.

work on *The Division of Nature*[1] has been appreciated as the one purely philosophical argument of the Middle Ages. It is for professed historians of philosophy to describe and criticise it: they have acknowledged the intellectual strength, the subtilty and daring of Erigena. He was called in by Hincmar of Rheims to strengthen the right cause against Gottscalc. They wanted a skilled apologist; they found one whose help, like that of the magic sword in certain fairy tales, might be dangerous for the side that used it. They asked him to oppose the excessive cruelties of predestination, as maintained by Gottscalc. But he would not be limited to the requisite amount of controversy, and before the Irish philosopher could be checked, he had refuted Sin and Hell. Neo-Platonist he is called, but in his case the name does not stand for eclectic oriental work; his mind is as clear as Berkeley's, with a vastly greater and more articulate system to explain and develop. For literature, the merit of his writing is that it expresses his meaning without hurry or confusion, and that his meaning, whatever its philosophical value, is certainly no weak repetition of commonplaces. It is to be noted that he takes a different view of Dialectic from what sufficed the ordinary professors. Dialectic is not a human contrivance. Dialectic is concealed in Nature by the Author of all the Arts, and discovered by those who look for it wisely. The proper study of Dialectic is the study of Reality. Erigena is discontented with abstractions. The current formulas

---

[1] Migne, *P. L.*, 122.

of the schools are not enough for him, in his Platonic quest for the Real. On the other hand, he saves himself from the more dangerous temptation of mysticism; he is not swallowed up in blind ecstasy. The world and its fulness is not dismissed as a shadow. He is rational, logical, though with a livelier and more imaginative logic than the common. If, like the mystics, he speak of the ineffable Unity, he has also, like Lucretius, an exultation in the welling energy of the world and its innumerable variety. Scripture, he says in one place, may be interpreted in endless ways, even as the colour shifts in a peacock's feather and there is this infinity of meaning because the world is inexhaustible. Although he makes little show of it, he was touched in imagination by the old poetic faith in the Soul of the World. He quotes, after a passage from the *Timœus*, the famous lines from the *Æneid*—

"Spiritus intus alit"—

which were taxed by Gibbon for their too close resemblance to "the impious Spinoza," and Erigena certainly cannot escape the same condemnation.

History flourished along with other learning at the court of Charles the Great. Paulus Diaconus and Einhard in different ways attained success, the one by liveliness and spirit, the other by discretion and sobriety.

Paul (*c.* 720—*c.* 790), son of Warnefrid, a Lombard, noted for his learning at the Lombard capital of Pavia before the fall of the kingdom, spent some time in the monastery of Monte Cassino after the triumph of the Franks, but was drawn by the generosity of Charles to *Paul the Deacon.* give the Frankish court the benefit of his learning. Towards the end of his life he returned again to the great Benedictine house, and there wrote his history of the Lombards.[1] He wrote much besides: a general history, to continue Eutropius, composed in the usual way by compilation from the usual authors, Orosius and others; lives of the Bishops of Metz; a life of Gregory the Great; a collection of homilies; Latin poems. But none of these have the value of the Lombard history, which, apart from its importance as a document and a record, is a book to be read for the stories in it. It is known to all students of Teutonic mythology and heroic literature on account of the legends it has preserved; the myth of the origin of the Lombard race, and still more impressive, from a different strain of tradition, the heroic story of Alboin. The tale of Alboin as given by Paul is translated and explained in *Corpus Poeticum Boreale* (vol. i. p. lii) and its relation to old Teutonic poetry discussed. The passages there quoted are of a kind which, in a general way, is not uncommon in mediæval and other history. Many historians—Herodotus, Livy, Saxo Grammaticus, William of Malmesbury—have drawn from popular tradition. The epic element in Jordanes, noted in the same context by the Oxford editors of the Northern poetry, has already been referred to here. The distinction of Paul is merely that he tells his stories with a peculiar zest,

[1] Ed. Waitz, 1878.

and also with an unfailing sense of what is properly heroic. Not even the Irish historians are more sincere in their enjoyment of adventures, nor the Icelanders more thorough in their respect for manliness. The language of course is inferior. It is not indeed the inflated Latin of Gildas or of Saxo, nor the disjointed grammar of Gregory of Tours: there is nothing in it to impede or disable the narrative. But it is flat compared with the idiomatic histories of Ireland and Iceland: one never forgets in reading it the incalculable difference between a conventional language such as this and the vivid, expressive, illustrious, vulgar tongue as used by Snorri Sturluson, or Villani, or Froissart. Yet the stories are there, and though they want the air and colour of a native language they do not want life.

Among the best, merely as adventures, are the episode of the sleep of Gunthram, and the Lombard story of the demon fly (with a wooden leg): they are variants of well-known types, but none the worse for that.

It befell one day that Gunthram King of the Franks went hunting in a forest, and, as often happens, his companions were scattered and he himself left alone with one loyal attendant. He was overcome with sleep, and slept with his head resting on his retainer's knees. As the king slept, the other in whose lap he lay saw a small creature like a lizard come out of his mouth and look for some way to cross a slender stream of water that was running near. He drew his sword from the sheath and laid it across the water;

and the little reptile went over it to the other side, and disappeared in a hole in the hill. It returned not long after and came back over the sword and into the king's mouth. When Gunthram awoke he described a wonderful vision. It seemed in his dream that he had crossed a river on an iron bridge and entered a mountain where he found a great treasure of gold. Then the squire told him what he had seen while the king was asleep. Search was made in the place, and great heaps of ancient gold discovered there. Of this the king had a paten made, of great size and weight, adorned with precious stones, which he intended to have sent to the Holy Sepulchre in Jerusalem, but he was prevented, and placed it on the shrine of St Marcellus at Chalons, the capital of his kingdom, where it is to this day.

The story of Cunincpert and the fly is even more remarkable.

Cunincpert, King of the Lombards, was standing at the window of the palace in Pavia consulting with his marshal[1] how to remove his enemies Aldo and Grauso.

A large fly settled on the window-sill before him : the king made a blow at it with his dagger, but only cut off a leg. Meantime Aldo and Grauso were coming to the palace, ignorant of the king's designs against them. When they were at the church of St Romanus near the palace, there met them a one-

---

[1] "Cum stratore eius, qui lingua propria *marpahis* dicitur." Paul uses a few Lombard words, like this : *marhpaiz* is the groom who bits and bridles the horse.

legged man who said to them that if they went to
Cunincpert he would kill them. They were filled
with terror at this, and took refuge behind the altar
in the church: this was told to the king. Then
Cunincpert blamed his marshal for publishing his
intention. But the marshal answered, "My lord king,
thou knowest that since this was spoken of in counsel
I have not departed from thy presence : and how could
I tell it to any one?" Then the king sent to Aldo
and Grauso asking why they had fled to sanctuary.
They answered, "Because it was declared to us that
our lord the king would have put us to death."
Again the king sent to ask them who had given them
these tidings, affirming that unless they told they
should never have grace. Then they sent to the king
to say that a lame man had met them, wanting a foot
and with a wooden leg, who had warned them of destruction. Then the king saw that the fly whose foot
he had cut off was an evil spirit, and had discovered
his secret. He brought away Aldo and Grauso from
their refuge, and forgave them, and took them into
his favour.

Stories like these show that it was neither want of
spirit nor material that prevented Paul the Deacon
from rivalling the masters of narrative style in the
later vernacular literatures. He had it in him to
write a Lombard prose Edda, Lombard Sagas not
much inferior to those of Iceland; and it would be
easy to find in Froissart, both in the heroic and the
less solemn passages (like the story "of the spirit
called Horton"), good parallels to the Lombard his-

tory.   But the Latin language, useful as it is, and not
without a character of its own, as Paul writes it,
is altogether outclassed in comparison with mediæval French or Icelandic.

The heroic stories of Alboin already referred to are
derived, it is hardly open to doubt, from epic lays.
In other parts of the history, later, one seems to find
a different sort of adventure, where Paul, like Froissart,
is dealing more directly with historical fact, and gives
the heroic quality to his composition not by translat-
ing from any poem but finding for himself and expressing in his own way the meaning of the events
described.   The life of King Grimwald especially, in
the fourth and fifth books of the history, brings out
the excellences of Paul as an arranger and interpreter
of memorable things: the imaginative value of the
story is not small, and it is secured by fair means.
The character and strength of the king is disclosed
without the arts and expedients of the rhetorical
showman: it makes its own impression, dramatically,
from the time when the child Grimwald kills his
Avar captor with his little sword to the day when his
persecuted rival Berthari, putting out to sea to escape
to England, is recalled by a voice from the French
shore, telling that Grimwald has been three days
dead.[1]   The interest is not confined to the chief

---

[1] A short specimen of Paul's Latin may be given here from this
part of his work : l. v. c. 33 : "Igitur, ut dicere cœperamus, Perctarit
egressus de Gallia navem ascendit ut ad Brittaniam insulam ad
regnum Saxonum transmearet.   Cumque jam aliquantum per
pelagus navigasset, vox a litore audita est inquirentis utrum Perctarit in eadem nave consisteret.   Cui cum responsum esset, quod

personages : there is a richness of heroic incident such as is found in the memoirs of the age of chivalry, in Barbour for example : as in the last chapter of Book IV. the simple man (parvus homunculus) who avenged his lord and took the life of the treacherous Garibald at the expense of his own : or in the story of the constancy of Seswald, a Lombard Regulus, though it was not for the state that he sacrified his life, but (more like a Dane than a Roman) to preserve his foster-son. The Greeks with all their engines were besieging Romwald, Grimwald's son, in Beneventum, and took prisoner Seswald, who was coming with news of reinforcement to the Lombards in the city. Seswald was led up to the walls and enjoined for his life to say that there was no hope of relief for the besieged. Seswald however called to Romwald his fosterling to hold out, for his father was near : whereupon his head was promptly cut off by the Greeks and sent over the walls from a catapult ("cum belli machina quam petrariam vocant in urbem projectum est "). Then the Greeks raised the siege. The heroic generosity which is shown in the tale of the youth of Alboin comes out as clearly in the history of Grimwald : especially in his behaviour after the escape of Berthari and his treatment of the loyal servitor who had managed it.

Perctarit ibi esset, ille qui clamabat subjunxit : Dicite illi revertatur in patram suam, quia tertia die est hodie quod Grimualdus subtractus est luce. Quo audito Perctarit post se reversus est veniensque ad litus invenire personam non potuit quæ ei de Grimualdi morte nuntiavit ; unde arbitratus est, non hunc hominem sed divinum nuntium fuisse."

"The king asked the chamberlain in what manner Berthari had escaped. He told the king the whole business just as it had taken place. Then the king asked his courtiers: 'What is your judgment on this man, who has done all this?' Then all with one voice replied that he deserved torturing to death. But the king said: 'By Him that made me! the man shall be rewarded, who for the faith he owed his lord did not refuse death.' And he gave him a place among his chamberlains, bidding him observe the same faith to him that he had shown to his former lord."

This sums up the whole rule of the heroic age; the moral is the same as in the poem of Byrhtnoth and countless other documents. It is part of the value of Paul that his Latin history is a record of the Teutonic heroic age; and it includes in its course both the earlier and the later periods; a period of Lombard history corresponding to that which is represented in Iceland and England by the Poetic Edda and by *Beowulf;* and also a more modern period, corresponding to that of the Sagas in Iceland, that of the Maldon poem in England, where the ethics of the old heroic poetry are proved to be applicable in real life, or what is thought of as real. Froissart is in the same position with regard to the heroic ideal and the actual life of his own time or near his own time. He has in his mind the doctrine of old French epic, as Paulus Diaconus has the Teutonic theory of honour: he finds it available for things that really happen, the old motives still working in the minds of living men. So Paulus Diaconus, without any forcing of the matter or any unfair adulteration of the facts before him, finds the story of the more recent things

in Lombard history shaping into something of the
same fashion as the earlier. It is an historical
achievement of some note to have put so much into
one compendious book—a story which if translated into
Icelandic terms would reach from the poems of the
Volsung cycle, or even earlier, down to the Saga of St
Olaf or of Harald Hardrada; if into French terms, then
from the song of Roland to Joinville or Froissart. No
doubt it is better to have the French or the Icelandic
books as they are: the product of different generations, maintaining the same spirit from the first days
of early epic to the time of later prose memoirs and
chronicles. But that does not discredit the Lombard
summary, which, short as it is, is not bare or abstract.

Although the liveliest parts of Paul's book may be
supposed to come from traditional story-telling, he
was not, any more than Snorri or Froissart, independent of previous written works. As Snorri based his
history of the Norwegian kings on the earlier lives
written by Ari the Wise, and as Froissart adapted the
Chronicles of Jehan le Bel, Paulus Diaconus acknowledges a debt to Secundus of Trent (+612) "who wrote
a brief history of the Lombards down to his own time"
—*qui usque ad sua tempora succinctam de Langobardorum gestis composuit historiolam;* and he makes use
also of another short history, still extant, the *Origo
gentis Langobardorum.*

Einhard's *Life of Charles,*[1] in comparison with Paul's
Lombard history, recalls to mind the antithesis between the romantic and the reflective historian, the

---

[1] Ed. Jaffé, 1867 (*Monumenta Carolina*).

types represented by Herodotus and Thucydides, by Froissart and Commines. In contrast

Einhard. to the discursive methods of Paul, Einhard composes his book with a regard to unity and proportion; he has a definite scheme, he studies arrangement. His book has a modern character, because it has learned the ancient rules of construction. His biographical motive is not the heroic interest in adventure, but a more self-conscious ambition, studious and deliberate. He aims at expressing the value of the Emperor Charles in an intelligent and careful literary description. He gets the pattern of his design from Suetonius; but he is really more classical than his model, because he puts more thought into his work and is more seriously interested in his subject.

Einhard's book was edited by Walafrid Strabo, who describes him in the Preface. He was a Franconian of the Maine, educated at Fulda, and sent by the abbot as a man of learning to the Palace of Charles. Einhard's contemptible bodily presence and mighty spirit made a theme for the other Palatines; Alcuin and Theodulfus wrote epigrams on "Nardulus," which was his name in that learned society—

> "Nardulus huc illuc discurrat perpete gressu
> Ut formica tuus pes redit itque frequens," &c.

So Theodulfus begins his poem. Another name was Beseleel, by reason of his skill in architecture.

Einhard derives nothing from the vague popular sources such as were known to Jordanes and loved by Paulus Diaconus. The "barbara et antiquissima carmina," the ancient Frankish poems on the wars of kings, were of value to him as extant documents on account of Charles's respect for them : they occur as a fact in biography, because he took care of them and had them written down. Nor does he, like some other historians, find an epic treatment desirable for the events of his own time. The disaster in the Pyrenees, where Hruodland fell, warden of the Breton marches, along with Eggihard, provost of the king's table, and Anshelm, count palatine, is told with clearness and dignity, in brief prose. Einhard's mind has little of the mediæval temper in it, and much of the Roman. The luxury of sentiment, the effusion, the excess, of mediæval literature at its best and worst have no part in his composition. His book is intellectually strong, and prosaic. Along with Bede, though of course in a way of his own, he shows how easy it was in the Dark Ages to write sensibly and strongly, when the sense and the strength were present to begin with. Out of the common accessible culture of the time, the learning and scholarship, he selects those elements and learns those principles which are suitable for his own genius—like every other scholar in any other age. The case of Einhard is only specially remarkable because of the common prejudice which believes that the spirit of the Dark Ages is enough to warp or oppress native talent, particularly when the talent is rational and positive. A comparison of Alcuin and Einhard might be of some use to correct this idea, and to show how the same kind of schooling leaves the original characters distinct.

Alcuin with all his learning is soft, wordy, sometimes inept: he could not attain by any study to the precision of Einhard.   On the other hand, Einhard could tell a story, when he chose, as well as any one ; nothing is better in its way than the remarkable adventures in the hunt for relics, as described in his *Translatio SS. Petri et Marcellini.*   The dignified reserve of his historical work was not mere dryness or want of spirit.

Nithard, the son of Angilbert and grandson of Charlemagne, wrote the history of his own time addressed to Charles the Bald; the first two *Nithard.* books come down to the battle of Fontenoy (841), where Nithard himself took part, and Charles defeated his brother Lothair; the third and fourth come down to 843, and include the famous oaths of Strassburg between Charles and Lewis the German, reported in the two languages — *Teudisca, Romana lingua.*   Nithard died Abbot of St Riquier in 844, defending the place against an attack, probably of the Danes.   He is a business-like unrhetorical narrator, comparable with Einhard for honesty and good sense, though inferior in political talent and historical art.   His place as a witness and partaker of the actions described is such as hardly could be taken by any one else.

The monastery of St Gall had a great affection for stories, and some of the most amusing memoirs of the *The Monk of* Dark Ages were written there.   Ekkehard *St Gall.* in the eleventh century succeeded both to the tastes and the liveliness of the earlier Monk of St Gall, identified by some with Notker of the *Se-*

quences, who wrote the life of Charles the Great from oral tradition, and put into it a number of irrelevant and entertaining matters.[1] He was an old man when the Emperor Charles the Fat visited St Gall, in 883. That visit prompted him to write down his reminiscences, the anecdotes of Charlemagne which he had heard from his teacher Werinbert the priest, and from Werinbert's father Adalbert, an old warrior in the battles of the great Emperor. His book is often referred to for evidence of the growing romance of Charlemagne; it is the Monk of St Gall who tells the story of Ogier and King Didier: "by that sign you may divine that Charlemagne is near." The Monk, "slower than a tortoise," as he says, had never been in France, but he had no scruples about confessing the glory of the Franks, in which all the nations were proud to share. He has a description of Charles, surrounded by the splendour of his court, like the host of heaven. It is significant that this is made an opportunity for humiliating the Greeks; there are other passages in the same context where the vanity of the Greeks is ridiculed; the Monk sharing in that opposition of Frank to Greek which is expressed so humorously in the poem of Charlemagne's pilgrimage. He gives from the life, as it would seem, a sketch of the fighting man of those days, a certain Eishere, a son of Anak, who came back from the wars with the Slaves, and expressed his opinion of the business: "Wends? what have I to do with the Wends? Frogs I call them—frogs. I used to carry

---

[1] *Monachus Sangallensis de Carolo Magno,* ed. Jaffé (*Mon. Carol.*)

13

seven, or eight, or nine, on my lance at once—spitted
on my lance, and all gabbling nonsense." The large
and sanguine heroes of epic poetry, not strict in their
ways of speaking, given to expand their own exploits,
are known to the Monk without their poetic dress,
and much admired by him. Whatever be the value
of his history of Charles, he has added much to the
stock of information about private life and manners.
He is not an historian like Einhard, but he can write
many pleasant things which Einhard would not have
thought of. The story of the Brownie and the Farrier
is an instance—beneath the dignity of history, of
course. The Brownie is *pilosus*, a Ragman, a Satyr—
the word is used in the Latin of Isaiah, where "satyr"
is now read in English—*et pilosi saltabunt ibi*, Is. xiii.
21. He is humorous and good-natured, like other
Brownies. He promised to fill the smith's bottle
with wine, if he would only give him leave to play
about in the workshop and not vex him with the sign
of the cross. The smith consented, and the Brownie
kept his bargain, going for wine to the cellar of a
miserly bishop, and wasting more than he carried
away. He was caught at last, but his thoughts were
unselfish even in that trial: "Pity me, I have lost
my gossip's bottle!" (*Ve mihi quia poticulam com-
patris mei perdidi.*)

The style of the Monk is not unlike that of Ekkehard : mediæval Latin in every line of it, with nothing
classical except an occasional patch of quotation. It
has something of the excessive ornament to which
one grows accustomed; but many better scholars

have more of it, and it does not seriously get in the way of the meaning. He uses German words on occasion, *e.g.*, *minima meisa*, "the smallest titmouse"; but his grammar is not unreasonable: the Latin of St Gall under Abbot Grimald and Abbot Hartmuot might be familiar and careless enough, but it was a different thing from the decrepit grammar of Gregory of Tours.

Asser's Life of King Alfred was written about the same time; a work regarding which there are many

Asser. disputes, historical and critical; to be noted here as another example of florid Latin encasing much good plain sense.[1]

The tenth century, the period of the Saxon Emperors, is perhaps less scholarly than the time of Charlemagne, but the name of Gerbert at the end of it proves that nothing had been lost through political distractions. And the Latin writers of the tenth century, especially the historians, are full of interesting matter.

The family of Otho the Great was fond of learning: his brother Bruno reading Latin comedies " for style"; his nieces Gerberg, Abbess of Gandersheim, and Hadwig, the capricious great lady of the Hohentwiel. And literary men of different sorts from different lands were encouraged by the Othos: Liutprand of Cremona, Ratherius of Verona, Gerbert, all of them were of strong character. The Saxons came out as authors under their own great kings; if only they

---

[1] *Mon. histor. Britann.*, i.; a new edition is in preparation by Mr W. H. Stevenson.

had thought of writing down carefully their own
Saxon poems, instead of leaving the romances of
Saxony to be picked up three hundred years later
by a foreign amateur! Hrotswith of Gandersheim,
and Widukind, however, are good representatives of
the country, in their own ways.

The long life of Rather of Verona[1] (c. 890-974) was
spent in many different occupations, teaching, writing,
the practical work of his bishopric, the
Ratherius.   political business that made him an exile
and a wanderer. He was deposed by King Hugh in
935 and imprisoned in Pavia : there he wrote his *Præ-
loquia*, on holy living, and incidentally on the profane
state of the Italian bishops. His *Phrenesis*, in twelve
books, was put together in a later time of trouble,
after he had been for the second time compelled
to give up the see of Verona, as also that of his native
Liége. For the third time he was restored to Verona
(by Otho the Great in his Italian progress), and again
he abandoned it. His writings are strong in common-
sense, and his Latin is eloquent. He was a great
preacher, and could make familiar ideas new again :
"O quam hic abyssus Veteris Testamenti abyssum
invocat Novi! O quam antiquiora recentioribus con-
cinunt." He is one of the first to make use of fables
in illustration of his sermons ;[2] with all his pride he
had something like Swift's regard for the ordinary
intelligence, and its claim to have things made palp-

---

[1] Migne, *P. L.*, 136.
[2] He refers to the Frog and Mouse, well known in the collections
of *Exempla Familiaria*, and in Dante.

able to it. He speaks expressly against swollen rhetoric.

Hrotswith, a nun of Gandersheim,[1] got her learning from Gerberg, daughter of Henry—the Heinric who *Hrotswith.* makes so great a part in the history of his brother Otho. That history was one of Hrotswith's poetical subjects—*De Gestis Oddonis I. Imperatoris*—down to the imperial coronation in 962. Beyond that she will not go—the subject is too high for her. According to Hrotswith, Otho was drawn to Italy by motives such as have their place in the story of Geoffrey Rudel and many other romances: the pilgrims brought back such praises of the distressed queen Adelheid. Hrotswith wrote a number of legends in verse—St Gingulphus, Theophilus, and others. The story of Theophilus was one of the most popular in all the tongues;[2] how the young archdeacon, disappointed of his promotion, consulted a Jewish sorcerer and was taken to a meeting of devils, and renounced God in a written document, and repented, and was rescued by our Lady. Hrotswith adds to the story, characteristically, the education of Theophilus in the seven arts:—

"De Sophiæ rivis septeno fonte manantis."

There is little, for that time, remarkable in her Latin verse: she uses the Leonine rhyme.

The best known and most original work of Hrot-

---

[1] *Hrotsvithæ Opera*, ed. P. von Winterfeld, Berlin, 1902.

[2] Several versions—Icelandic, Low German, &c.—were collected and edited by Dasent in 1845.

swith is her imitation of Terence—six comedies, in prose.   Terence, she says, in her preface,[1] is read by many who are taken by the charm of the style, and corrupted by acquaintance with abominable things. Her comedies were to take the place of Terence in the studies of Gandersheim.   But her themes are still love-stories, because that is proper to this kind of poetry (*hujusmodi specie dictationis cogente*).   The names, it may be remarked, — *Gallicanus, Dulcitius, Callimachus, Abraham, Paphnutius, Sapientia,*—have been given by editors; there are no titles in the original.   To do justice to them here is impossible. No abstract can describe their simplicity, the gentle pride of learning in them (shown for example in the scene of Paphnutius and his scholars), much less the comic effect of their stories.   Dulcitius stricken with illusion, embracing the pots and kettles in the kitchen, while the three holy maidens, Agape, Chionia, and Irene, are saved from his villany; Dulcitius frightening the watch with his blackened face, detected by his wife, is like an importation from the City of Laughter in Apuleius, but turned into pure innocence.

Flodoard of Rheims (894-966) is one of the chief historians of the century, in his Annals and his *Historia Remensis Ecclesiæ*.   He is respected for his sober methods and his independent use of documents.

Liutprand of Cremona,[2] though not careless about

---

[1] Hrotswith, like Aldhelm, knows the Saxon meaning of her name ; in the preface she is *Clamor validus Gandersheimensis.*   Compare also Ermoldus Nigellus on the etymology of "Hludovicus," above, p. 56.

[2] Ed. Dümmler, 1877 (Pertz, *Scriptores*).

historical facts, is in manner a contrast to Flodoard.
Liutprand. The Dark Ages are not dull, with Liutprand. He has levity enough to weigh up
shiploads of encyclopedias and homilies; he escapes
like Ariel from all rules. The accidents of his
birth and nation have prevented him from taking
the place which his abilities would warrant, as an
illustration of the Celtic genius. Irish literature
contains nothing more wilful and irrepressible. Some
other historians in the Dark Ages may have a greater
fund of adventure: the tales of Paulus Diaconus are
better in themselves than those of Liutprand; there
is a greater variety, and more of them; but Liutprand
has no one near him in his gift of pure mischief. He
has contributed to the footnotes of Gibbon, but it is
his manner more than the value of his stories that
makes him delightful.

It comes partly from the general circumstances of
education that his style is so remarkable. The con-
fusions and the excesses of rhetoric, so often referred
to already, produced many wonderful things in the
Dark Ages, from Martianus Capella to the Hisperica
Famina, from Cassiodorus to the polite Latin of the
old English charters,—things that look as if the
whole business of their language had been directed
by the genius of Rabelais himself, with the help
of a committee of the court of Pantagruel, and the
Limousin scholar added. It is of course an accidental
unconscious Pantagruelism that has made the rich
motley of so much early mediæval literature; but
every now and then, in Ireland more than elsewhere,

but not exclusively in Ireland, the Pantagruelic Idea
comes to a consciousness of itself in some of the finer
spirits, and they use the resources of variegated diction
with a sense of its value. Liutprand is one of these:
not that even he can be supposed to have understood
how wonderful his style is: but he had a mercurial
gift or passion for words, a vituperative genius not
inferior to that of Mac Conglinne himself, and no
ambition stronger than that of doing as he pleased.
This pleasant character is expressed in the very
opening words of his history:—

"In nomine Patris et Filii et Spiritus Sancti incipit liber
antapodóseos αντατοδόσεως retributionis regum atque principum
partis Europæ a Liudprando Ticinensis ecclesiæ diacone en ti
echmalosia autû ἐν τῇ εχμαλοσια ἀυτοῦ in peregrinatione ejus ad
Recemmodum Hispaniæ provintie Liberritanæ ecclesiæ epis-
copum editus."

That is his way: the original manuscript now in
Munich has these Greek spices scattered over it
in Liutprand's own writing; the amanuensis who
made the fair copy having left the proper blanks
for the author to fill in when he revised the book.
The spelling and accents are authentic; the motives
are sometimes intelligible, as where he is quoting
the words of a Greek—"filanthrope vasileu"—*i.e.*,
"humanissime imperator"; or where he himself explains it, for the sake of the sound. "Et quia sonorius
est, grece illud dicamus. Ἀδελβέρτος κόμις κουρτης
μακροσπάθης γουνδοπιστις. Adelbertos comis curtis
macrospathis gundopistis quo significatur et dicitur
longo eum uti ense et minima fide," ii. c. 34. This

"quia sonorius est" must be taken to justify all the cases where there seems no other reason for the ornament. He quotes in full, in Greek, the story of Jupiter, Juno, and Tiresias, "secundum Grecorum ineptiam" (iii. c. 41) on a chance association: the word "blind" is enough to set him off. He quotes in Greek, with a transcription as usual (like Panurge's Greek), the text of the camel and the needle's eye— "eucopoteron gar estin camilon dia trimalias rafidos iselthin i plúsion is tin basilian tu theu." But Greek is not his only resource. He intersperses Latin poems of his own. He tags his sentences out of any author he has read, Horace or Ezekiel. "Quousque tandem abutere, Hulodoice, patientia nostra?" is a speech put in the mouth of Berengar.

Berengar was the adversary: and Liutprand's title *Antapodosis* is explained by him at the beginning of the third book as meaning retribution to Berengar the tyrant and the second Jezebel. "Such bolts of falsehood, such extravagance of robbery, such blows of impiety have they bestowed on me and my house and kindred without a cause, as neither tongue avails to express nor pen to write down." It is also a return, he explains, to his benefactors; but the other motive is clearly the stronger one, and it is because he has this score to pay and a good unforgiving temper that there is so much spirit in his history.

Liutprand's father had been employed before him in diplomatic affairs, and had visited Constantinople as an envoy of King Hugh. Liutprand himself, not long after his father's death (*c.* 927), was brought as a boy to the court of Pavia and there well educated. After the fall of Hugh and the rise of Berengar, Liutprand was still kept at court; in 949 he went as Berengar's envoy to the Emperor Constantine Porphyrogenitus. On his return he incurred the misfortunes spoken of above at the hands of Berengar and his wife Willa, and took refuge with Otho the Great. His *Antapodosis*, dedicated to Bishop Recemund of Elvira, was begun at Frankfort in 958 and finished in the isle of Paxos, in another journey in Greece, which is the *echmalosia* spoken of in the preface, *v. sup.*

He was made Bishop of Cremona in 961, took part in the dealings between Otho and the Romans, and interpreted the Emperor's speech at Rome in 963: "quia Romani ejus loquelam propriam hoc est Saxonicam intellegere nequibant." In the following year he wrote the history of Otho's Italian journey. An original manuscript in his own writing precedes that of the *Antapodosis* at Munich. In 968 he went again to Constantinople to negotiate with the Emperor Nicephorus a marriage between the Emperor's daughter Theophano and the younger Otho. His account of this legation is another exercise of his satiric power. Nicephorus is treated with the same skill as Berengar in the *Antapodosis*, and with much more leisure and attention to details. Liutprand died in 971 or 972.

The life of Liutprand was well filled: he saw history being acted; he knew the most notable men of his time, and had the confidence of the greatest. He took part in high politics with judgment and dignity. But he could not extinguish the mocking genius in his nature, the spirit of freedom which makes the Bishop of Cremona akin to many less reputable and equally untamable authors. Among the most characteristic specimens of his style is the story of the Frolicsome Emperor in the first book, introduced in a significant way with the remark that, speaking of the Eastern Emperors, he may be pardoned for relating two adventures of Leo son of Basil, "worthy of record and of laughter."[1] Leo went about his capital in disguise, like Haroun Alraschid, and Liutprand tells how he fared, with more enjoyment than he shows in the more serious parts of his narrative. In his book about Otho, though it is written with spirit, there is less opportunity for his peculiar ways: he avoids digressions, and refrains from his Greek decoration. In the narrative of his embassy to Nicephorus he finds exactly the subject that suits him. It is all his own: he speaks of what he has seen; he has accounts to settle with the arrogance and vanity of the Greeks in general, and especially with their disgusting Emperor, who is described in terms that would have pleased an Irish professional satirist and enriched the vocabulary of Dunbar.[2]

---

[1] Nunc autem non pigeat libellulo huic res duas quas ejusdem Basilii filius memoratus Leo imperator augustus memoria risuque dignas egit inserere. *Antapod.*, i. c. 11.

[2] Liutprand's Greek is not exceptional. The *Corpus Glossariorum Latinorum*, vol. iii. (*Hermeneumata Pseudodositheana*, ed. Goetz) contains a number of Greek-Latin dialogues, some of them in MSS. of the time of Liutprand, others older or younger. A specimen

Widukind, monk of Corbey, in his history of the Saxons[1] is not unlike Paulus Diaconus in scope and method: he is writing about his own nation, *Widukind.* he has the same affection for popular songs and stories, and the same kind of historical learning. If Widukind the Saxon has less variety of narrative than Paul the Lombard, in compensation he deals more fully with his own times and with greater personages. His history is dedicated to Matilda, daughter of Otho the Great, and the Saxon emperor is his hero. The book was finished in 968; after the death of Otho in 973 a short continuation was added. The traditions of the Old Saxons (as Bede and the Anglo-Saxons generally called them) are fairly represented by Widukind in the early part of his book: at least one can trace there the ancient German simplicity which the Saxons retained longer than other Teutonic nations except the Northmen: they keep, as Bede remarked, a simple political system, with equality

from a Munich MS. of the twelfth century may be admitted here, to illustrate not Liutprand merely, but the culture of the Middle Ages :—

epidioro : quoniam video.	difficultatem.
pollus : multos.	*kai poliplithian :* et multitud-
epithimuntas : cupientes.	inem.
romaisti : latine.	*rimaton :* verborum.
dealegeste : disputare.	*tiemi cacopathia :* meo labore.
kai ellinisti : et grece.	*kai filoponia :* et industria.
mite eucheros : neque facile (quo-	*ucefisamin :* non peperci.
que MS.)	*tumi piise :* ut non facerem.
dinaste : posse.	*oposentrisin :* ut in tribus.
diatis discherian diatin : propter	*bibliis :* libris, &c.

[1] Ed. Waitz, 1882 (Pertz, *Scriptores*).

among the chieftains, and no king over them, except occasionally for purposes of war. The Irminsul, the sacred pillar of Saxon religion, is mentioned, and the tragedy of Iring, who slew his lord Irminfrid and then purged his treason, is a relic of some value from the lost heroic literature of the Saxons. Widukind had the national love of ballads, though he made no such profit out of them as was made three centuries later by the Norwegian who collected in Saxony the lays of Theodoric. It is not difficult to find in his work the traces of popular romance, and he quotes the popular satire of the ballad-singers, who chanted after a victory, "Where is there a roomy Hell, big enough to hold the French?" Widukind also has the skill of the writer of memoirs, and notes the same sort of things as Froissart, such as the "subtilties" of warfare, the cunning devices and stratagems: one of these practical jokes, founded on knowledge of pigs and their natural affection, is repeated in Froissart.[1]

In dealing with the principal theme, the life of Otho, Widukind is drawn away from the attraction of stories to a graver interest more like that of Einhard's Life of Charles; and he shows himself capable of understanding and explaining the character and work of the Emperor.

Richer, monk of St Remy, a pupil of Gerbert, in-

[1] "Augebat quoque indignationem ducis grex porcorum ab Immone callide captus. Nam subulcis ducis cum contra portas urbis transirent, Immo porcellum pro porta agitari fecit et omnem gregem porcorum apertis portis in urbem recepit. Quam injuriam dux ferre non valens coacto exercitu obsedit Immonem."—Widukind, ii. c. 23.

cluded something of Gerbert in his four books of
Histories : a description of his teaching and

Richer.

a remarkable account of a scholastic debate at Ravenna in 980 between Gerbert and Otric
the Saxon philosopher, in presence of Otho II. It
lasted too long for the Emperor.[1] One of the most
interesting passages in the memoirs of that time, not
inferior to the stories of Ekkehard, nor except in
language to Froissart, is Richer's narrative of his
troublesome journey from Rheims to Chartres for the
sake of learning (iv. c. 50):—

"I had been thinking much and often of the Liberal
Arts, with an eager desire for the Logic of Hippocrates
the Coan, when one day in Rheims I met with a
traveller on horseback come from Chartres. I asked
him his name and his duty, whence he came, and for
what motive. He answered that he had been com-
missioned by Herbrand, a clerk in Chartres, and
charged to find out Richer, a monk of St Remy.
When I heard my friend's name, I declared myself
as the person he sought, gave him the kiss of greeting,
and brought him where we might talk undisturbed.
He produced a letter urging me to read the Aphorisms of Hippocrates. This gave me great pleasure,
and I determined to set out for Chartres along with
my envoy and a boy to attend me. From the Abbot
at departing I received no more than the gift of one
palfrey. Without money or letters of credit I reached

---

[1] "Augusti nutu disputationi finis injectus est, eo quod et diem
pene in his totum consumserant et audientes prolixa atque continua
disputatio jam fatigabat."—Richeri, *Hist.*, l. iii. 65 ; ed. Waitz, 1877.

Orbais, a place renowned for charity; and there was much refreshed in conversation with the Abbot, and munificently entertained. I left on the morrow for Meaux. But the perplexities of a forest which I and my companions entered were not without their evil fortune: we went wrong at cross-roads, and wandered six leagues out of our way. Just past the castle of Theodoric (Château Thierry), the palfrey, which before had appeared a Bucephalus, now began to drag like the sluggish ass. Now the sun had passed the South, and, all the air dissolving into rain, was hastening to his setting in the West, when that strong Bucephalus was overcome by the strain, failed and sank beneath the boy who was riding him, and as if struck by lightning expired at the sixth milestone from the city. What was my anxiety they will easily judge who have been in like fortune. The boy, not used to this kind of travelling, lay utterly worn out by the body of the horse; the bags had no one to carry them; the rain was pouring; the sky all cloud; the sun nearly set. However, Heaven gave counsel among these troubles. I left the boy there with the baggage, told him what to answer to questions from passers-by, bade him beware of falling asleep, and, along with the Chartres messenger, got to Meaux. I pass on to the bridge, with scarcely light to see by. Then looking more narrowly I was assailed by new mischances. There were so many large gaps in the bridge that the visitors of the townsfolk can only have got over that day with hazard. The man of Chartres, full of quickness and of good sense likewise for the difficulties of the journey, after looking all about for a ferry and finding none, came back to the perils of the bridge: Heaven granted him to get the horses safe over. For in the gaping places he sometimes put his shield under the horses' feet, sometimes laid loose planks over, stooping and rising and coming and going till he had brought the horses, and me with them, safe across. The night lowered and veiled the world in darkness and gloom when I entered St Faro's; the brethren were just preparing the loving-cup. That day [? Mid-Lent] they had dined in state, and read the chapter of the Rule 'Concerning the Cellarer of the Monastery,' which was the cause of their late potation. By them I was received as a brother, and restored with pleasant conversation and a plenteous repast. I sent back the man from Chartres with the horses to pass again the perils of the bridge and find my boy. He crossed as before, and after some wandering came to the boy in the second watch, calling often before he found him. He picked him up, and brought him back to the bridge; but knowing enough of its dangers by this time, turned aside to a cottage near, where after a day of hunger they spent a night of sleep. What a sleepless night had I, racked with what cruel pain, they may imagine who have been kept awake by anxiety for their friends. With the morning, not too early, they appeared. They were nearly perished with hunger, and food was brought them. The horses also had provender and straw. Leaving the boy, horseless, in care of the Abbot, I went on with all speed to Chartres, and then sent back my travelling companion with the horses to bring the boy on. All ended well, all anxieties passed away; I studied diligently in the Aphorisms of Hippocrates with Dan Herbrand, a man of great liberality and learning. In the Aphorisms I found only the prognostics of diseases, and as a simple knowledge of ailments was not enough for my ambition, I obtained from him further the reading of the Look entitled *Harmony of Hippocrates, Galen and Suranus:* Herbrand was proficient in medicine, and neither pharmaceutics, botany, nor surgery was beyond his range."

The year of this was 991.

Ekkehard's memoirs of the monastery of St Gall [1] are like a College history, with the gossip of successive generations better preserved than it *Ekkehard.* usually is, and also with a strain of heroic and romantic adventures such as has not been common in our Universities, at any rate for the last century or two. Some of the matter of Prideaux's letters is very like much of Ekkehard, who would have understood very well the disagreements between a Head of a College and the Fellows, and could have appreciated the humour of such incidents as the visit of Cornelis Tromp to Christ Church. The local knowledge of Ekkehard is all important for his history; it gives him a literary advantage over even such lively writers

---

[1] *Ekkeharti Casus S. Galli,* ed. G. Meyer von Knonau, 1877 (*St Galler Geschichtsquellen,* iii.) There were four Ekkehards of St Gall; the first and the fourth are best known. Ekkehard I., the author of *Waltharius,* died in 973; Ekkehard IV., the historian, about 1036.

as Paul the Deacon or Liutprand. His stories, whatever their historical value, are charged with the reality
of the place. His theatre is not like the vague geo-
graphical scenery of ordinary history. The walls of
the monastery and the familiar landscape of St Gall
are never out of his mind; the scriptorium, the cellar,
the old men's corner, where the good Abbot Thieto sat
after his resignation, all the well-known buildings are
a sort of authority for his narrative; they are his
sources, in no merely figurative or fanciful sense.
They have the same effect with him as the knowledge
of their country in the Icelandic sagas, where the
historians can rely on their heaths and valleys to
confirm the story, and the travelling of Gunnar or
Gisli comes to the reader's mind like his own memory
of the same places. There are other resemblances
in Ekkehard to the Icelandic sort of history: his
book is a Saga, a family history, a story of individual
men and their fortunes. He does not need the larger
political interests in his biographical sketches: the
portraits come out all the clearer because he is not
a profound historian. There are no generalities, no
abstractions to deface or blur them. His characters
are not spoilt, because there is nothing in the author's
mind more interesting than character.

Ekkehard continued the earlier work of Ratpert, *De
Casibus Monasterii S. Galli.*[1] Ratpert is one of his
first heroes, but not alone: there are three friends,
Ratpert, Tuotilo, and Notker, and the story of the
three inseparables, as Ekkehard calls them, is one of the

---

[1] Ed. G. Meyer von Knonau, 1872.

passages of mediæval history that may stand comparison with anything modern; the real life in it comes out unimpaired through all the quaintnesses and awkwardness of the Latin prose. The three friends are as distinct, their characters as vividly expressed, as any three in history: Tuotilo the strong man of genius, a sanguine temper; Ratpert the scholar, not eminently devout, attentive in his work as a teacher, but rather negligent otherwise; Notker the stammerer, gentle and shy, except when the Adversary was to be resisted. These three senators of our commonwealth, says Ekkehard, like all learned and useful men, suffered detraction and backbiting (*dorsiloquia*) from the vain and idle, particularly Notker, because he was the least dangerous. Of this base sort we will bring forward a specimen to show what power Satan assumes in such people. There was in our house a *refectorarius* named Sindolf, who afterwards, by fawning and flattering and talebearing, obtained from Bishop Solomon the office of dean of the works. Before this, while he was sewer and had charge of the table, he used to render disservices where he dared, especially to Notker. Bishop Solomon was much occupied, and not able to give much attention to details in St Gall [Solomon was abbot there, and Bishop of Constance at the same time]. The victuals and drink were poor and nasty, and there was complaint made, in which the three took part. But Sindolf, knowing where the source of this heat lay among these fellow-scholars, applied himself to the ear of the Bishop as though to tell him something that concerned his honour, and the Bishop heard him, though he must have known that there is nothing more injurious for a prelate than to listen to such whisperings. Sindolf told him that those three were used to speak evil of their abbot, and had yesterday said blasphemous things against God. Solomon took this for truth, and showed rancour towards the three, groundlessly; they guess themselves circumvented by the devices of Sindolf (*Sindolfi se tegnis ariolantur fuisse circumventos*). The matter was discussed in public before the brethren; the evidence of all was in their favour. They ask for vengeance on the false witness. Solomon would not disclose him, and there was nothing for it but to endure in silence.

It was the custom of those three inseparables, with leave of the prior, to pass the interval of lauds at night in the scriptorium, finding passages in the Scriptures meet for that hour. Sindolf knew this, and one night crept up outside to the window of glass at which Tuotilo was sitting, to listen for something that he might distort and carry to the Bishop to injure them. Tuotilo detected him, and being a strong courageous man, he spoke thus to his fellows in Latin, so as not to be understood by Sindolf. "He is here," says he, "with his ear at the window. But do you, Notker, because you are not overbold (*quia timidulus es*), go to the church: Ratpert, take the scourge that hangs in the chapter-house, and come round from without. When you are near him I will fling the pane open and take him by the hair and pull him inwards. Do you, my soul, take comfort and be strong; lay into him all your might with the scourge, and take vengeance for God on him." Ratpert was never too lenient in his discipline, and went out quietly, took the scourge, and ran; and when Sindolf was held fast by the head and drawn inward, dealt a storm of scourging from behind. Sindolf fought and spurned, and caught the scourge in his hands: Ratpert caught up a stick that lay handy, and continued his strenuous strokes. Sindolf thought it no time for silence, and after begging for mercy in vain, cried out with a loud voice. Some of the brethren came with lights, amazed at the voice at that unwonted hour, and asked what it meant. Tuotilo kept repeating, *I have hold of the Devil*, and asked them to bring a light that he might see in what shape he appeared. Then Sindolf's unwilling head was turned this way and that for the brethren to see. *Can it be Sindolf?* asked Tuotilo: and when the brethren answered that it was he indeed, and begged him to be released, let him go, saying: *Wretch that I am, to have laid hands on the auricular friend of the Bishop!* Ratpertus, meantime, had withdrawn. Nor could the sufferer tell from whom his lashings came. Some asked Tuotilo where Notker and Ratpert had gone. *Both*, said he, *when they had wind of the Devil went to do the work of God, and left me alone to deal with the walker in darkness. But know ye all, it was an angel of God that with his own hand dealt the scourgings.*

However, there was debate on this matter in the brotherhood.

The three friends are well known in literary history, but it will be seen that Ekkehard has other things to tell of them besides the facts, to which he gives proper weight, that Notker was the famous author of the *Sequences*, and that Tuotilo, scholar, artist, and musician, taught gentlemen's sons the flute, when he had leisure for it.

Ekkehard is so good that it is scarcely possible for any modern rendering to take his place. Even Carlyle could hardly have done for him what he did for Jocelin of Brakelonde; because in Ekkehard the imaginative work is done already. Scheffel's historical novel, the hero of which is the elder Ekkehard, the Dean, the author of *Waltharius*, is almost all derived from the younger Ekkehard's Memoirs, and not without success. But no one who knows the original can think of the novel as anything but a dilution of it.

There is no room here for the variety of the book, and no summary can represent it. There are two sections of it which may perhaps be preferred to all the others, after that of Notker and his two friends. These are the account of the Hungarian invasion, and the scenes at the Hohentwiel, the castle of the accomplished and rather dangerous Duchess Hadwig. The Hungarians are thought by some to have influenced the poem of *Waltharius;* it is not improbable that the revels at the court of Attila in the poem may have been drawn from the experience of St Gall when the Hungarians were there. Ekkehard's account is one of the most humorous things in mediæval literature, describing particularly the adventures of an obstinate monk Heribald, who refused to leave the monastery when the monks went to a fortress. *The chamber-*

*lain has not given me my shoe-leather for this year,
and I will not move.* The Hungarians were good-
natured ogres. Heribald cried out to them to stop
when they were breaking the cellar-door : " What are
we to drink when you are gone away ? " At which
they laughed and spared the cellar, to the great
surprise of the Abbot when he returned. They had
plenty of drink otherwise, and used to give it kindly
to Heribald. His account of them dwelt most on
their kindness and their want of the monastic virtues.
" They would talk in church, and when I warned them
not to make a noise, they beat me : then they were
sorry, and gave me wine to make up for it ; more than
any of you would have done," said Heribald.

Hadwig, widow of Burchard, Duke of Swabia, niece
of Otho the Great, daughter of Henry of Bavaria, is
more like a scholarly lady of the sixteenth century
(Queen Elizabeth, for example) than the heroines of the
Middle Ages. She was a near neighbour of the monastery, and a benefactor. Her character is given in
one of Ekkehard's phrases, where, mentioning her fine
needlework done for St Gall, and especially the rich
alba with the wedding of Philology on it, he goes on
to, " also a dalmatic and a subdeacon's tunicle in gold
thread, which afterwards, when Abbot Ymmo had
refused her a book of antiphones, she took away
again, with her usual quick and variable humour "
(*acutia sua versipelli*).

With that we may leave Ekkehard, or rather break
off this hopeless attempt to describe his inexhaustible
memoirs. They will not bear any form except their own.

This account might well be brought to an end with Richer's hero Gerbert. a great man and the chief representative of Latin learning just before the new age of Scholasticism. His letters [1] are those of a man for whom there were other interests besides rhetoric and philosophy; some of his short notes have the same kind of reality as Cicero's, being not records or reflections but practical agents in a great revolution. Gerbert got the name of a king-maker, and seems to have deserved it. Though simply *Scholasticus* (Master of the School) at Rheims, he did more than any one else to help the child Otho and his mother, the Empress Theophano, against their enemies. He was among the first authors of the Capetian monarchy. In a hurried unsigned letter, written in the thick of troubles and danger, he points out that Hugh Capet is virtually king of France. If it was not owing to this sentence of Gerbert's that Hugh was crowned and consecrated shortly after, Gerbert at least foretold his power. The letters admit one to a close acquaintance with the very life of that obscure time, and a knowledge of actual motives and character. Gerbert's care for learning comes out plainly in his correspondence, generally in requests for particular books to be sent him, not in the expansive style of Cassiodorus or Alcuin.

Gerbert.

Gerbert is followed in literary history by Rodulphus Glaber, like a hero with a comic squire: Rodulphus represents the permanent underlayer of medieval absurdity above which Gerbert rises so eminently; the two together make it impos-

Rodulphus Glaber.

[1] Ed. Julien Havet, 1889.

sible to arrive at any easy generalisation about the culture of the Dark Ages.[1]

Rodulphus was one of the unfortunate children of whom Rabelais speaks, put into a monastery at twelve years old, not having then, nor ever acquiring, any fitness for the religious life, beyond frequent visions of the Devil. He was expelled, after he had made himself a nuisance to every one, and became a vagrant from one monastery to another, picking up odd jobs. But he had some liking for books, and settled down towards the end of his life, and wrote his history. He had few historical sources, besides tradition; and his book is one of the most authentic renderings anywhere to be found of the average mind of the time—both in the contents of the mind, visions, portents, stories, and in its artless movement from any point to any circumference. He has sometimes been treated too heavily, as if the whole Middle Age were summed up in Rodulphus Glaber. That is not so, but he is nevertheless a true son of his time, and has some claim to speak the epilogue at the close of the Dark Ages.

No literary work in the Dark Ages can be compared for the extent and far-reaching results of its *The new forms* influence with the development of popular *of Latin verse.* Latin verse. The hymns went further and affected a larger number of people's minds than

---

[1] *Raoul Glaber ; les cinq livres de ses histoires* (900-1044) publiés par Maurice Prou, 1886. Cf. Gebhart, *l'état d'âme d'un moine de l'an 1000—le chroniqueur Raoul Glaber :* in *Revue des deux Mondes*, Oct. 1, 1891.

anything else in literature. They gave the impulse
to fresh experiment which was so much needed by
scholarly persons; provided new rules and a new
ideal of expression for the unscholarly. Those who
had no mind to sit down and compose an epithalamium in hexameters or a birthday epistle in elegiacs,
might still write poetry in Latin,—unclassical Latin,
indeed, but not dull, not ungentle—a language capable
of melody in verse and impressiveness in diction.
As Bede says, the ear in rhythmic verse will observe
a measure of its own, and scholarly poets will use
in a scholarly way the forms that the common makers
use rudely : "quem (*sc.* rhythmum) vulgares poetæ
necesse est rustice, docti faciant docte." The most
beautiful things in Latin rhyme belong to a later
period, it is true, and will be appraised by the Editor
of this series in the following volume; but the
Dark Ages began it. Also the free Latin verse is
the origin of all the rhythms and measures of modern
poetry in the Romance languages, and in English and
German too, where they are content, as Shakespeare
and Milton generally were, with the Romance types
of versification.

There seem to be two different ways in which
Latin was made available for popular poetry. Irregular Latin verse might be either (1) in the classical forms used irregularly, or (2) in forms not
classical at all. But in both cases, whether, for
example, an iambic trimeter is written without respect for quantity, or whether on the other hand the
irregular poet takes a line of his own, not imitating

any classical pattern of verse, there is the common feature that quantity is neglected, or at any rate not treated under the old rules. In both cases there is a rebellion against the Greek tradition of prosody, introduced at Rome by the founders of Latin poetry under the Republic. This emancipation from the Greek rule of good verse sometimes but not always went along with a strong metrical emphasis on the accent, like that which in Greece itself was replacing the old verse-measures with the new "political" line, the verse of the Greek ballads.[1] In Latin there was more excuse for it than in Greek, because it was a return to the natural genius of the language. This of course does not make things any better from the classical point of view; but it increases the dignity of accentual Latin among the modern forms of verse, if it can in any way be traced back to the Saturnian age. A pedigree of this sort has been attempted by some scholars.[2] Whatever may be the true history of the Saturnian verse, whether it died out after the beginning of classical Latin poetry, or survived in country places and came back in a new form in French and Provençal, it is certain that the old Latin rhythms, before the Greek forms were introduced, had more likeness to modern verse in their accent than Greek verse has. It is known also that the common people when they adopted classical measures used them accentually: "the popular poetry of the Republic as well as of the Empire was markedly ac-

[1] See below, p. 343.
[2] See Stengel, *Romanische Verslehre*, in Gröber's *Grundriss*, ii. i.

centual."[1]   Just as in English poetry there is a continual dissension between the naturalised French measures, decasyllabic, octosyllabic, &c., and the licentious spirit of the language, which will not count the syllables exactly, so in Latin the tunes of common speech interfered with the strict use of prosody. The analogies between English and Latin poetry are striking, when their histories are compared. The Latin Saturnian, it has often been thought, had the same fortune as the English alliterative verse; Chaucer is "our English Ennius," and his contemptuous allusion to the older fashion of poetry—

"I cannot geste ROM RAM RUF by lettre,"

is in the same spirit as the slighting reference to Nævius in the younger poet's *Annals*:—

"Scripsere alii rem
Vorsubu' quos olim Fauni vatesque canebant."

Ennius is all for the Greek prosody in Latin, as Chaucer is for the French metres in English. But there is a closer resemblance than this analogy of Saturnian and alliterative English, in the practice of the English and Latin poets who adopted the foreign models and did their best to be regular. Chaucer's verse is not the same as his French masters wrote; it does not keep the French rules exactly, and its graces and beauties are not those of the French. The Latin poets wrote like Homer, as near as they could, but they could not

[1] W. M. Lindsay, *The Accentual Element in Early Latin Verse: Transactions of the Philological Society*, March 2, 1894.

escape from their language: in Virgil and Ovid there
are traces of the Italian Faun—vestiges of the old
poetical diction, an emphasis which is not Greek, but
comes down from the ancient days, before the *vates*
and the Camenæ had made way for the Greek Muses.
Greek metres were brought into agreement with the
accent of Latin speech. One of the marvellous things
in Latin at the end of the classical age is the effect
of the accent in the *Pervigilium Veneris*—

"Cras amet qui numquam amavit, quique amavit cras amet,"

and in the poem of Tiberianus—

> "Amnis ibat inter arva valle fusus frigida,
> Luce ridens calculorum, flore pictus herbido :
> Cærulas superne laurus et virecta myrtea
> Leniter motabat aura, blandiente sibilo." [1]

From this poem it is some distance in time to the full
beginning of modern verse in the Romance languages;
but there is no difficulty in making the passage from
the rhythm of Tiberianus to that of the Count of
Poitou—

> "Qu'una domna s'es clamada de sos gardadors a mei"—

in which the accentual effect is the same, and the
regard for quantity equally distinct, though not quite
so thorough-going. In the interval there were many
poets who kept the same sort of measure—Prudentius,
Fortunatus, and others. In this particular kind of
trochaic verse it proved to be fairly easy to adapt the
Greek form to popular use without spoiling its original

---

[1] Baehrens, *P. L. Min.*, iii. 264 ; cf. Mackail, *Latin Literature.*

character altogether.   It was the favourite verse for popular songs, like the sufficiently quoted lampoons of Cæsar's army; it was much employed in hymns.[1] From William of Poitou to *Locksley Hall* and a *Toccata of Galuppi,* and later ("Where the dawn comes up like thunder"), it has been at the service of modern poets, and yet it has never lost its ancient character.   The trochaic verse is such—so widely distributed and so much at home—that Latin verses of this sort appeal to every one familiarly.   The Latin poets very early gave them their modern character, by trusting a good deal to the accent.

In other kinds of verse there may be something like the same successful transition from classical to mediæval forms.   The iambic dimeter becomes an octo-syllabic line without strict rule of quantity: yet for all that it may preserve its identity.   Between the correct verse,

"A solis ortus cardine,"

and the irregular "rhythmical" verse, as Bede calls it,

"Rex æterne Domine,"

there is indeed an enormous technical difference. but not such as to destroy the identity of type at the back of both; not even though the rhythmical verse drop

---

[1] Bede, in his notice of this verse, says that it is divided into two versicles—that is, he treats it like the "eights and sevens" of the hymn-books :—

"Hymnum dicat turba fratrum,
Hymnum cantus personet;
Christo regi concinentes
Laudes demus debitas."

out the opening syllable and put spondees where
they ought not to be. And here again there is continuity from early Latin times: "It has been remarked
that lines from some of the early Tragedians read
almost like lines from a Christian (accentual) hymn
—*e.g.*, Ennius, 163 R.:

> ' O mágna témpla cáelitum | commíxta stéllis spléndidis.' "[1]

The hymns of St Ambrose and his school, in iambic
dimeter, are in the same position with regard to later
accentual hymns in this verse as the *Pervigilium
Veneris* in relation to later accentual trochaics—that
is, the Ambrosian hymns began by respecting quantity
and accent together, and were followed by "rhythmical" poems which neglected the classical quantities.
There are four great hymns of St Ambrose, written
probably about the time when he baptized Augustine,
Easter 387:—the Evening Hymn—

> "Deus creator omnium";

the Morning Hymn—

> " Æterne rerum conditor";

Tierce—

> "Jam surgit hora tertia";

Christmas—

> " Veni redemptor gentium."

In these opening lines the coincidence of accent and
quantity gives the example for all the later Ambrosian

---

[1] W. M. Lindsay, *op. cit.*

hymns in which quantity is left out of account. The author of the "rhythmical"

"Rex æterne Domine"

thought that he was using the same verse as

"Deus creator omnium,"

and he was right, though he had added to the principles of St Ambrose a new rule as to quantity, and rejected the classical precedent. St Ambrose, it should be observed, does not consistently make the accent fall as it does in his first verses: variations are frequent. But just as in English blank verse the regular lines are sufficient in number to control the rhythm, without forcing it into the "drumming decasyllabon" of the early monotonous poets, so in the hymns of St Ambrose there is a perfectly distinct preponderance of lines such as

"Tu lux refulge sensibus,"

and

"Te vox canora concrepet;"

while such a line as

"Pontique mitescunt freta,"

where all the accents fall otherwise than the metrical ictus, is exceptional. The practice of St Ambrose is analogous to the practice of Milton: there is no absolute rule about the accent, but it agrees in so many cases with the regular pattern of the metre that the exceptions are recognised as exceptional. In

"Póntique mitéscunt fréta

the word-accents all fall on syllables which metrically

are in the weak places of the line. But in the great
majority of verses the word-accents fall on the strong
syllables of an iambic foot; there are few lines in
which the fourth syllable is not accented. This respect for accent, and general agreement in principle
with the *Pervigilium Veneris*, is the more surprising in
St Ambrose's hymns, because there was another influence at work tending to the equal neglect of both
accent and quantity. St Ambrose was a poet; he
wrote to please his own ear. But these poems were
not intended for readers of poetry; they were meant
to be sung, they were part of an innovation in Church
music, "according to the use of the East." Authors
less poetical than St Ambrose found that practically
there was no need to be careful about either accent or
quantity; the hymn-tune could make the syllables anything it pleased, as it does for example in *Adeste fideles*,
a hymn which in the books, and apart from the tune,
has no rhythm of its own. A large amount of mediæval Latin verse is really not verse in either of the two
great classes used by Bede, neither "metrical" nor
"rhythmical," but simply a provision of syllables to
fit a tune, leaving it to the tune to impose its own
quantity and accent. The famous hymn of St Augustine against the Donatists, written not long after his
baptism at Milan, was composed with an object not
unlike that of St Ambrose — namely, to give the
common people something to sing, not too complicated, not learned, not remote from their own natural
language. It is one of the first precedents for un-
metrical popular Latin verse, and it is interesting to

remark how it differs from the Ambrosian form. St
Augustine says[1] that he would not adopt for this
purpose any regular poetical measure, lest he should
be forced into the use of learned words not familiar to
those for whom it was written. It is an alphabetical
poem, in stanzas or tirades of twelve lines each, and
a refrain (*hypopsalma*)—

> "Omnes qui gaudetis pace modo verum judicate."

Each line has sixteen syllables, and there is a
division in the middle: it is irregular trochaic verse,
longer by a syllable than that of *Cras amet*. Quantity,
as the author says, is neglected: thus St Augustine
goes further than St Ambrose in complying with the
popular voice. But, on the other hand, he does not go
as far as St Ambrose in respect for the accent of the
ordinary language. Many lines are accentually right
according to the mediæval usage—*e.g.*, the first—

> "Abundántia péccatórum | sólet frátres cónturbáre."

But the second and the third are—

> "Propter hoc Dominus noster | voluit nos præmonere
> Comparans regnum cœlorum | reticulo misso in mare"—

where the rhythm is much less marked. The writer
trusts to the tune to carry it through, and does not
feel himself obliged to keep a poetical rhythm distinct
from the music. He is not under the rules of either
prosody; neither the classical nor the modern rule is

---

[1] *Retractationum*, i. 20: "Non aliquo carminis genere id fieri volui,
ne me necessitas metrica ad aliqua verba quæ vulgo minus sint
usitata, compelleret."

binding, though he has in his head what may be called a modern rhythm, which comes out in many verses—

"Maledictum cor lupinum | contegunt ovina pella."

St Augustine's experiment has in a sort of nebulous shape the principles of two different orders of modern verse,—that which takes account of the accent, as is done in Italian, Spanish, and English verse, and that which does not, like French and Irish. A phrase like *Maledictum cor lupinum* sounds to men of the first group like the verse of their own country; each hears in it his native accents. But the following verse sounds out of tune—

"Junxerunt se simul omnes | crimen in illum conflare"—

though probably to French or Irish hearers it is neither more nor less correct than the other. *Maledictum cor lupinum* is an example of that instinctive though not classically regular quantity which Bede observed in the rhythmical verse; *Junxerunt se simul omnes* wants the proper "modulation," though it keeps the number of syllables. St Augustine thus gives two different types, one putting the stress generally on the syllables where, according to the old prosody, the metrical beat would fall, the other apparently indifferent to accent, and generally more indifferent to quantity also than is necessary even in irregular verse. In time, as the barbarian languages shape themselves, and the several provincial rules of verse come to be determined, it is possible to distinguish local peculiarities in the treatment of Latin. Thus,

to take an instance about which there can be no
mistake, an Icelander writing Latin verse will often
keep the Icelandic prescription of the three alliterative
syllables. Less obviously, but still in a demonstrable
way, the Latin of an Englishman will differ from that
of an Irishman, and between Irish Latin and French
Latin there is often a close agreement.   St Columba's
Altus generally avoids the stress that would be found
natural in Bede's kind of modern Latin :—

> " Altus prosator vetustus | dierum et ingenitus
> Erat absque origine | primordii et crepidine
> Est et erit in sæcula | sæculorum infinita."

In accent it is like Baudelaire's Latin poem *Franciscæ
meæ Laudes,* which is sometimes iambic, sometimes
trochaic, never consistently either : —

> " Quem vitiorum tempestas
> Turbabat omnes semitas
> Apparuisti Deitas
> Velut stella salutaris
> In naufragiis amaris
> Suspendam cor tuis aris."

The French poet has no rhythm in his octosyllabics.

> " Labris vocem redde mutis,"

which is regular according to the school of Bede, is
an accidental regularity here ; and

> " O castitatis lorica "

rhymes with

> " Aqua tincta seraphica "

in the same poem.   Abelard shows the same indiffer-
ence.   The following verses are intended to be in the

same measure as *Pange lingua gloriosi,* but Abelard loses the rhythm towards the end of each line, and the rhymes are as impossible as *lorica* and *seraphica :—*

> "Angelorum stupent cantu admoniti pastores
> Magos nova ducit stella metu languet Herodes
> Dat mandata magis stulta loquens eis in dolo,
> Sed illusus fuit dolus fraudulento fraudato."

It is of course difficult to arrange the irregular imitations of classical verse according to degrees of irregularity. Where the classical number of syllables is kept, and where nothing is kept of the classical rules of quantity, it may seem superfluous to look further for any more precise division. Yet Bede's principle is never irrelevant in reading the mediæval Latin poets: the ear distinguishes those who have a sense for quantity and accent together from those who ignore the natural Latin rhythm.

On the other hand, it is easy to distinguish the new lengths of line, the new stanzas, from the imitations of classical types of verse. Some of the classical lines, like the measure of *Cras amet* and the short iambic line, were proof against any change; the taste of all the nations found them in different ways congenial. But the new Latin also required new measures, especially for rhymes, and the most famous Latin rhymes are in verses not of the classical order. The new forms are adaptations of classical verse, however, like the hexameter without cæsura and with internal rhyme—

> "Hora novissima tempora pessima sunt : vigilemus."

Even for this rhythm there may be some precedent in the line of Ennius,[1]

"Poste recumbite, vestraque pectora pellite tonsis."

But the ancestry was not known, and the new hexameters were practically a new invention. Other favourite forms are more remote from classical poetry. The two commonest, which it is not inconvenient to quote under their Goliardic titles of *Mihi est propositum* and *Quid dant artes*, are modifications of the tetrameter :—

   (1) "Ridet florum gloria, fructibus formosis
       Locus in quo lilia præparantur rosis,"

an iambic tetrameter, wanting the opening short syllable of each half-line.

   (2) "Ave cujus calcem clare
       Nec centenni commendare
       Sciret seraph studio."

This is from the trochaic tetrameter, with the first half repeated : it is one of the forms of *rime couée* —caudate or tail rhyme, the tail being made by the old-fashioned way of bracketing the first two lines and setting off the third to the right of the page :—

"Quid dant artes nisi luctum } Fert genus et species ?"
  Et laborem vel quem fructum }

"Olim multos non est mirum } Et *Fraternas acies.*"
  Provehebant *Arma virum* }

Another common line, though not so common as

---

[1] Quoted by Professor Lindsay, *op. cit.*

these, was made by cutting the iambic trimeter at
the sixth syllable, the proper cæsura being ignored :—

> " O Roma nobilis urbis et domina
> Cunctarum urbium excellentissima
> Roseo martyrum sanguine rubea
> Albis et virginum liliis candida
> Salutem dicimus tibi per omnia
> Te benedicimus salve per sæcula." [1]

This is of the tenth century, Veronese. The verse
is borrowed from an older piece—

> " O admirabile Veneris idolum "—

which also belongs to Verona, and the metre seems to
have been common there. Both these poems have
musical notes attached to them, and so has the popular
song of Modena, which, however, does not divide the
line in the middle like *O Roma nobilis*, but after the
fifth syllable, keeping something like the classical
cæsura :—

> " O tu qui servas armis ista mœnia
> Noli dormire, moneo, sed vigila."

The same verse is found in the poem of Paulinus of
Aquileia on the death of Erich, Marquis of Friuli
(799); it is used, in quatrains, with a refrain additional, in a lament for Charlemagne :—

> " A solis ortu usque ad occidua
> Littora maris planctus pulsat pectora :
> Ultramarina agmina tristitia
> Tetigit ingens cum mœrore nimio :
> Heu mihi misero."

---

[1] See Traube, *O Roma nobilis*, in the Munich Academy's *Abhand-
lungen der philosophischen-philologischen Classe*, vol. xix. (1891).

Another stanza with the same sort of line appears in the poem on the destruction of Aquileia, attributed to Paulinus, and in the lament for the abbot Hugh, a bastard son of Charles the Great, who fell at Toulouse in 844, in the war between Charles the Bald and Pippin—

> " Hug dulce nomen, Hug propago nobilis
> Karli potentis ac sereni principis
> Insons sub armis tam repente sancius
> Occubuisti."

One of the most interesting of the new types is a trochaic line of eleven syllables, which appears in many different places and times.

> " Where the quiet coloured end of evening smiles "

in Browning is identical in scansion with a Provençal verse used by Count William of Poitou. That same measure is found in Provence in the tenth century, in Latin, along with a Provençal burden. The poem where it occurs is commonly known as the first *alba*, the oldest extant morning song of the kind, which afterwards was to be so famous : " The dawn over the dark sea draws on the sun : she passes over the hill, slanting ; see, the darkness is clearing." So the difficult refrain has been interpreted.

> " Phœbi claro nondum orto jubare,
> Fert aurora lumen terris tenue ;
> Spiculator pigris clamat : Surgite !
> *L'alba part muet mar atra sol ;*
> *Poy pas abigil ; mira clar tenebras.*"

This trochaic Latin verse is used earlier in a comic poem on the abbot of Angers, which also has a refrain, though not in the vernacular—

> "Andecavis abbas esse dicitur
> Ille nomen primum tenet hominum
> Hunc fatentur vinum velle bibere
> Super omnes Andecavis homines.
> *Eia eia eia laudes, eia laudes, dicamus Libero.*"

This belongs to the ninth century; the *Lorica* of Gildas has the same measure in the sixth, if that poem be authentic, as Zimmer thinks, and Mommsen denies :—

> "Subfragare trinitatis unitas,
> Unitatis miserere trinitas,
> Subfragare mihi quæso posito
> Maris magni velut in periculo."[1]

As used by William of Poitou, it is found in combination with the trochaic tetrameter,—

> "Compaigno, non posc mudar qu'eu nom esfrei
> de novellas qu'ai auzidas e que vei,
> qu'una domna s'es clamada de sos gardadors a mei."

The Irish poet of the court of Charlemagne, "Hiber-

---

[1] Compare the hymn of Gui de Basoches, twelfth century, Mone, ii. 6 :—

> "Dei matris cantibus
> sollemnia
> Recolat sollemnibus
> ecclesia:
> Vota tuis auribus
> concilia,
> Te devotis vocibus
> laudantia
> digna dignis laudibus.

nicus Exul," makes use of a rhyming measure with many Irish characteristics:—

> " Carta Christo comite per telluris spatium
> Ad Cæsaris splendidum nunc perge palatium
> Fer salutes Cæsari ac suis agminibus
> Gloriosis pueris sacrisque virginibus
>
> . . . .
>
> Dic regales pueri per prolixa spatia
> Sint sani sint longevi salvatoris gratia
> Sint coronæ regiæ digni dic honoribus
> Felices ac victores genitoribus moribus."

It is like *Mihi est propositum*, with a trisyllabic rhyme. The half line of seven syllables is the commonest type of Irish verse in the vernacular; and this poem of "Hibernicus Exul," along with similar verses later by Sedulius Scottus, has been of interest in connection with the problems of Irish metre.[1]

There is a short kind of verse in a poem of the ninth century which strikes the ear with a modern ring:—

> " Sancte sator, suffragator,
> Legum lator, largus dator
> Jure pollens es qui potens
> Nunc in æthra firma petra
> A quo creta cuncta freta
> Quæ aplustra ferunt flustra
> Quando celox currit velox
> Cujus numen crevit lumen
> Simul solum supra polum."

It is probably Anglo-Saxon in origin, to judge from

---

[1] Cf. Ebert, *Litteratur des Mittelalters*, ii. 324 ; Thurneysen, in *Revue Celtique*, vi. 345.

the vocabulary,[1] not to speak of the alliteration. A comparison with Anglo-Saxon rhymes like *blissa bleoum, blostma kiwum* shows how easily the forms of the two languages might be brought to correspond: while the resemblance to certain Icelandic rhymes is also notable. It is hard to dissociate the form of Egil's *Ransom* poem, with its short rhyming lines, from this Latin specimen.

"Quando celox currit velox"

is much the same in form as the Icelandic

"Brustu broddar, enn bitu oddar."

In the song written by Gottschalk (about 846 ?) the trochaic measures are in a way less regular; the effect is singularly unlike anything in the old Teutonic languages, and not far from some of the melodies of French and Spanish verse, with the "broken" trochaic half-line:—

"O quid jubes, pusiole,
Quare mandas, filiole,
Carmen dulce me cantare,
Cum sine longe exul valde
Intra mare ?
O cur jubes canere ?"

Gothschalk's adversary Hraban has nothing so good, but his poem in octosyllabic couplets on Paradise Lost and Regained is of some interest historically, considering the future fortunes of that sort of measure. The Latin poem on the story of Placidas (St Eustace),

---

[1] Müllenhoff and Scherer, *Denkmäler*, v. lxi ; Mone, i. 365 ; Braune, *Althochdeutsches Lesebuch*, v. xi.

which belongs to the ninth century also, is in a drawling verse suited to professional story-telling, and near akin to much of the common minstrelsy later.[1] It goes in stanzas of five lines; for example, in telling about the happy meeting of Placidas with his wife and his two sons:—

> "Exivit mater eorum, ivit ad principem
> Ut suggereret illi quomodo capta est :
> Dum ad vestigia ejus se vellet sternere,
> Agnovit eum et collum ejus amplexa est,
> Et cum lacrimis marito cepit dicere"—

which is not an unfair specimen of the style and method of this narrative. No legend has more of the character of mediæval romance than that of St Eustace, and few were in greater favour. A comparison of the different versions—Ælfric's prose, the Northern *Placitus Drápa*, and many more—would bring out very clearly the differences of taste in story-telling all over the Middle Ages. The story of *Sir Isumbras* is nearly the same as *Placidas*, though it does not end in martyrdom. From the Latin *Placidas* of the ninth century to the English *Sir Isumbras* there are many stages to pass through; but the Latin version has already the simple unaffected pleasure in adventure which makes up for so much else in the stories of the minstrels and the less courtly romances, the companions of *Sir Thopas*.

The *Sequentia*,[2] or *Prosa*, which comes into favour in

---

[1] Edited, along with other poems of the Carolingian period, by Dümmler in the *Zeitschrift für deutsches Alterthum*, xxiii.

[2] F. A. Wolf, *Ueber die Lais, Sequenzen, und Leiche*, 1841; K. Bartsch, *Lateinische Sequenzen das Mittelalters*, 1868.

the ninth century, chiefly through the school of St
Gall, is a new kind of Latin poem, with a
The Sequences. new principle of verse—or rather an old
principle rediscovered and applied in a new way. The
sequence was a tune before it was a poem, and the rule
of the sequence, as poem, is to follow exactly the notes
of a melody. It came from the *Alleluia*, which concluded the *Graduale* between the Epistle and the Gospel. It was the fashion to prolong the *Alleluia* in a
"jubilant" song—without words—which was often
long and musically elaborate. The tunes were found
hard to remember, and experiments were made in
fitting words to them, possibly by Alcuin among
others. But the first attempts were soon made
obsolete by the rapid development of the sequence
under the direction and example of Notker[1] of St
Gall (+912). The music of the sequences had come
to be studied at St Gall through the presence there
of one of the two Italian musicians who had been
called northward by Charlemagne to improve the
psalmody. Some of the early experiments in fitting
words to the sequence tunes had been brought thither
also, by a priest from the ruined monastery of
Jumièges. Notker found fault with the composition
of these hymns—the syllables were not well placed—
and set himself to supply words for the melodies
according to a strict principle, giving a syllable to
each note. *Psallat ecclesia mater illibata* was his

---

[1] Called Balbulus, to distinguish him from others of the same
name later—Notker, surnamed "Peppercorn" (*Piperisgranum*), the
doctor of physic, and Notker Labeo, the great translator.

first sequence, and this was followed by many more, until, in 887, a book of sequences was complete. But the ideas of St Gall were accustomed to spread rapidly; all the world knew at once whatever was being done or thought in the great monastery. Almost before Notker was ready, the form of the sequence had established itself, and had even imposed itself on vernacular French, in the poem of *St Eulalia*.

The sequences are not to be scanned according to any classical rule, nor yet by the methods accepted for the "rhythmical" poetry, as explained by Bede. They follow the melody exactly, and the tunes of that time were not in accordance with any of the known poetical measures, either classical or popular. In principle, the sequences are governed by the same general law as Pindar—namely, that words follow music. But as the music was of a new kind, the words obeyed no established poetical rule. Their measures are hard to understand with only the words to judge by. One kind of regularity they indeed profess on the face of them. As the melody fell into periods, each of which repeated the same notes, the poetical sequence takes the form of a series of couplets or stanzas, each couplet or stanza having its own pattern. In some sequences, as in those of the Northern French school, to which the *Eulalia* poem belongs, there is a duplicate series — strophe and antistrophe.

It is perhaps as one of the forms invented and taken up at a time when the new languages were stirring, and new literary ambitions awake, that the sequence is chiefly memorable. It was the right thing in its own day; it agreed with the musical taste of the time, and had the enormous advantage of musical support, of alliance with new tunes that went everywhere, and carried the poetical form along with them. It was open to any one to supply words for any tune. The first problem, " Why not fit Latin religious words to the sacred melody ? " had been raised and solved by Notker. But then came other suggestions: (1) Why religious words ? (2) Why Latin? And the result was prolific in many ways when the new languages added this to their poetical resources. In Germany in the tenth century it was common to write fresh Latin words to well - known tunes— *Carelmanning, Liebing, Modus Florum,*—and it became commoner to fit the tunes with German words, and to make new tunes of the same kind with German words appropriate to them. The Leich of the Middle High German poetry is descended from Notker's Latin sequence. The old French Motet, an irregular form of free verse, different from the common stanzas, whether of the courtly or the mere popular orders, appears to have had the same kind of origin as the Leich, though less closely connected with the sequence. The Motet, like the sequence, came after the tune, and depended upon it: it had no fixed pattern of stanza, but followed the windings of the music.[1]

[1] See W. Meyer in *Gött. Nachrichten*, 1898 ; G. Raynaud, *Recueil de Motets français*, 2 tom. 1881-83. The manuscript of Valenciennes containing the *Eulalia* poem is one of the most significant things of its day with regard to the polyglot experimental character of literature, the great variety of tastes, the immense possibilities of new

The popular interest of many mediæval Latin poems is so strong that they may naturally find a place here, half-way between the ancient and the modern languages. The chief of these is *Waltharius.* the poem of Walter and Hildegund, the fullest extant rendering of a famous German story. *Waltharii Poesis*[1] was written as a school exercise in Latin hexameters by Ekkehard of St Gall, the first of that name (+937).

discovery, the intercourse of different languages at the end of the ninth century. It contains a Latin sequence on St Eulalia; the old French poem on the same subject, written to the same music; after the French poem there follows, on the same page in the same hand, the opening of the *Ludwigslied.* French and German are written by the same scribe, and both the French piece and the German are novelties. Some couplets of the Latin *Eulalia* are added here, in illustration of the method of the sequence:—

1. Cantica virginis Eulaliæ
   Concine suavisone cithara

2. Est operæ quoniam pretium
   Clangere carmine martyrium

3. Tuam ego voce sequar melodiam
   Atque laudem imitabor Ambrosiam

4. Fidibus cane melos eximium
   Vocibus ministrabo suffragium

5. Sic pietatem sic humanum ingenium
   Fudisse fletum compellamus ingenitum

6. Hanc puellam nam iuventæ sub tempore
   Nondum thoris maritalibus habilem

7. Hostis æqui flammis ignis implicuit
   Mox columbæ evolatu obstipuit

8. Spiritus hic erat Eulaliæ
   Lacteolus celer innocuus.

In the second part, the measures of the four stanzas 3 to 6 are repeated. See P. von. Winterfeld, *Z. f. d. A.*, xlv.

[1] Grimm and Schmeller, *Lateinische Gedichte des X. und XI. Jh.*, 1838; ed. Peiper, 1873; ed. Althof, 1899.

One might expect the worst result from that sort of task—incongruous ornament, a discord of Latin and Teutonic manners, the ordinary barbarism. But though *Waltharius* is faulty in many respects, it succeeds as a story. The German idiom breaks through (*e.g.*, *Wah! sed quid dicis?*) and the *Gradus* phrases are quaintly out of keeping with much of the matter.[1] But Ekkehard (like Ermoldus with his siege of Barcelona) has got at the heart of the epic mystery. Virgil is his master, but what the German student finds in the *Æneid* is not anything commonly called Virgilian; no gentle grace, nor the style that Dante learned, but the spirit of battle poetry. Virgil, in fact, is really Homer for the time; it is nothing but Homer that Ekkehard discovers in him. So Ermoldus rediscovered the true Homeric simile under the conventional ornaments of the grammar-school — the simile which is not a piece of rhetoric but a gift of the imagination.

How much of *Waltharius* is due to a lost German poem is hard to make out. The story was certainly given, not invented. Much is due to the fable; the story of Walter and Hildegund is hardly inferior to that of Rodrigue and Chimène in natural dignity.

It is simple enough, as told by Ekkehard. Hagen, Walter, and the princess Hildegund are hostages with Attila for the Franks, Aquitanians, and Burgundians respectively,—Hagen taking the place of Gunther, son of Gilbicho, who was too young for a hostage when

---

[1] *Waltharius* was edited by the author's namesake, the historian of St Gall. But the later Ekkehard's Latin, which is never dull, is not that of a sound philologist.

the Franks first submitted to the Huns. Hagen and Walter grew up together, sworn brothers in war: Walter and Hildegund are plighted lovers from their childhood. Hagen escapes; and, later, Walter and Hildegund flee togeher, after a feast in which the Huns are left helpless:—

"Heroas validos plantis titubare videres."

Attila's headache the next morning is well described. The fugitives took plenty of treasure with them— golden rings, the usual heroic form of wealth—and made their way to the Rhine at Worms. There they were discovered by Gunther; for Walter, who had a fishing-rod with him, caught more than was wanted for the pot, and gave some to the ferryman, who in turn made a present to the king's cook: so Gunther came to hear of the stranger and the lady along with him, and the rings. "My father's treasure returning from the Huns," cried Gunther; and "he took the table with his foot" (*mensam pede percutit*) like other excited heroes. Gunther set out to find Walter, though Hagen tried to dissuade him, "mindful of the old covenant and the former companion." Then comes the great fight in the Vosges, the Wasgenstein of later accounts, with Walter, in his camp among the rocks, a natural stronghold only approached by a narrow way—the right place for an epic battle. Hagen would not go against Walter. At the end of the day, when Walter had killed all his men, and only Gunther and Hagen were left, Gunther tried to stir up Hagen against his old friend; but Hagen refused, and they withdrew. Walter and Hildegund remained in their fortress, taking turns to watch, Hildegund singing to keep herself awake. In the morning, as they were moving away, the Franks returned, and the attack was renewed. After all three chieftains had been wounded, peace was made. Walter and Hildegund reigned long in Aquitaine, but their later triumphs belong to another story. The poem ends with an apology for the writer's youth.

Ekkehard's similes are hardly as striking as those of Ermoldus, but they are often good: the host of Attila, a forest of iron, gleaming like the sun on the morning sea :—

> " Ferrea sylva micat, totos rutilando per agros,
> Haud aliter primo quam pulsans æquora mane
> Pulcher in extremis renitet sol partibus orbis."

It is as a story of adventure that *Waltharius* is notable. There is no fumbling about the composition; everything is in its place, and clearly seen. The author, or his original, knew how his people behaved. Their rudeness is little disguised, their motives are not elaborate, but (one is thrown back to the old formula) there is Nature in their story. One example of it is the conduct of Walter at night, after the battle, when he first builds his fence and then looks to his fallen enemies, placing the severed heads by the bodies, and praying for them toward the east with his sword drawn in his hand, like a good knight. Then he goes out to catch and hobble the horses left behind by Gunther. The fence for the night encampment was regular, as is shown in the wanderings of

Sturm the missionary in the forest before he settled at Fulda.[1] The business with the horses is thoroughly practical, and would have been approved (perhaps before the religious ceremony) by Ulysses or Grettir equally. But the respect for the slain enemy is not a new thing, nor purely Christian. As Grimm points out, Arrow Odd after the fight in Samsey buries Angantyr and his brothers. Other Icelandic references might be easily multiplied, and compared with the chivalrous romances where the true knight gives housel to his enemy after mortally wounding him.

About the same date as *Waltharius* appears the *Ecbasis Captivi*,[2] one of the forerunners of *Reynard the Fox*, inasmuch as it is a satirical story with the beasts as actors: it was written by a monk of Toul. A hundred years later came the fragments of the curious romance of *Ruodlieb*,[3] very hard to arrange and explain: the story of an adventurer, like many another in the tales of chivalry. The verse, like that of the *Ecbasis*, is leonine hexameter; German words are found in it:—

Ecbasis Captivi.

Ruodlieb.

(*The* LADY *speaks.*)

Dixit: "Dic illi nunc de me corde fideli
Tantundem *liebes*, veniat quantum modo *loubes*,
Et volucrum *wunna* quot sint, tot dic sibi *minna*,
Graminis et florum quantum sit, dic et honorum."

There is a pretty scene with a dwarf or elf, true of word, as those wights always are; and this, with the

---

[1] The passage is quoted by Ebert, ii. 105, from Eigil's Life of Sturm.
[2] Ed. Grimm and Schmeller, *Lat. Ged.*, 1838.
[3] Ed. Grimm and Schmeller, ibid.; ed. Seiler, 1882.

name of King Ruotlieb, has been found again in the
Eckenlied of the German *Heldenbuch*. More remarkable are the anticipations of the French romantic
school—*e.g.*, the elaborate descriptions of works of art
are such as were fashionable with French poets in
the next century.

The Comic literature of Germany has never had
much credit from other nations, though they have been
Modus Liebinc: ready to live on it without acknowledg-
Modus Florum. ment, borrowing Till Owlglas and other
jesters. In the Middle Ages, Germany is ahead of
France in a kind which is reckoned peculiarly French;
the earliest fabliaux are in German Latin, with
Swabians for comic heroes,—the story of the *Snow-
Child*, and the other, *How the Swabian made the King
say 'That's a story.'* These are written to well-known
tunes, which give them their titles, *Modus Liebinc* and
Modus Florum. They are good enough: the former one,
with considerable elegance in phrasing, tells a story
fit for the *Decameron;* the other, with less ambition,
gives one of the well-known popular tales—a
monstrous lie rewarded with the hand of the king's
daughter. The malice of the *Snow-Child* is something different from anything in vernacular literature
till the time of Boccaccio and Chaucer; the learned
language and the rather difficult verse perhaps helping
to refine the mischief of the story. It is self-conscious,
amused at its own craft: a different thing from the
ingenuous simplicity of the French "merry tales,"
not to speak of the churlish heaviness of the worst
among them.

CHAPTER IV.

THE TEUTONIC LANGUAGES.

RULES OF VERSE—OLD HIGH GERMAN POETRY—'HILDEBRAND'—'MUS-
PILLI'—OTFRID—SAXON AND ANGLO-SAXON POETRY—'BEOWULF'
AND 'BYRHTNOTH'—CÆDMON—THE SAXON GENESIS—CYNEWULF—
THE ELEGIES—NORSE AND ICELANDIC POETRY—THE 'ELDER EDDA,'
AND OTHER NORTHERN POEMS—COURT-POETRY IN THE NORTH.
GERMAN PROSE—GOTHIC, HIGH GERMAN, ANGLO-SAXON, ICELANDIC
—ULFILAS—THE ENGLISH 'CHRONICLE'—ALFRED—ÆLFRIC—ARI
THE WISE—NOTKER THE GERMAN.

THERE is extant a considerable body of poetry in the old
Germanic tongues, especially in Icelandic and Anglo-
Saxon.   In addition, there are many historical facts on
which to base conjectures about what has been lost,—
and that much has been lost is certain.   The measures
taken by Charlemagne and Alfred to preserve the Frankish and the English poetry were frustrated by the prejudices and the negligence of their successors.   It is by
chance only that anything has been preserved.   The
Anglo-Saxon poems and the "Elder Edda" have come
through fire.   We know the hair-breadth escapes of the
text of *Beowulf*, of *Finnesburh*, and of the *Lay of Maldon;* and there is nothing fanciful in believing that

fires, rats, librarians, or Protestant enthusiasm may
have dismissed from the world an Old English heroic
poem on the Nibelung history, with even less mark of
its having once existed than there is for the lost story
of Wade, or for the English version of Hildebrand.[1]

It is proved, and it scarcely needed proof, that the
old Germans had the popular kinds of poetry which
were not wanting even to the founders of Rome.
They had spell-songs, they had gibing verses, they
had riddles,—kinds that belong to the whole world,
and of which there are remnants and reminiscences
current still.

They had a common form of verse which was used
for any purpose, and which early in historical times
was already developed as the proper form of expression for a noble kind of heroic poetry.[2]

---

[1] See the *Academy*, February 15, 1896. A fragment of verse was
found by Dr James, and interpreted by Mr Gollancz, in a thirteenth
century Latin homily : *Ita quod dicere possunt cum Wade :*—

> Summe sende ylues
> and summe sende nadderes :
> summe sende nikeres
> the bi den watere wunien
> Nister man nenne
> bute ildebrand onne.

[2] The Teutonic alliterative verse has in recent years been pretty
fully explained, mainly through the learning and skill of Dr Edward
Sievers of Leipzig, whose *Altgermanische Metrik* gives his results in a
summary but not too contracted form. These have been in some
points exposed to criticism and in some points supplemented ; see
especially for exceptional rules in the Old Northern Scaldic verse
Mr W. A. Craigie's ingenious demonstration in the *Arkiv för Nordisk
Filologi*, vol. xvi. (of the new series, xii.), p. 341 *sq.* (Lund, 1900).
But Dr Sievers's theory has not yet been damaged in its central
positions—being indeed not hypothesis, but mainly statistics.

Some of the principal rules of the old verse are
Teutonic Verse. retained in England in the alliterative
poems of the fourteenth century, among
which *Piers Plowman* is the chief:—

"Ac in a Máy mórning | on Málvern hílles."

The line is divided into two sections, with two strong
syllables in each, and with alliteration in three out
of the four. The varieties of rhythm have been reduced to five chief types for the half line, taken
separately, which in their simplest form are as
follows. The examples are from Anglo-Saxon, Old
Saxon, and Icelandic:—

A. $-'\smile\ |\ -'\smile$: *béne biddan, skarpun skúrun, bauga
dregna.*

B. $\smile-'\ |\ \smile-'$: *in helle grund, an morgantíd, af sárum
hug.*

C. $\smile-'\ |\ \smile'\smile$: *on hranráde, an ér dagun, of grásilfri.*

D. $-'\ |\ -'\smile'\smile$ (a secondary stress after the second chief
stress): *beorht blœdgifa, hard harmskara, folks
oddviti.*

E. $-'\ |\ -'\smile-'$ (a secondary stress between the two chief
stresses): *fyrngidda fród, gramhudig man, end-
langan sal.*

Rules of quantity can be clearly made out from
the common usage of all the languages. The chief
stress is always on a long syllable, or on a resolution
of a long syllable (*sĭgŏră dryhten*), with one exception: a short syllable may have the chief stress
when it comes immediately after a long syllable
which has either a major or a minor stress. This

exception is especially common in the *C* type, *e.g.*, *of léodhĕte.* Icelandic differs from the other languages in admitting short syllables at the end of *B* and *E.* The Icelandic verse was more exclusively dactylic or trochaic than the Anglo-Saxon.

In some parts of the line the number of unaccented syllables may be increased without spoiling the measure; the greatest licence in this respect is at the beginning of half lines of the *B* type. The languages came to vary considerably in their tastes with regard to number of syllables. Icelandic poets became more and more correct; the alliterative verse tended more and more to strict observation of syllables, four in each short line. The Old-Saxon poet of the *Heliand* shows the opposite tendency —towards an increase in the number of unstressed syllables and a diffuse and irregular habit of verse. The later English alliterative line of the great fourteenth century school is licentious as compared with Cynewulf, unrestricted in the number of syllables. But the old rhythm is not lost. The verse of *Piers Plowman*, quoted already—" Ac in a Máy mórning "—preserves the old measures well enough; and much later, the poem of *Scotish Field*, on the battle of Flodden, follows the same rule, in most essential points, as the poem of *Maldon:—*

"Which foughten full freshly while the feild lasted."

Scotish Field refuses the common anapæstic canter of the "tumbling verse"—

"A notable story I'll tell you anon"—

and keeps to the ancient variety of cadence which makes the charm of the Anglo-Saxon and the old Norse epic poetry. But it is the last of its noble race, in Britain at any rate, and the ancestral splendour is the worse for wear.

This metre, which is used in a poem on the battle of Flodden by an English writer, is found in one of the oldest Teutonic inscriptions, with grammatical inflexions older than the Gothic of Ulfilas, on the golden horn of the Copenhagen Museum.[1] It was found near Gallehus in Sleswick, in the country that the English came from. The artist (about 300 A.D.) has left his name in a verse—

> "Ec Hlewagastiz Holtingaz horna tawido."
>
> (I Hlewagast Holting the horn fashioned.)

Between this and *Scotish Field*—not to speak of the use of the verse by the poets of Iceland at the present day—there is a long history.

By far the greater part of the poetry that has survived in the older Teutonic languages and in the old verse is narrative; it may be called *epic* without forcing the term too much. That the alliterative verse was originally used in strophes or stanzas meant for singing, and that the continuous narrative verse grew out of the lyric form, is a theory generally accepted; and though " the similarity of two hypotheses

---

[1] The golden horns—there were two of them—are lost. They were stolen in 1802 ; and by a further stroke of bad luck, the gold copies of them were lost at sea. Fortunately there were drawings, from which the existing models were made. See Stephens, *Runic Monuments*, and Steenstrup, in *Danmarks Riges Historie*, i. 99.

does not prove both," yet it is convenient to remember that the same sort of evolution is supposed to have taken place in the epic of Greece and of France. Of strophic or lyric poetry in Germanic tongues there remains, for example, the old English poem called *Deor's Lament*, with a repeated burden, while the Icelandic narrative poetry is always strophic in form. The metrical rules, it has been seen, are to a great extent common to High and Low German, English and Icelandic alike. But in what may be called poetical syntax there are considerable divergences. Two principal types are represented by the Icelandic and the old English poetry respectively; the English manner being more or less the manner of the Continental poems that are extant in German dialects, the Hildebrand lay and the Old Saxon *Heliand*. The difference is that in the English or Continental type the sentence is generally continued from one line to another, and as often as not begins in the middle of a line, while in the Icelandic type the lines and phrases coincide, the grammatical construction does not cut across the middle of the verses, and the verses fall regularly into quatrains in which the sense is concluded. The English verse is narrative, the Icelandic verse goes into lyrical staves. The old English type agrees in much of its grammar and rhetoric with the practice of blank verse: it makes paragraphs where the sentences are distributed unequally, and where rhetorical swell and cadence are freely varied. The Icelandic type, more obviously regular, more emphatic and formal, is not adapted for the long rolling recitative of the other school; it is quicker, more alert, more pointed.

Alliterative poetry by its nature requires a large supply of synonyms, and this remains its character down to the latest examples. The alliterative poem on Flodden uses not a little of the poetic dictionary of *Beowulf;* the fighting man has a variety of names beginning with different letters, that fit into different alliterative schemes: *burne, freke, leedes, rinck, sege, wye* are the terms of *Scotish Field,* A.D. 1513; *beorn, freca, leode, rinc, secg, wiga* are the words of the old English epic school, which are common also to the poets in the other Teutonic languages, part of the common *Gradus.*

Richness of vocabulary belongs of right to all alliterative poets, good or bad; it is a kind of literature that tends to extravagance. With the profusion of many names for the same thing goes the love of metaphor. Similes are little used. The epic simile of Homer is scarcely adopted in modern poetry before Dante, but the Teutonic epic not only does without this kind of ornament, it uses even less of simile than is common in ordinary story-telling or in the most unpretending talk. It looks almost like wilfulness in a battle poet not to say that a hero went through the enemy "as runs a hawk through flocks of wild birds, or a hound through flocks of sheep," but comparisons of this sort are of the rarest in Teutonic epic.[1]

[1] The chief exceptions are in Cynewulf, *Christ,* l. 851 *sqq.,* and in Gudrun's lament for Sigurd, *C. P. B.,* i. 326; cf. ibid., p. 141; p. 54 ('I am left alone like an aspen in the wood'); p. 330.

The figurative decoration goes almost altogether into epithets and descriptive phrases. The temper of the poets or the tradition of their school induces them to put out more of their strength in diction than in illustration. Instead of the pictures that in Homer, Virgil, Dante, and Chaucer illuminate the story, both distracting and quickening the attention of the reader, there is found in the old German heroic school a kind of rich rhetorical incrustation of gems over the plain narrative: the art of poetic diction is thoroughly understood, and used " without remorse or mitigation of voice," sometimes gloriously, sometimes mechanically. But whatever the art or talent of the poet may be, the language of his poetry is unlike that of prose, and the invention and disposition of separate jewels of speech is always a chief part of his task.

With this conception of poetry there was an obvious danger that the brocading work of epithets might hamper the narrative, or again that it might be learned as an art for its own sake by people with nothing to say. A well-established conventional diction made it easy for a moderate wit to dress up any story or sermon. Much of Anglo-Saxon poetry is compounded on the same general principles as Milton's translation of Psalm cxiv., "done by the Author at fifteen years old," turning "When Israel came out of Egypt " into poetical diction: "When the blest seed of Terah's faithful son," and so forth. The details of the process are different, but the ambition is the same as in the Anglo-Saxon poetical embroidery. The periphrastic demon reappears in different ages

with new clothes.   Give a sentence to an Anglo-
Saxon poet and an eighteenth-century moralist, and
they will develop it in different ways, but both will
be ready for the business, and well supplied with
formulas.   The Anglo-Saxon makes nine lines of the
sentence "Almsgiving quenches sin as water quenches
fire."   In the school of "Terah's faithful son" one
finds the same sort of proportion:—

> " Happy the man to whom the Heav'ns impart
> A soul of sympathy, a gen'rous heart :
> Honour from men the liberal spirit knows ;
> A Higher Judge a nobler meed bestows.
> What Virtue can with *Charity* compare,
> The healing Effluence, the Bounty rare !
> As quenching stream the fiery pest allays,
> Quells the fierce embers and prevents the blaze," &c.[1]

But in spite of this tempter the Anglo-Saxon epic
and its counterpart in Germany, taken altogether,
show a truly admirable power of narrative; the best
things of the school are magnificent in the right sense
of the word.   There is a balance and compromise
between two different sorts of excellence such as is
only found in a grand style: the Anglo-Saxon love of
swelling oratorical periods, of grammatical variety, of a
continuous onward movement in discourse, was enough

---

[1] Wel bið þam eorle, þe him on innan hafað
reþehygdig wer rume heortan !
Þæt him biþ for worulde weorðmynda mæst
and for ussum Dryhtne doma selast !
Efna swa he mid wætre þone weallendan
leg adwæsce, þæt he leng ne mæg
blac byrnende burgum sceððan,
swa he mid ælmessan ealle toscufeð
synna wunde, sawla lacnað.—(*Cod. Exon.*)

(at least in the case of the good writers) to save the poetry from stiffening under the rich vocabulary. With many differences, the same kind of power is shown in the great alliterative poems of the fourteenth century.

There are very few remains of the old heroic poetry or of the old alliterative verse in the German languages *Old High German Poetry.* of the Continent. The High German dialects especially made an early surrender to the attractions of rhyme. They show scarcely anything of the old verse except the *Muspilli*, a poem on the Day of Judgment, and a few fragmentary prayers and charms. The Low German tongues of Northern Germany kept the old rhythm longer, as the Saxons likewise kept a livelier interest in the old stories. It was in Saxony that a Norwegian traveller in the thirteenth century picked up and collected the stories of "Didrik" of Bern, which are extant now in their Norse prose form as he translated and adapted them. The Lay of Hildebrand, the only surviving poem of the old school on the Continent,—the only poem *Hildebrand.* which uses both the old verse and the old heroic tradition,—is properly Low German, though the language of the existing manuscript has been altered and made to conform roughly to High German usage by the two High German clerks who copied it. Damaged and timeworn as it is, the Lay of Hildebrand and his son Hadubrand has still preserved the character of true heroic poetry.[1] To call

---

[1] The fragments of Old High German, verse and prose, are collected in *Denkmäler deutscher Poesie und Prosa aus dem VIII.-XII. Jahrh.*, by Müllenhoff and Scherer.

it epic is not to strain the term too far, if "epic" be allowed to denote quality, even when the proper length of story is not attained.   For the story is only a single scene, though it is a scene which in itself completes a tragedy.   Shortly, it is the encounter between father and son, in which the son is slain—an old and favourite theme for tragic authors in different countries.   It is here told with a variation from the common type; for while in other stories of the sort the father kills the son in ignorance, here he discovers who his son is, and is driven to fight with him because his son will not believe him.   Hildebrand and Hadubrand met between the hosts in some great battle of the Huns, and the older warrior asked the name and lineage of his opponent.   They were on opposite sides, and did not know one another, because Hildebrand had been long in exile with Theodoric, escaping from the wrath of Odoacer.   When he fled, leaving "bride in bower," his son was an infant.   Now Theodoric comes back with his Easterlings (*ôstar liuto, Ostrogoths*) in the army of the Huns, and Hildebrand is in his company.   Hadubrand will not listen to his father's story; he is sure that Hildebrand is dead.   His father's offer of gifts is rejected: "with spears shall the gift be welcomed, point against point." The speech of Hildebrand when he finds that he is being driven against his will into the combat is a good specimen of the dignified oratory which belongs to epic:—

[Hildebrand spake, Heribrand's son] "Wellaway, Lord God, sorrowful fate cometh on.   Thirty summers and thirty winters have I been a wayfarer, and always I was chosen to the company of the fighting men, and never yet, by any town of men, has my slayer found me. Now shall my own child smite me with the sword, lay me low with his brand, or I am to be his death. Yet well and lightly, if thy valour be strong in thee, mayst thou win spoils from this old man, plunder his war-gear, if thou canst make good thy claim. Let him be the craven of all the Easterlings who now shall keep thee from battle, now that thou desirest it, from the communion of war : let him put it to the touch, that cannot do else, whether he is to-day to strip his trappings from him, or to be lord of the armour of twain."

The poem breaks off in the description of the combat, where the fighting is in a well-accepted style—as in the *Battle of Maldon*, a poem composed two hundred years after this one was copied. First go out the lances, the ashen spears that are caught in the shields: then they take to their swords:—and then the fragment ends, and nothing more is known of the old Lay of Hildebrand.

It is full of phrases that illustrate the common character of the Teutonic poetry, its reliance on tradition and the traditional fashions of speech. There are not seventy lines in the fragment, but at every turn there is something analogous to something else in Old English or Icelandic poetry. Not only in the separate phrases, such as might be put together in a poetical Teutonic dictionary, but equally in the general temper, in the principles of style, the *Hildebrand Lay* proves itself of the same kin as *Beowulf* and the *Elder Edda;* with a much closer relationship to *Beowulf* than to the Icelandic poems. The grammar is that of the English, and definitely not that of the Northern

17

school.   It may be seen in the passage translated
above how the phrases are doubled: "smite me with
the sword, lay me low with his brand;" "keep thee
from battle, from the communion of war." The
phrases thus rendered are double phrases, such as
are required by the verse when it is used in the Old
English manner; the repeated synonymous phrases
serve to ride over the breaks between the lines.
They are the regular device for obtaining continuity
in the discourse, and preventing the staccato effect
which, on the other hand, was admired by the
Northmen.

Besides *Hildebrand*, there are a few fragmentary
High Dutch poems in the old measure.   The Bavarian
verses, commonly called the Wessobrunn Prayer (*Das
Wessobrunner Gebet*), are often quoted for their likeness to some phrases of the *Volospá*:—

"That is known among men for the greatest of marvels. Earth
was not, nor high Heaven, nor hill nor tree. The sun shone
not, the moon gave not light, nor the glorious sea. Then there
was naught, unending unwending, and there was the one Almighty God, mildest of men, and there were also many with
him, righteous spirits."

Even these few lines show their accordance with the
poetic traditions.   They begin with the formula "I
heard tell," like *Beowulf*, *Hildebrand*, and so many
others—

"Dat gafregin ih mit firahim."

Of *Muspilli*, a poem on the Last Judgment, there
are more than a hundred lines, and here, again, the
regular pattern is observed, the formulas are repeated

(*daz hôriih rahhôn*, "that heard I tell"). The system of parallel phrases is found here, as in Anglo-Saxon

Muspilli.   poetry, also the extended verse and the occasional use of rhyme. The lines on Paradise have a faint resemblance to the Anglo-Saxon description in the *Phœnix;* the battle of Antichrist and Elias and the flaming of the world are given with the spirit and energy that properly belong to the old alliterative rhetoric. The Court of Heaven is described in the terms of familiar law and politics: the King holds an assembly (*mahal*) summoned by his ban which none may neglect (*furisizzan*). The doctrine is like that of many English poems, especially the old "Moral Ode";[1] the condemnation of Meed agrees with *Piers Plowman.*

The most considerable of the Old High German poems, Otfrid's version of the Gospel history,[2] is as

Otfrid.   distinct from the alliterative order and the heroic tradition as the *Ormulum* in England from Layamon's *Brut.* It resembles the *Ormulum* in many points besides their community of subject. Like the *Ormulum*, it is the careful work of a student, who has chosen a new measure to write in, and is proud of his achievement and his distinction from the common minstrels. But Otfrid, though much occupied with the technicalities of his literary workshop, is happily less precise than the English Orm, whose book is indeed without a rival in its peculiar virtues, its deliberate and pious monotony.

[1] In *An Old English Miscellany*, ed. Morris, E.E.T.S.
[2] Ed. Kelle, 1856; Piper, 1878; Erdmann, 1882.

Otfrid wrote in rhyming verse; his poem was meant for singing, and has notes, in places, to give the tune. The measure corresponds to the musical period of sixteen bars, which comes by nature more universally than reading and writing to the whole human race. The chief syllables are marked with accents, which in one of the manuscripts probably come from Otfrid's own hand. The rhyme is always on the last syllable, even when the rhyming words are such as *harme, barme;* or *lindo, kindo* — *i.e.,* these which look like ordinary feminine rhymes do not end in light syllables. Both syllables are stressed, though not equally :—*líndò, kíndò.* This forced accentuation is explained by the fact that the verse is meant for singing, not for recitation: the tune dwells on syllables that are passed over more lightly in speaking.

The same kind of verse appears in England at the close of the Anglo-Saxon period, and is found in large quantities in the *Brut* of Layamon, along with the common alliterative measure. Layamon did not know Otfrid, and there are other reasons in contemporary literature to make it probable that Otfrid was not the inventor of the form which commonly goes by his name. Rhyming German verse is common about that time. The *Rithmus Teutonicus* of 881, in honour of King Lewis—the *Ludwigslied*— may have been copied from Otfrid's pattern; but it is on the whole easier to suppose that what is common to both was derived from older practice. There are rhyming accidental lines in the narrative poetry, like those in *Muspilli*—

> "diu marka ist farprunnan ; diu sêle stêt pidungan,
> ni uueiz mit uuiu fruaze : sâr verit si za uuîze "—

which differ not only in rhyme but in rhythm from the common verse, and which agree in rhythm with Otfrid.

At Fulda Otfrid was the pupil of Hraban : thus his poem represents the tastes and ideas of the chief educational tradition. The teaching of Hraban, like that of Bede and Alcuin, like that of Hilary, Ambrose, and Gregory the Great, thought less of philosophy than of the needs of the flock. It was natural that exposition of the Scripture should be given in the language of the common people; and at least two German versions of the Gospels, besides Otfrid's, are connected with the School of Hraban. About 830 a copy, still to be found at Fulda, of the Harmony of the Gospels, derived from Tatian, was translated there into German prose. The Saxon *Heliand* is based on Tatian also, and on Hraban's commentary on St Matthew. Otfrid's work is thus not an isolated experiment, but falls in with the general movement of the time.

He completed his work about 868 in the monastery of Weissenburg, where most of his life was spent. A Latin epistle explains his motive. Some reverend brethren and an honourable lady Judith made a petition to him that he would turn the Gospel into

their own tongue.   The brothers complained that
their ears were offended by the gross songs of the
laity, and that their native tongue ought not to be left
to the profane.   So he wrote, he says, part of the
Gospels in Frankish (*franzisce*), adding occasionally
moral and spiritual interpretations.   The first chapter
of his poem is headed *Cur scriptor hunc librum
theotisce dictaverit,* and gives his reasons in his
own German verse.   They are the motives of the
Renaissance: Otfrid acknowledges the supremacy of
Greek and Latin art, of the ancient poets whose composition is as smooth as ivory.   He has no hope of
attaining with his Frankish tongue to the pure, exact,
and perfect measure of the ancients; but why should
not the Frankish tongue do as well as it can?   This
is in the proper spirit of humanism, reverent, but not
abashed, in the presence of the old masters.   There is
nothing wrong with Otfrid's good intentions.

Connected with Otfrid's verse and manner there
are several short poems in Old High German—a song
in honour of St Peter, a longer ballad of St George
(with a refrain, but without the dragon), a rhyming
piece on the woman of Samaria.   The German poem
of Ratpert in praise of St Gall is lost, but it was
translated into Latin by Ekkehard the chronicler,
as near as possible in the original rhythm—

"Cursu pergunt recto Cum agmine collecto
    Tria tranant maria   Celeumant Christo gloria."

The most famous of all this set—*Rithmus Teutonicus
de piæ memoriæ Hluduico Rege, filio Hluduici æque*

Regis—follows immediately on the Old French sequence of *Eulalia*, written by the same hand, in the Valenciennes manuscript.[1] It is commonly known as the *Ludwigslied*, and praises Lewis III. for his victory over the Northmen at Sancourt in 881. Lewis died the next year, but the poem was composed before that, immediately after the battle. The adventures of King Lewis became a favourite subject in French epic;[2] and the *Ludwigslied* at one time was made into evidence that French epic was derived from German. But this has been given up: the French song of King Lewis is otherwise descended, and the pious well-meaning verses of the *Rithmus Teutonicus* have no share in its ancestry. The German poem is absolutely sincere and right in its sentiments: the Lord was helper and nursing-father to the orphan king; the Normans plagued the people for their sins; the young king brought deliverance; God save the king! But there is scarcely a thought in it that is not abstract and fit for prose; a phrase of one of the old heathen spells might buy the whole of it.

The Anglo-Saxons have acquired (probably through the association of King Alfred with blameless heroes like George Washington) a name for respectability. Their extant literature is largely moral. But Anglo-Saxon tameness is fury compared with the High German, if the remains of High German literature are any evidence. In both cases, probably, the people are misrepresented by these relics.

The Saxon *Heliand*[3] is in great part derived from

[1] Above, p. 221, note.   [2] See below, p. 351.   [3] Ed. Sievers, 1878.

the same sources as Otfrid, about the same time; it
belongs, of course, to a different school. But
Heliand.
although it preserves the language and form
of the old heroic poetry, it is not a primitive thing; it
is a pupil of the Northumbrian school, the artistic
narrative poetry of England, and it is not less ambitious than Otfrid in its literary scope. The merit
of the Saxon poem is that it runs freely; it has fewer
brilliances than the English poetry, and nothing like
the imaginative force of the Saxon *Paradise Lost*
which has been preserved in the old English *Genesis*.
The morality is that of the epic tradition, especially
in the motive of loyalty: the disciples accompany
their Lord like the thanes of Beowulf or Byrhtnoth.
The language is full of phrases that belong to the
common stock—"bitter breast-care," "mickle mood-
care," "grim and greedy," and so forth—well known
in Anglo-Saxon verse. Yet this conventional language
is used with spirit, and there is much energy in the
story, perhaps none the worse for the want of novelty
in the diction. The prophecy of the end of the world
(ll. 4294-4377) may be referred to as an example
of the style, with its poetical use of common words—
"by this ye shall know that summer is nigh, warm
and winsome and weather sheen" (*warm endi wunsam
endi weder sconi*). The descriptive parts of the story
are seldom elaborate, neither are they untrue. The
Lord "*sat and was silent and looked long at them,*
gracious in thought, mild in mood; then he opened
his mouth and declared to them many a glorious
thing." It is an Old Saxon counterpart to the de-

scription in the *Iliad* of Ulysses speaking.[1] The two
poets have both known the same kind of eloquence,
when the orator is slow to begin: the elementary
Saxon phrasing, though not exactly Homeric, is
sound and effective.

Anglo-Saxon poetry has the characteristics of an
accomplished literary school, with a fully developed
Anglo-Saxon language and a regular traditional method
Poetry. of expression. The greater part of the extant poetry, it is true, has been transposed from the
Anglian dialect of the North to the language of
Wessex, but this translation has not changed the literary character of the original. The shifting of the
literary centre from Northumbria to the Wessex of
King Alfred did not break the tradition of English
poetical style: indeed, the English school takes in not
only the Anglian and Saxon dialects of England, but
also the Old Saxon of the Continent; the *Heliand* and
the fragments of the Old Saxon *Genesis* being very
closely related in their poetical style to the narrative
poetry of Northumbria. This English school differs from
the High German alliterative poetry most obviously
in its fecundity; the High German poetry was wither-
ing and drying up, being displaced by new rhyming
forms, when the English poetry was flourishing and
exuberant, and not in the least inclined to part with
its native habiliments in exchange for rhyming verse.
It differs again from the Northern school, from the
Elder Edda, in its preference for continuous narrative;
the detached couplets of the Norse poetry are not

[1] *Il.,* iii. 216 *sqq.*

favoured by the English poets, who use a freer kind of rhetoric, more voluminous, less lyrical, allowing their sentences to run on from line to line. Old English poetry has, in fact, over against the Icelandic, much of the quality of Miltonic verse as compared with the couplets of Waller, or of the *Excursion*, contrasted with the *Holy Fair*. The two modes, of continuous eloquence and of ringing phrase, are not limited to any one dialect or country, but represent different habits of mind, which repeat themselves mysteriously in different parts of the world, like types of character or physical feature.

Very little has been preserved from the Anglo-Saxon period of what may be called the experimental stages of the poetry. The poems are all of a class which has got through the 'prentice time; the ways are ascertained and sure, the patterns are authorised. Popular poetry is not well represented, though there are some spell-songs that show what style was current where there was less literary ambition. For the most part, the Anglo-Saxon poetry may be taken as belonging to a period more like that of Chaucer and Gower than that of the confused and adventurous thirteenth century in England. There is nothing in Old English like the rich irregular experimental Middle English literature, or like the period of Marlowe, Greene, and Peele in the history of the Drama. Taken generally, Anglo-Saxon poetry has rather the look of respectable maturity than of any promise. It has its subjects and its methods well in hand, its resources are large; but at the

Contrast of English and Icelandic.

same time there is a certain complacency and slowness in its gait, as if it had finished its education and was inclined to rest on its achievements. It is different in the Norse country, where the old poetry gives way indeed and is displaced, but never loses its springiness. If the *Elder Edda* is the last of it, it shows up to the last a relish for new attempts, a spirit of progress, a desire of new beauties, not like anything in the better equipped and more contented Anglo-Saxon.

The Old English epic poetry, with *Beowulf* as its chief extant work, is properly valued by historians *Old English Epic.* as giving the only narrative poems in an old Teutonic dialect that in respect of their scale can be compared with the epics of other lands. Though there may be Homeric analogies in Germany and Iceland, yet *Hildebrand* is too short, Northern lays too lyrical, to be brought into close comparison with the *Iliad* or the *Chansons de Geste*. In Anglo-Saxon poetry there is not only the heroic spirit and tradition, there is the taste for stories with a certain amount of room in them. Size counts for something in an epic. *Beowulf* musters 3000 lines, enough to put it in a different class from *Hildebrand* or the Northern poems of Sigurd and Attila. Among the fragments, those of the Anglo-Saxon *Waldere* plainly belong to a story of some considerable size, of about the same scale as *Beowulf*.

It is difficult to judge the importance of this epic poetry for the times when it was composed. Undoubtedly a vast amount has been lost irrevocably; in this there must of course have been many different grades of value, and at least as much variety as in the English romantic literature of the thirteenth and fourteenth centuries, which has been better preserved. The extant remains of Anglo-Saxon epic, and particularly a comparison of the *Finnesburh* poem with *Beowulf* and *Waldere*, seem to prove at any rate the existence of two well-marked and accepted types of heroic poem: one not far removed from the pattern of *Hildebrand*, the other more amplified and more ambitious. The *Finnesburh* poem, judging from what remains of it, was a short epic with one definite adventure in it, an episode of heroic defence, treated boldly and without much ornament. The plot of *Waldere* is one of the same sort, but the treatment is different, the rhetorical speeches in the extant fragments, with their digressions and illustrations, belong to a different and more sophisticated kind of work. The adventures in *Beowulf* also are treated with more ornament and more digression than was found suitable by the poet of *Finnesburh*. As it is the less restricted manner which is found prevailing in the narrative poems on Christian themes, both in English and in Old Saxon, it is justifiable to take this as the proper characteristic Anglo-Saxon type; to make *Beowulf* rather than *Finnesburh* the specimen of Anglo-Saxon epic style.

Beowulf and *Waldere* are the work of educated men, and they were intended, no doubt, as books to read. They are not, like the *Elder Edda*, a collection of traditional oral poems. It may be accident that has made it so, but it is the case that the Anglo-Saxon books in their handwriting and their shape have the air of libraries and learning about them, of wealth and dignity. The handsome pages of the Junius MS. in the Bodleian (the *Cædmon* manuscript) belong to a learned world. The book of *Roland* lying near it is different—an unpretending cheap copy, not meant for patrons of learning to read, but more probably for the minstrel who chanted it. The *Beowulf* MS., though not so fine as the Junius one, is intended as a book to be read, and is got up with some care. From the look of it, one places it naturally in the library of a great house or a monastic school; and the contents of it have the same sort of association; they do not belong to the unlearned in their present form.

One would like to think of the Anglo-Saxon epic, with *Beowulf* its representative (out of a number of lost heroes), as naturally developing to its full proportions from earlier ruder experimental work, through a course of successive improvements like those that can be traced, for instance, in the growth of the Drama or the Novel. And one wishes there were more left to show how it came about, and also that the process had gone a little further. But not only is there a want of specimens for the literary museum; there is the misgiving that this comparatively well-filled narrative poetry may not be an independent product of the English or the Teutonic genius. There is too much education in *Beowulf*, and it may be that the larger kind of heroic poem was attained in England only through the example of Latin narrative.

The English epic is possibly due to Virgil and Statius; possibly to Juvencus and other Christian poets, to the authors studied by Aldhelm and Bede. It may be that *Hildebrand* for the Western Germanic group, that the *Atlamál* for the North, fixes the limit of epic size in the old Teutonic school; that it was difficult or impossible to get beyond this without the encouragement of Latin poets, showing how to amplify and embroider, to compose orations for combatants, and to discriminate the particulars of their wounds.

Yet while there may be about the Anglo-Saxon epic this suspicion of foreign and learned influence, the Anglo-Saxon, or rather the West German type, was capable of growth, for all its slowness, as the Norse type of poetic story was not, for all its energy and curiosity. The old-fashioned poem of *Hildebrand* is so constructed as to leave room for expansion; the loose jointing, the want of restriction in the form, might easily tempt a poet to the fuller mode of treatment found in *Waldere*.

A reasonable view of the merit of *Beowulf* is not impossible, though rash enthusiasm may have made too much of it, while a correct and sober taste may have too contemptuously refused to attend to Grendel or the Firedrake. The fault of *Beowulf* is that there is nothing much in the story. The hero is occupied in killing monsters, like Hercules or Theseus. But there are other things in the lives of Hercules and Theseus besides the killing of the Hydra or of Procrustes. Beowulf has nothing else to do, when he has killed Grendel and Grendel's mother in

Beowulf.

Denmark : he goes home to his own Gautland, until at last the rolling years bring the Firedrake and his last adventure. It is too simple. Yet the three chief episodes are well wrought and well diversified; they are not repetitions, exactly; there is a change of temper between the wrestling with Grendel in the night at Heorot and the descent under water to encounter Grendel's mother; while the sentiment of the Dragon is different again. But the great beauty, the real value, of *Beowulf* is in its dignity of style. In construction it is curiously weak, in a sense preposterous; for while the main story is simplicity itself, the merest commonplace of heroic legend, all about it, in the historic allusions, there are revelations of a whole world of tragedy, plots different in import from that of *Beowulf*, more like the tragic themes of Iceland. Yet with this radical defect, a disproportion that puts the irrelevances in the centre and the serious things on the outer edges, the poem of *Beowulf* is unmistakably heroic and weighty. The thing itself is cheap; the moral and the spirit of it can only be matched among the noblest authors. It is not in the operations against Grendel, but in the humanities of the more leisurely interludes, the conversation of Beowulf and Hrothgar, and such things, that the poet truly asserts his power. It has often been pointed out how like the circumstances are in the welcome of Beowulf at Heorot and the reception of Ulysses in Phæacia. Hrothgar and his queen are not less gentle than Alcinous and Arete. There is nothing to compare with them in the Norse poems : it is not till

the prose histories of Iceland appear that one meets
with the like temper there.   It is not common in any
age; it is notably wanting in Middle English literature, because it is an aristocratic temper, secure of itself, and not imitable by the poets of an uncourtly
language composing for a simple-minded audience.

This dignity of the epic strain is something real, something in the blood, not a mere trick of literary style.
It is lost in the revolution of the eleventh
Byrhtnoth.
century, but it survives at any rate to the
days of Ethelred the Unready and the Battle of
Maldon. The Maldon poem, late as it is, may claim to
be of an old heroic stock.   It uses the old traditional
form and diction. But more than that, the author has
seen his subject—the modern contemporary battle of
Maldon—with the imagination of an epic poet, with
a sense of tragedy and tragic nobility, with a perfectly
right proportion of action and dramatic speech.
There is no stronger composition in English till the
work of Chaucer; there is nothing equally heroic before *Samson Agonistes*.

That the Maldon poem should have been written,
so fresh and strong, so long after the old style had
passed its culmination, may be a warning
Widsith : Deor.
against neat theories of development in literature. The close of an artistic period may sometimes
miraculously regain the virtues of directness and force.
Far older, there are two poems not properly epic yet
belonging to the heroic age — *Widsith* and *Deor's
Complaint*, the former vaguely lyrical, the latter
definitely so, with a repeated burden, and something

like the Northern stanza, as it is found, for example, in the Lament of Gudrun. *Widsith* is a sort of fantasy on a number of the favourite historical themes, as if the epic poet's mind had gone for a discursive holiday, skimming over the ground which for narrative purposes would require a closer attention to business. *Deor's Lament* also makes use of legendary material for illustration of a lyrical theme: but here the lyrical motive is stronger; it is not mere fanciful recollection. The passion of the singer is comforted by the heroic examples. The refrain makes good the argument, "That old distress passed over, and so may this woe have ending."

The religious poetry of the Anglo-Saxons and the Old Saxons is part of their heroic literature; it uses *Religious Poetry:* the measure, the formulas, the ideas, of *Cœdmon.* German heroic verse. In quantity it is considerable, and it is not all of the same class. There are two names of poets, Cædmon and Cynewulf: the first of them regarded by Bede as the founder of Christian poetry in England; the second, by his own signature, the author of some of the finest extant poems.

Of Cædmon's own verse probably nothing remains except the lines quoted in Latin by Bede and separately preserved both in a Northumbrian and a West Saxon version.

Long ago, the subjects of the poems in the great Oxford MS., *Genesis, Exodus, &c.,* suggested to Francis Junius that they were the work of Cædmon. But the variety of authorship manifest when these poems

18

are more closely studied has left the name of Cædmon
only a conventional value in relation to them, like
the title of "Elder Edda," sometimes convenient,
whether accurate or not.   And here the gain is small,
for the texts are easily quoted under their several
proper names.

The *Genesis* has been the ground of some of the acut-
est criticism and a most brilliant philological victory.
The Anglo-Saxon The poem is easily detected as by different
Genesis.   hands.   Milton patched upon Blackmore and
Glover might represent in more modern terms the incongruity of it.   Great part of *Genesis* is mere flat commonplace, interesting as giving the average literary
taste and the commonplace poetical stock of a dull educated man.   But some of it—the story of *Paradise Lost*
in it—is magnificent.   This part of the poem, studied
by Dr Edward Sievers,[1] appeared to him to be mani-
festly not English in its origin, but an English version
from the Old Saxon, from an Old Saxon *Genesis*
belonging to the same school as the Old Saxon
Heliand.   So the theory rested, and was accepted or
denied or explained away according to the taste
of scholars, until the learned Heidelberg librarian
found in the Vatican, in a book that once had belonged to Heidelberg,[2] some considerable passages of
Old Saxon verse, written on fly-leaves and blank
spaces by some one in the ninth century who admired

---

[1] *Der Heliand und die angelsächsische Genesis* (Halle, 1875).

[2] Karl Zangemeister und Wilh. Braune, *Bruchstücke der altsächs-
ischen Bibeldichtung ans der Bibliotheca Palatina*, 1894 (**Neue**
Heidelberger Jahrbücher, **iv. 2**).

the poetry, and including, besides a passage from the *Heliand*, three from the unknown hypothetical Old Saxon *Genesis* of Sievers—one quotation coming from the part of the Anglo-Saxon *Genesis* which had been detected by Sievers as Old Saxon.[1]

The Saxon *Paradise Lost* is more imaginative and more eloquent than anything in *Beowulf;* it may be inferior to the *Maldon* poem in sincerity and gravity, not stronger than *Judith* in poetic spirit, but it surpasses all these in freedom and in dramatic force. Descriptions of Hell are frequent in all the tongues, in verse and prose: the Saxon *Genesis* is not commonplace, though it uses the favourite ideas, interchange of heat and cold, for example, which Dante and Milton knew, and which was supposed to be indicated by the distinction in the Gospel between weeping (in the fire) and gnashing of teeth (in the cold); and also the common idea of fire that gives no light, "the derke light that schal come out of the fuyer that ever schal brenne," as Chaucer puts it. But the common descriptions are recast and made new:—

"Therefore the Almighty God set them where the light was evil, in the nether parts of earth, baffled in the darkness of Hell. There at eventide is fire new kindled, long abiding; and at morning comes an eastern wind, felon cold; fire or the shaft of frost, cruel torment is upon them all. This was their punishment; the fashion of their world was changed. . . ."

---

[1] This Heidelberg fragment corresponds to *Gen.*, ll. 790-817. The Old Saxon quotation has unfortunately been mutilated, the page on which it was written having been shorn across. The other passages not represented in the Anglo-Saxon book are from the stories of Cain (124 ll.) and Sodom (187 ll.)

And again—

"They sought another land, that was empty of light and full of flame, fire, and the terror thereof."

The speeches of Satan in their copious language recall the speeches in Virgil and Ovid, which Virgil and Ovid wrote with the examples of Greek tragedy as well as Greek epic before them. The complaint of Satan will always be a remarkable thing in literature; in style it escapes from the besetting difficulty of the Teutonic poetry, the danger of the repeated formula, the temptations of the *Gradus*. The poem of *Judith*, generally so admirable, is not quite free from this excess; it sometimes is tripped by its vocabulary, as *Beowulf* is also. In *Judith* the same complimentary [1] phrase is used within 30 lines of Holofernes and of God : in *Beowulf*, the hero and the dragon, under the influence of literary convention, pass together from "this transitory life." [2] This slowness of sense and readiness to take the current phrase is not found in the *Fall of the Angels*. The language, which in the other part of *Genesis* is so stiff and formal, here is pliant and free; instead of fixed phrases, the words here seem to have a living meaning of their own, proper to the context,—

"hafað us God sylfa
forswápen on þás sweartan mistas."

(God himself has forswept us into these swart mists.)

---

[1] "Þearlmod þeoden gumena."
[2] "Hæfde æghwæðer ende geféred
Lǽnan lífes."—Ll. 2844, 2845.

And when Satan's angel passes through Hellgate (for here it is not Satan himself who undertakes the voyage to Middle-Earth),—

"Swang þæt fýr ontwá féondes cræfte."—L. 449.

(The fire swang in two, as the Fiend ruled it.)

Both imagination and good sense are shown, as Sievers has brought out, in the view taken of the temptation. The ordinary theological motives, gluttony and vainglory, did not seem sufficient. The poet would not so degrade the Protoplast. Adam and Eve are beguiled by the lies of the serpent, who brings them word that the Lord has revoked His prohibition, and that for their good they are to eat of the fruit of the tree. Dramatic grace is not wanting here, either. Eve speaks, after she has taken the apple:—

"Adam, my lord! this fruit is so sweet, so glad to my breast, and this messenger so bright, God's good angel: in his garb I see that he is our sovran's envoy, from the King of Heaven. Better his favour for us twain, than his anger against us. If to-day thou spake aught grievous against him, yet he will forgive it, if we render him homage. Why this vexing strife against the servant of thy Lord? We have need of his grace; he can bear our errand to the King of Heaven. From this place I can see Him where He sits to the South and East, in His goodliness enfolded, who was the Maker of this world. I see in compass round about Him His angels flying with their wings, a mighty host, a gladsome company. Who could give me this knowledge, but if God sent it straight to me? I hear unhindered, and far and wide over the broad creation I look upon all the world; I hear the mirth of Heaven. Light is my thought without and within me, since I ate of the fruit."

The *Exodus* is a good poem, with a distinct character. It is not a tame paraphrase; it is not

historical; the author has taken for his subject not
the story of Moses, nor the controversy with Pharaoh,

Exodus.   nor the plagues, but simply the escape
out of Egypt and the destruction of the
Egyptian host; and this is treated with all available
power of rhetoric to bring out the magnificence of the
adventure.   It is like *Judith* in the way the author is
possessed by the sublimity of his theme; but, unlike
Judith, it is impersonal: it describes the mighty work,
not the human actors.   Moses is praised; he is not a
dramatic character like Satan in the Saxon *Genesis*.
The pillar of cloud and of fire, the pageant of war,
and more than all, naturally, the overthrow of
Pharaoh in the Red Sea, make the stuff of the
poem.   It is full of the conventions of the old
school;—commonplaces, like the wolf and raven of
battle; conceits, like the description of the protect-
ing cloud as a sail, "but no man knew of the tack-
ling nor the sailyard, how it was set."   The union
of conceits and other rhetoric with genuine poetic
energy in this poem is akin to many later things in
different schools; Dryden's *Annus Mirabilis* is one
example, and the poetry of Dryden's century offers
many more.   The *Exodus* was written by a man who
was full of the traditional forms, with fire enough
of imagination to make them do what he wanted.
The result is no mean thing; not to speak of its
eloquence, few mediæval poems are more effectively
concentrated on the right points in the story.   It
is true that as the text stands there is one intoler-
able digression, but no reader will hesitate to cut

this out as an interpolated passage. The author in one place allows himself the use of a Latinism (*ne wyllað = nolite*), but there is no pedantry in his work, or if there is, it is the pedantry not of the Latin school but of the North. The children of Israel, for example, are consistently treated as if they were companions of Beowulf, and are called "Sea-vikings," *sæwicingas*, contrary to history. *Daniel* is one of the inferior pieces, with nothing original in its method and little distinction in its phrasing. There are

Daniel.

occasional beauties, as in the appearance of the Deliverer along with the three holy children in the fiery furnace, like dewfall and fresh summer winds. The Song of the Children is well rendered ; it goes easily into the forms of Anglo-Saxon poetry, which delighted in all the works of the Lord. There is another version of this part of the story, in the *Exeter Book*, commonly quoted as *Azarias*, which greatly amplifies the rendering of this canticle— another instance of the common pernicious verbosity.

Much has been written about the conjectural biography of Cynewulf, and some of the worst logic in the world has been applied to the sub-

Cynewulf.

ject. One eminent scholar having to choose between Northumbria and Mercia for Cynewulf's country, argues to the following effect: "Poetry will not flourish in the middle of raids and plunderings ; poetry needs quiet. Now in the eighth century there were many more kings of Northumbria than of Mercia ; which proves the comparative unrest and insecurity of Northumbria : therefore Cynewulf was a Mercian."

It used to be generally held that the first riddle in the *Exeter Book* was an allegorical device for the name of Cynewulf. But better interpretations have been found, and the old reasons for attributing the Riddles to Cynewulf have disappeared, taking with them the inferences as to Cynewulf drawn from the language of those poems.[1]

Four poems contain the name of Cynewulf as their author—*Crist, Elene, Juliana,* and the short piece in the Vercelli manuscript called the *Fates of the Apostles.* This last is probably not a separate poem, but an epilogue to *Andreas,* which in that case is also claimed by Cynewulf. There are several other poems which have been assigned to him on internal evidence—*Guthlac, Phœnix, the Dream of the Rood.* Even if the evidence fail to prove this, it is not denied that these poems belong to the same order: "the school of Cynewulf" is a justifiable term.

Cynewulf is an artist. He does not go for his subjects beyond the accessible sources of religious history; he has the same religious motives as Otfrid and the English and Saxon poets who versified the Bible. But his style is distinguished by a sensitive use of language, a rhetorical grace, not unconscious: he is a correct poet. Most probably he had studied literature: his masters may have shared in the love of words so characteristic of Anglo-Saxon culture.

---

[1] Napier in *Zeitschrift für deutsches Alterthum,* 33, p. 72 *sqq.*; Sievers in *Anglia,* xiii. (against Cynewulf's authorship of *Andreas*); Skeat in *An English Miscellany;* Trautmann, *Kynewulf, der Bischof und Dichter,* 1898.

His own taste, and also doubtless the stronger elements in the native poetry, saved him from the "garrulous verbosity" of Aldhelm. As it is, the danger in his verse is that fluency and sweetness may be carried too far. Like Alcuin, he is sometimes over-gentle. Grimm's phrase about the autumnal beauty of *Andreas* and *Elene* remains in the mind; there is not much promise in them. It would not be misleading to compare Cynewulf with Marini, if it were not that Marini's faults have been exaggerated by the critics. There is the same regard for melody, the same sort of effusive eloquence in both poets, the same attainment of a perfection that leaves no hope beyond it for anything but a new beginning with different ideals. Cynewulf could not be bettered. The good things in the later poetry, especially *Judith* and *Byrhtnoth*, succeed by forsaking Cynewulf and strengthening themselves in a more heroic school.

Cynewulf is a romantic poet. He is related to the older epic poetry as the French romances of the twelfth century are to the *chansons de geste*. His interest is in the expansion and decoration of the theme more than in the action itself or the characters. It is true that embroidery and amplification are allowed in *Beowulf;* that the plot is more or less epic in *Andreas* and *Elene*. But in *Beowulf* the characters have an independent value not found in the personages of the saints' lives; in the latter poems, as in all purely romantic work, the characters and the story are subordinate to the incidental beauties. The tone, the poetical moral, the drift of the general argument, take up more of the poet's mind than the dramatic situations. *Andreas* is a poem of strange adventures, a romance of the sea. So in the third *Æneid* the story is more important than the hero, and the scenery more than the story; though St Andrew is a better hero than Æneas. The division of interest is otherwise arranged in epic poetry; the *Lay of Maldon* shows how, as clearly as the *Iliad*.

In his verse Cynewulf uses many variations, not in a casual way, but as distinctly as Pope under the principles stated in the *Essay on Criticism*. There is some mannerism, perhaps, but there can be no doubt of the art, in the crashing emphasis of the lines on Doomsday—

> "Hu þæt gestun and se storm and seo stronge lyft
> Brecað brade gesceaft ! "

Or again, where the repeated iambic ending of the first hemistich is contrasted with a different cadence in the second :—

> " Þæt on þæt deope dæl deofol gefeallað
> in sweartne leg, synfulra here
> under foldan sceat, fæge gæstas,
> on wraþra wic, womfulra scolu."

The effect is like the changing stress of French Alexandrines.

Some of Cynewulf's modes seem to have become conventional, like the use of rhyme for the "Paradise" motive—

> " Ne forstes fnæst ne fyres blæst
> ne hægles hryre ne hrimes dryre." [1]

---

[1] *Phœnix*, l. 15. Cf. *Guthlac*, l. 801 ; *Andreas*, l. 857.

But this was found out by an artist, before it was repeated by the school.

The religious poetry of Northumberland is not to be dismissed as mere paraphrase of mediæval commonplaces. *The Dream of the Rood* is a poem on a common theme—the cross regarded as a tree, the noblest of the forest—

"Crux fidelis inter omnes arbor una nobilis."[1]

But the rendering in the English poem is not commonplace. It is hard to describe it justly, but there is one simple beauty in it which makes a vast imaginative difference; it takes the story as if it were something new, and thinks of it as a mystery acted in some visionary place, not on any historical scene. It is not the solemnity of Passion Week in the ritual of the Church, but a sorrow unheard of before, scarcely understood.[2]

In other poems much less remarkable there is the same sort of independence. The *Phœnix*,[3] for example, is taken from a well-known Latin poem; but this is used as a theme for original fancy, not merely paraphrased in the easy conventional manner.

The Anglo-Saxon genius for poetry is best shown in the elegies—*The Wanderer, The Seafarer,* and others— to which there is nothing corresponding in Germany

---

[1] Fortunatus.

[2] Passages from this poem, in Northumbrian, on the Ruthwell Cross, were read and interpreted by Kemble before the discovery of the West Saxon version in the Verceli MS.

[3] Attributed to Lactantius, but possibly not Christian (Baehrens, *Poetæ Latini Minores,* iii. 249)

or Iceland. The English invented for themselves a form of elegy, much more modern in character, or more *Anglo-Saxon* classical, than the ordinary types of medi-*Elegies.* æval poetry. They seem to have been more readily touched by motives of regret and lamentation than other people. Their poetry is sometimes censured as too fond of pathos. But they could give a dramatic setting to their laments. The Wanderer and the Seafarer are imaginary personages, not the poet himself; the dramatic form is a safeguard; it requires a free imagination not overwhelmed in sentiment. *The Wanderer* is the best preserved, and formally the most complete, of these idylls; *The Seafarer* is obscure and much less regular, but there is more variety in it, and a hearty poetical enjoyment of the grievous weather.

The *Ruin* at first looks like a more direct attempt to make a profit out of the *Vanity of Human Wishes*—" I passed by the walls of Balclutha, and they were desolate." There is really much more than this: it is a poem of imagination rather than sentiment. The author has his eye on the object, and is fascinated by his own picture of the deserted city, as the Seafarer is by his recollection of hail and frost, cliffs, breakers, gannets, and sea-gulls.

There are some signs of degeneracy in much of the later poetry, stale ideas and flat verse, like the drowsy leavings of the old alliterative school in Germany. The uncertainties of Layamon's prosody are already found two hundred years before him in Anglo-Saxon. But *Judith*, more warlike than anything in Cynewulf, yet with full command of the art of verse, belongs most probably to the tenth century: *Byrhtnoth* to the very end of it. The poem on Brunanburh, which is earlier, is a conventional panegyric, quite different in scope from the Maldon lay.

There is much good phrasing in the Anglo-Saxon Gnomic Verses, which it is interesting to compare with the Northern moralisings, shortly to be spoken of.

The collection of Northern poetry which it is still occasionally convenient to call the " Elder Edda " was *Norse and Ice-* made in Iceland, and is contained in one *landic poetry.* famous manuscript book belonging to the King's Library in Copenhagen (*Codex Regius*), written at the end of the thirteenth century. The name *Edda*, which properly belongs to the prose treatise of Snorri Sturluson, was given to the poems by Bishop Brynjolf of Skalholt (+1674), who called it "Edda Sæmundi multiscii," the *Edda* of Sæmund the Wise. Brynjolf's theory was that he had discovered the poetic original on which Snorri's prose mythology was based, and that this poetical or "elder" *Edda* was the work of Sæmund the Learned (+1133). The name is unjustifiable, but like "Anglo-Saxon" and some other terms not approved by philological reason, it saves a good deal of trouble. There is extant also part of another copy of the poems, which contains one not found in *Codex Regius*—the *Dreams of Balder*, which is Gray's *Descent of Odin*.

The "Elder Edda" is not merely a heap of poems put together without order. They are arranged in

an intelligible scheme, and the original editor has
given prose notes to explain them, and in some cases
has filled in the connection with prose narrative. He
puts the mythological poems first, headed by the
Volospá or *Sibyl's Prophecy*, the noblest work of the
Northern imagination in dealing with the themes of
the Northern faith. After the mythology come the
heroic poems, with the lay of Weland the Smith
as a kind of link between the myths of the gods
and the tragic history of the Volsungs and Niblungs.
The editor's sense of order is proved by the way in
which he interposes a kind of poetical summary of the
fortunes of Sigurd—the *Grípis Spá* — *i.e.*, "Gripi's
Prophecy" — before the separate poems in which
successive episodes of the story are presented. Before
this, and following *Weland*, come certain poems, the
Helgi lays, which are connected indeed with the
Volsung cycle, but are not required in the main
part of the story, and have nothing to do with the
sorrows of Gudrun.

The mythical poems are of different kinds. They
are not all in the same form. Some are in the
narrative measure that corresponds to the epic verse
of Anglo-Saxon poetry ; others, again, are in stanzas
which are related to the common epic verse, much
in the same way as the elegiac couplet to the hexameter. They differ, again, in the nature of their
design. Some are simply narrative ; some, like the
Volospá, lyrical ; some didactic, like the body of
proverbial morality that goes by the name of *Hávamál*,
or the poems in which mythological doctrine is ex-

pounded in dialogue, the *Grímnismál* and others. Thus the "Elder Edda" gives specimens of many different artistic aims, various degrees of poetic talent and opposite schools of rhetoric. This variety belongs to it throughout, though it is more pronounced and more obvious in the mythological than in the heroic division. The reader finds himself appealed to by a number of minds, not contemporary with one another, and possessed of different ambitions and ideas. The poems have the widest range—from the ordinary works and days of the Norway fells to the splendours of Asgard and the horror of the Judgment. The tempers of the poets and their rhetorical canons differ not less than Polonius and Horatio, or Hamlet and Laertes. The ordinary morality of the North is delivered in the maxims of the *Hávamál;* the fantasies of untold generations and their reflections on the origin and end of the world are recorded in sublime and enthusiastic prophecy. The lyric rapture of the *Sibyl's Prophecy* goes beyond all other poems in this tongue ; the clear and temperate excellences of the *Grímnismál* are admirable in a different way, and perhaps equally surprising to readers who expect Gothic confusion here. One does not reckon on finding elegance and lucidity in authors so remote from academic tradition. But it is impossible to go far in Icelandic literature without discovering that it is habitually rational and clear. These virtues, which have their proper place in the Sagas, are well represented in some parts of the "Elder Edda."

Naturally and rightly, the Northern poetry, ever

since it was recovered in the seventeenth century, has conquered readers with the fascination of its glorious visions, its splendid courage. Possibly its reputation may have suffered, like other favourites of the romantic schools, by the indiscreet enthusiasm of its admirers. But any one who submits to the fair preliminary conditions, such as are required in all reading of poetry, any one who understands the language and the literary conventions, will find in the small volume of these poems many days' provision of stories and of noble verse. The most grudging pedant might be forced to acknowledge the technical skill of the rhetoric; the most careless fancy might well be kept attentive by the passion of Brynhild or Gudrun.

The title *Hávamál*, "Discourse of the High One," covers a miscellany of moral precepts which offer a view of life in the heroic age uncoloured by myth-

Hávamál.

ology or by the "wavering flame," the shifting streamers of Northern romance. The title is not appropriate : it belongs to one section in the group, the mystical form of the devotion of Odin,[1] which in subject and spirit is quite unlike the sententious practical teaching of the rest of the collection. The book of Proverbs, as it may be called, comes undoubtedly from Norway, and not from Iceland or the Western Islands. The wood-cutting, the wolves, the reindeer, the birch-bark shingles used for roofing the house, are all Norwegian. At the same time, apart from these local touches, the life described is common to the whole of the North,

[1] See above, p. 49 *sq.*

and the teaching does not need much adaptation to make it suitable for Icelandic conditions. The life represented and criticised is the ordinary substantial prosaic basis from which the brilliant adventurers of the North set out, with which Olaf Tryggvason and Harald Hardrada were familiar in their domestic intervals. It is the daily life of the Northern homestead, such as is recorded incidentally in the Icelandic Sagas,—the ordinary traffic between house and house, with the perpetual tasks and difficulties that rise wherever people meet, "every man in his humour," and every man with his own game to play. For the moralist here is mainly ethical, not political: the state has no existence, and the point of view is generally that of Bacon's *Essays*, for the benefit of a man with his fortune to make, and therefore with rivals to be outdone.

The book begins with the *Guest's Wisdom*, as it is called in the Oxford edition,[1] consisting of about eighty quatrains in the Northern gnomic verse (*ljóða háttr*). At the opening a traveller comes into the house and greets his hosts. The moralist provides first of all for his bodily comfort, a fire, food, clothing, water, and a towel. From this basis of living he proceeds to the doctrine of good life. It is the life of a prudent man without illusions, courageous and self-reliant, sceptical, acquainted with the weaknesses and perils of human nature, not sanguine. The guest in this poem is not one of the daring adventurers of the Viking Age: his travels are inland, among the fells, from

[1] *C. P. B.*, i. 2 *sqq.*

one garth to another in the ordinary way of business. But he has at the same time one of the strong Viking motives—the desire to know the world, and the sense that home-keeping wits are dull. "Anything will pass at home" (*dœlt es heima hvat*), and "a man that has travelled far and seen many lands will know what moves in the mind of the wise." Moderation is taught, much as it was by the Wise Men of Greece, and by the Preacher in Jerusalem. "A man should be wise and not too wise, for the heart of the wise is seldom glad: let no man know his fate; his head will be free of care." Silence is good: the wise man does not readily give himself away. But he knows how to speak: the fool either sits glum or talks too much. "Archdunce (*Fimbulfambi*) is he who can speak naught, for that is the mark of a fool." Like all sound moralists, the Norwegian proverbs give different sides of their matter, and are not scrupulous about contradictions. The prudent wary character is admired. "A fool thinks all that smile on him are his friends." But there is also a contemplative fool, "awake all the night, troubled about all things, and in the morning he is weary and all his vexation is as it was before." The wise man renders to others their own measure, "laughter for laughter, and leasing for lies." But also it is well to be free, and not too careful. "Silent and thoughtful should a king's son be, and daring in war: glad and blithe should every man be, till his death-day come:" the two opposites of caution and frankness are here recommended together, in the same stave of the poem. If in its general scope the instruction is a philosophy of competition, there is also some regard for apparent or partial failure. It is better to be alive than dead, better to be blind than (funerally) burned; a lame man may ride a horse, a handless man may drive a herd, a live man may always get a cow. While, on the other hand, this set of prudent maxims includes also in its theory the heroic motive, worldly prudence confesses the higher power of something beyond it. "Wealth dies and kindred die, and a man himself dies at the last: but glory and fame die never, whoso may win them."

Part of the Northern proverbs, as the Oxford editors remark, is like the Hebrew "Instruction of Lemuel," and forms a separate chapter—the Lesson of Loddfafnir—each stave beginning with the same formula in the mouth of the Preacher, "I counsel thee, Loddfafnir." The substance has the same general character as the rest of the book; the doctrine of the Mean is taught again: "Be wary, but not too wary." "No man is so good as to be blameless; none so bad as to be worth nothing." In another part of the book the opinion of Solon, which Aristotle discusses, is given in a Norwegian form: "Praise the day when it is ended, the ale when it is drunk, ice when it is crossed, a woman after the funeral fire."

Other didactic passages belong to a different kind of science, and are associated with the *Hávamál* properly so called, the mystic doctrine of Odin, "The Discourse of the High One." This is mainly the theory of the virtue of Runes: charms that blunt the sword of the enemy and disable his shooting, that will shake off fetters, avert fire, calm the sea, call down the felon from the gallows, win the mind of a woman, turn the adversary's magic against himself. Much of this kind of learning appears also in a poem of the Volsung cycle, the *Sigrdrifumál*, where Sigurd wakes the Valkyria from her sleep, and she tells him of the Runes and their power. Moral passages also, resembling the Guest's Wisdom, are found here and there in other of the heroic poems; for example, the sentence in *Fafnismál* (the dialogue of Sigurd with Fafnir the Worm), quoted by King Sverre of Norway, "Few are keen in age that in youth were craven."

Gnomic poetry is not usually poetical; it tends to prose, naturally—sometimes to the language of Benjamin Franklin, sometimes more happily to that of Sancho Panza. But proverbial wisdom is not unfit for poetical expression; it can be kindled into generous admiration and scorn that require the fit poetical phrase to render them. There is to be found in the Norwegian teaching an austere dignity and fortitude which give a distinct character to the moral verse.

The didactic poetry of the "Elder Edda" includes
Didactic besides these moralisings a number of ex-
Mythology. positions of mythology, quite different in tone and intention from the poems with stories in them.

The *Vafþrúðnismál* [1] has a dramatic opening: Odin,

[1] *C. P. B.*, i. 61.

setting out to challenge the giant Vafthrudnir to a match of wit and knowledge, dissuaded by his wife, who warns him of the power of the Adversary, and then sped on his way with her good wishes when she finds that it is of no use to argue with him. Odin comes to the giant's hall uninvited and challenges his wisdom. "Who is this that casts his words at me in my house?" says the giant: "out thou comest not from our halls except thou show thee the wiser." Then Odin, keeping his disguise, gives his name as Gangrad, one of the many assumed names in his wandering explorations, and the questions begin. "We shall each wager his head in this game of learning," the giant says. The giant's knowledge was afterwards turned to profit by Snorri in his account of the origin of things, in his *Edda*. Vafthrudnir is an authority for much of the strange antique cosmogony in the Northern mythological tradition; for the son and daughter that grew under the hand of the Frost-giant; for Bergelmer in his ark (saved from the flood); for the Giant in an eagle's coat that sits at the heaven's end and sends winds over the earth with the beating of his wings. Vafthrudnir knows also the diversions of the heroes in Odin's hall, and the end of the world, the death of Odin himself, and the vengeance to be taken for him when the Fenris-wolf shall be slain by Vidar. But he cannot answer the last question, in which Odin is revealed, and the match is lost and won.

Odin says: "Much have I travelled and much inquired, and much have I proved thy powers: what spake Odin himself in the ear of his son Balder before he was set on the funeral fire ? "

The Giant answers: " No wight knows what thou spakest in the ear of thy son in the olden days. With death-doomed mouth [1] I uttered my ancient stories, the tale of the Fate of the Gods. Now have I matched my lore against Odin: thou art ever wiser than all."

The *Grímnismál* [2] is founded on another story of Odin's wanderings, given in a prose introduction in *Codex Regius*. Odin, in disguise under the name of Grimnir, is put to the question, in the painful sense of that phrase, by a king in whose character Odin is interested. This King Geirrod had been mischievously warned by Odin's wife of coming danger from a wizard, and naturally took the vagrant blue-mantled Odin for his enemy, especially as Odin refused to explain what his business was. Odin bore the torment for eight nights, sitting between two fires, till the king's son, Agnar, had pity on him and gave him a drink. Then Odin recited the Discourse of Grimnir, a summary of mythology, describing all the worlds, the homes of gods and men, ending with the revelation of Odin himself and of all his various names. The poem includes the description of the tree Yggdrasill, which is spoken of also in *Volospá*, though naturally there without the detail proper in a circumstantial didactic poem like *Grímnismál.*

In *Alvíssmál* [3] the parties in the dialogue are Thor the god and Alvis the dwarf, who has come to claim

---

[1] *Feigum munni,* fey mouth.
[2] *C. P. B.,* i. 69. [3] Ibid., 81.

Thor's daughter as his bride. Thor holds him in conversation till the day breaks, and then tells him that he is lost and beguiled: for the sun shines into the hall and the dwarf is stricken lifeless. The learning of Alvis is not mythological but rhetorical; he gives Thor the names for things—Earth, Heaven, Sun, Moon, Fire, Corn, Ale, &c.—which are called one thing by men, another by gods; Men, Gods, Elves, Dwarfs, and the mysterious race of Vanir supply a variety of terms to serve as a kind of literary vocabulary. It is the interest in synonyms, always strong and growing stronger in the Northern poets, that has produced this dialogue: though the dialogue of Alcuin and Adrian and Epictetus shows that the taste is not specially Northern, nor even the form in which the lesson is given.

By far the strangest of all the dialogue poems is the *Loka Senna*—the Railing of Loki[1]—where Loki (who is nothing if not critical) thrusts himself into a banquet of the gods and tells each of them pointedly the scandals of their past lives; till Thor, who had been at his usual work among the trolls in the East country, comes home in the middle of it and prevails on him to go away. It is Old Comedy of the most genuine sort, founded on the perennial delight in the conflict of strong language that leads in one country to the deadly iambics of Archilochus and the eloquence of the Sausage-seller, in another to the Flyting of Dunbar and Kennedy.[2] Interludes

Loki.

---

[1] *C. P. B.*, i. 100.
[2] *Equites* of Aristophanes, ed. R. A. Neil, Introduction.

of the same comic character are found among the heroic poems also: the contention of Atli and the giant's daughter (which like the *Loka Senna* is in gnomic verse) and of Sinfiotli and Gudmund, in the ordinary epic measure; both included in the Helgi Lays.

The *Volo Spá*, or *Sibyl's Prophecy*, is, unlike all the other mythological poems in the "Elder Edda," not didactic, not narrative, but an enthusiastic

Volospá.

ode. The popular beliefs about the gods and the fate of the world had in them a crude imaginative power; they required and found a poet to express them. The author of *Volospá* knows the glory and tragedy of the life of the world: he is affected by the mythical vision of the universe and the rhythm of its progress much as Lucretius was when the abyss and its cataracts were laid open when the disclosure of Nature filled him with divine pleasure and fear. It was not left to modern authors to discover the value of myth. The *Volospá* is an imaginative rendering or interpretation of old traditions; it is not itself a mere recital of beliefs. Beliefs are its material, but they are transformed and turned to something new in the lyrical energy of the poem. The story of the birth of Athena is one thing for the mythographer, another thing for Pindar; and the author of the *Sibyl's Prophecy* is Pindaric in the way he takes his subject.

Unfortunately the poem is ill preserved,—incomplete, disarranged, interpolated. There are two versions of it, and the two versions do not agree. Neither the number nor the order of the stanzas is the same in both, and the theories of scholars have hardly yet cleared up the full intention of the poem. But it does not require to wait for full interpretation to make its poetical impression. The poet has his way, in spite of the faults and difficulties of the text.[1]

There are two difficult and fragmentary poems, not in the "Elder Edda," which are in some relation to *Volospá*. One of them is referred to by Snorri as the "Short" *Volospá*; the other is the *Lay of Hyndla*, into which fragments of the short *Volospá* have been introduced. The *Lay of Hyndla* is a genealogical poem with a mythological introduction; the short *Volospá* appears to have been, like the great poem of that name, a summary of the creation and fall of the universe.[2]

Another poem not found in *Codex Regius*, but in one of the manuscripts of the prose *Edda*, may be taken along with the mythological and the didactic poems: the *Rígsthula* is a kind of allegory of the ranks and occupations of men.[3] The story is that the god Heimdal, under the name of Ríg (probably derived from the Gaelic), went abroad on his travels and begot three sons, who with their families

Rígsthula.

---

[1] See *Volospá Reconstructed*, in *C. P. B.*, ii. 621. The Oxford editors have gone on a sound principle: that Snorri's prose para-phrase of the mythological matter of *Volospá* was based on a good text, and would naturally follow its order; therefore the prose *Edda* may indicate how the sections of *Volospá* are to be arranged. The two extant texts are compared, *ibid.*, i. 379-381, and should be considered by all students who disapprove of rearrangements by editors.

[2] A plausible reconstruction of both poems is given in the second volume of the Oxford edition, pp. 515, 629.

[3] *C. P. B.*, i. 234.

represent the three estates of men in civil society— Thrall, Carl, and Earl. Thrall is described with something of the contempt for the villain which is expressed more emphatically and cruelly in a poem of Bertran de Born. Carl is the busy franklin, a man of substance, ploughing, shaping timber, building barns. Earl knows such arts as Harald Hardrada professed; he can string the bow and use it, ride, and wield a sword, and swim. The poem is full of matter of this sort, neatly and humorously versified. In temper it is a contrast to the proverbial wisdom of *Hávamál*, where the tasks are not meted out so distinctly according to birth. Its chivalrous philosophy is more precise and exacting than was common in Norway or Iceland, even as late as the thirteenth century. In real life, as shown in the Sagas, the Earl, even the King, might turn his hand to many trades besides the gentle arts. But the poem is not to be considered too seriously as a political document: being satirical, it chooses definite types and keeps them apart. All the same, its method is strikingly different from the unconventional freedom of the proverbs, and their sympathy with ordinary life.

There are different kinds of narrative poem in the old Icelandic, and variety is shown in the treatment *Fashions of Narrative.* both of mythical and heroic subjects. One kind of story is given almost entirely in dialogue, rather difficult to understand without prose explanations, and making one inclined to accept the theory that the original narrative method in the North was like that which is favoured in Ireland, a prose tale with dramatic lyrics interspersed. The dialogue verse, appropriate for comic debates, is hardly enough to work out a story clearly where there are changes of scenes and persons as in *Frey's Wooing* (*Skírnismál*); so in that poem the introduction and the stage directions, as they may be called, are given in prose.[1] In *Balder's Dream*, on the other hand, the dialogue is intelligible by itself, and here there is no prose: an introductory passage in three stanzas is enough to explain the story (" Up rose the King of men with speed," &c.) In some cases explanations in prose have been added because the transcriber's recollection of the poems is imperfect.

It is plain from the documents as they stand that the Northern poetry was far from having reached the stage of fixed forms and orthodox patterns. It was making experiments: it was, one is inclined to say, trying to get the right proportions of narrative. In this process several devices were tried, none of them without interest. There was no want of spirit in the stories themselves. The adventures of Thor and of Sigurd had everything in them to fire the imagination and prompt the ambition of quick-witted people with a taste for poetry. In some things they succeeded almost beyond criticism. Accepting the manners, the language, the prosody of the Northern race, there is nothing for any one to find fault with in the poems

---

[1] The use of dialogue in Teutonic poetry is studied and discussed by Professor Heusler of Berlin (*Zeitschrift für deutsches Alterthum*, xlvi.), who regards the prose explanations as unessential in poems like *Skírnismál*.

of *Thor's Hammer* and *Balder's Dream*, or in the idyll of Gudrun weeping over the body of Sigurd. These poems have done what they set out to do. They take an adventure, an episode, a moment, out of a cycle of familiar stories, and give it exact and complete expression, in short compass. But there were difficulties when the task was changed, when the poets found themselves called upon to deal with larger matters, with the whole tremendous course of the Nibelung history, or the more complex parts of it. They have few rivals in the art of short poetic narrative.[1] But the talent for selection, for compression and reticence, is not enough for a long story: the lyrical cast of the phrasing in the Northern poems is too difficult. There is too much meaning in them; the masters of narrative in other languages are more diffuse and leisurely than was ever possible in Icelandic verse. Unhappily the manuscript of the poetic *Edda* has lost the pages which are known, from the prose paraphrase in the *Völsunga Saga*, to have contained the noblest part of the story, the farewell between Sigurd and Brynhild.[2] Even the passion of Brynhild after the death

---

[1] One has appeared lately, Bacchylides with his ballad of Theseus and Minos, and the lyric dialogue in which the coming of Theseus to Athens is told indirectly, with a curious suspense and abruptness.

[2] " Homer has no such scene, no such ideas. The mastery of love in Brunhild's heart, her scene with Sigurd, where he ranges through every choice before them, to live as friends, to live as lovers, her disdainful rejection of friendship, her Northern pride of purity, his anguish, her determination to slay him and follow him, her one laugh as she hears Gudrun's first moan over the dead, her death, the mourning of the horse Grani, as of Achilles's horse Xanthus, the lament of Gudrun—all this is mere perfection, all is on the loftiest

of Sigurd, which is one of the great things in the extant poetry, is simpler than this, being monologue, and less intense, being memory, not the immediate conflict of will with will.

The difficulties and limitations of the Northern form are proved most curiously when there is anything like adventure to be described. The poets cannot spend time in story-telling. The persons, their wills and thoughts, are more interesting than their exploits. The best of the narrative poems, such as the *Lay of Thor's Hammer*, are comparatively light and simple; where there is weighty historical matter, such as the fall of the Nibelungs, hardly any space at all is given to the fighting. The Northern poetry does not know the Homeric method, which is not wanting to the Anglo-Saxons, French, or Germans, to the poets of *Waltharius, Byrhtnoth, Roland,* or the *Nibelungenlied.* It was not for want of interest: it was because the available poetical forms were not adapted for description or history. By reason of this there is a cramped and rather uncomfortable effect about the poems on the fighting in the house of Attila. The heroic spirit of Gudrun and her brothers is within the comprehension of the poets, and they have the right means to bring it out in their verse; but they are not allowed the proper space, they do not choose to employ the regular formulas, for epic battles. The slaughter "grim and great" at the close of the *Nibelungenlied*

level of Shakespeare, and has no parallel in Greek or Roman poetry." —A. Lang, *Homer and the Epic*, p. 396. Cf. Heusler, *Die Lieder der Lücke im Codex Regius der Edda*, 1902.

is told by the Austrian poet in the same way as the killing of the Suitors in the *Odyssey* ; but in the poems of Attila in the " Elder Edda " it is treated much as Burbage and Shakespeare treated their scenery on the stage : it is taken as something understood.   One result of this economy of narrative in the Northern poems was that narrative had to find another channel.   The Icelandic Sagas are the complement of the poetry ; they have the breadth and freedom that the poems have not, an Homeric literature in " the other harmony of prose."

With the incomplete and tentative character of so much of the poetry there is naturally also the beauty

Thor.

of the young art that has not grown too perfect, that still has something to learn ; and among all the variety of experiments in form and style there are some that cannot be bettered : they are accomplished and perfect work, according to the ideas of the Northern school.   The *Lay of Thor's Hammer* [1] has already been mentioned as one of these successful things.   It is not a tragic poem, nor is there too much solemnity in the companion to it, *Thor and the Sea-serpent*.[2]   These two, the former most of all, are clear and slightly ironical versions of well-known myths. Snorri's humorous method in prose was partly derived, no doubt, from these tales in verse.   To go to them from *Volospá* is something like passing from Dante to La Fontaine.   Both in matter and style they have affinities with more enlightened and more critical periods of literature than that to which they belong. Indeed throughout the Northern poetry the style is

---

[1] Þrymskviða, *C. P. B.*, i. 175.   [2] *Hymiskviða*, ibid., 219.

capable of neatness, dexterity, and point, often in a delightful contrast to the terror and wonder of the themes. It was this that attracted Gray, doubtless: he translated the *Descent of Odin* and the *Fatal Sisters* because of their style, and not on account of their romantic qualities merely. Gray had mythology and romance at heart, no doubt: he had visions in his own poetry—"down the eastern cliffs afar"—that come as near as anything in English to the sublimities of the *Sibyl's Prophecy*. But he had not the romantic vagueness, he had not the insecurity of phrase, that haunted the discoverers of romance in his day; he required something more than wonder. When Gray read the original of the *Descent of Odin* in Torfæus or Bartholinus he must have known that it was really classical in expression ; that the Northern author had done what he, Gray, was engaged in doing—using precise terms, deliberately and effectively, for romantic ideas. Vague and grand imagination along with definite terms of expression—this paradoxical thing was known to Gray in his own mind and writings, and he found it in the poems he translated from the Icelandic. These translations are a piece of criticism and of literary history—mainly for Gray's own benefit —as well as a romantic diversion.

Other poems of the Northern mythology have more mystery in their themes and a less modern character in their style, especially the two love-stories

Frey.

of Frey [1] and of Svipdag—the latter not being part of the *Codex Regius.* Both are in the

---

[1] *Skírnismál, C. P. B.,* i. 110.

dialogue measure, and in neither case does the poem make the story quite clear. The second (Svipdag) is in two parts, which have a curious philological history.[1] They are found in nothing earlier than seventeenth-century MSS., and the two separate por-

Svipdag.

tions of Svipdag's story, *Grógaldr* and *Fjölsvinnsmál*, kept distinct in the MSS., were first proved to belong to one another through the Danish and Swedish ballads, in which the matter of both is united, and the story runs on from one to the other unbroken. It is the story of the quest for the princess over sea, the love of destined lovers before their first meeting, which was told in Norway, Ireland, and Wales long before the time of Geoffrey Rudel and the Lady of Tripoli.

The *Song of Weland*, which is placed intentionally between the mythical poems and those of the Nibelung

Weland.

story, essays to give the history of Weland from the beginning down to his vengeance on King Nidad—the story that is touched upon in the old English *Lament of Deor*, and illustrated on the famous whalebone casket.[2] It is one of the poems in which there is little attempt at proportion ; one of the least artistic in design : belonging to an older region of poetical taste than the ballads of Thor. There were probably many heroic lays of the same sort, giving the adventures of a hero from his birth. With a more diffuse and eloquent school of epic, the subject of Weland might have been made to fill as much room as *Beowulf.*

---

[1] *C. P. B.*, i. 92.

[2] Ibid., 168.   See Napier on the *Franks Casket*, in *An English Miscellany* (Oxford, 1900).

The next poems in the book, with Helgi as the name of their hero, are in many respects difficult to *Helgi and* make out; but among them the tragedy of *Sigrun.* Helgi and Sigrun is intelligible. It is told in two versions, one called *The Lay of Helgi*, the other *The Old Volsung Lay*. Helgi was the son of Sigmund the Volsung, and his fortunes belong to that great epic branch, though they have not much connection with the more famous history of Sigurd. The tragic plot has the strength which is so often found in early legends, seldom bettered, as far as the mere dramatic problem goes, by later invention. Helgi had to protect Sigrun against a detestable marriage arranged for her by her father; her father was killed by Helgi in the conflict with the bridegroom; her brother killed Helgi and took vengeance for her father's death. *The Lay of Helgi* is one of the most ambitious of the Northern experiments in epic. It has a largeness of scale at first that seems to promise something grander than any extant Icelandic lay; but this is not kept up. The poem is certainly notable as a magnificent thing wrongly designed. The theme is the deliverance of Sigrun from the undesired wedlock (leaving out the after-history, the tragical part of it); but this is introduced with a fine prelude about the hero's birth, and a summary passage about his early victory over King Hunding, which do not seem to be well proportioned. The author appears to have been distracted between his rather exceptional talent for amplification and the contrary and more common tendency to abridge a long story after the fashion of *Weland's Lay*. However that may be, this is one of the finest of the heroic poems: the appearance of Sigrun the Valkyria in the air, riding with her company of armed maidens to take Helgi for her champion, is one of the magical adventures that make these romances of the North so different from the Anglo-Saxon stories.   There is no elf-queen in *Beowulf*.[1]

The second version of *Helgi and Sigrun*, called the old Volsung Lay, goes beyond their wedding to the tragedy of Helgi's death and his return from the dead; ending in one of the finest passages of the Northern poetry, where Sigrun watches in the twilight for her lover coming back to her: "Thy hair, Helgi, is all rime-laden, the prince besprent with the dew of the slain; cold are the hands of Hagen's kinsman; how may I win healing of this, O king?"   And Helgi answers: "Thou alone, O Sigrun of Sevafell, art cause that Helgi is folded in deadly dew: or ever thou go to sleep thou weepest cruel tears, O gold arrayed, sunbright lady of the South, and every tear falls in blood on the breast of the king, piercing cold, stricken with mourning."

The epic poet is here in the same world as some of the later ballads, one of which, the Danish ballad of *Sir Aage*, is possibly derived from *Helgi and Sigrun*.[2] The ballads have generally a truer knowledge of the

---

[1] The meeting of Helgi and Sigrun is like one of the stories of Finn, in the Gaelic tradition, where the daughter of the King beneath the Waves appeals to Finn to save her from wedlock with a hated suitor (*Book of the Dean of Lismore*).   Compare also the story of Pwyll and Rhiannon in the *Mabinogion*.

[2] Cf. *C. P. B.*, i. 502, and *Grimm Centenary Papers*, by Vigfusson and Powell, Oxford, 1886.

land of the dead than the more ambitious heroic literature desires or obtains. Heroic poetry is too magnificent for such motives as those of *Clerk Saunders* or
The Wife of Usher's Well. The mystery, the suspense
and sorrow in the fragmentary lyrical verses of *Helgi
and Sigrun,* would have been lost in the finished
periods of a regular epic. But the Northern poetry
has many varieties of style, and is not always self-
conscious and rhetorical.

The original editor of the Helgi poems did his best
to arrange and explain them, but there were too many
difficulties. He found three separate stories of a hero
named Helgi; besides that of Sigrun, which is fairly
full, there are fragments of two others, *Helgi and
Swava,* and *Helgi and Kara,* the latter hardly more
than a name. The editor has a distinct theory, which
cannot be ignored—namely, that Helgi and Sigrun
were thrice born: "Sigrun was Swava born again,"
and "Sigrun was born anew as Kara, Halfdan's
daughter, as is told in the songs of Kara." "It was
a belief in the old days that men were born again,
but that is now reckoned old wives' fables." Whatever the value of this belief, there is good poetry in
what remains of *Helgi and Swava,* a sound dramatic
motive. Helgi's brother, Hedin, is betrayed into a
vain oath that he will wed his brother's bride: he re-
pents, and confesses, and is forgiven. Helgi, mortally
wounded in a duel, gives a message to Swava that she
should marry Hedin. The end is Swava's speech of
unchanging loyalty to Helgi, and Hedin's leave-taking
as he goes to avenge his brother. The temper of this

is less romantic than in the story of Sigrun; the poem
has the strength "that is not passion's slave"; the
truth of Swava and the penance of Hedin are rightly
understood by the author.

Then follow all the poems of the "Elder Edda" belonging to the Volsung story properly so-called, the
story of Sigurd. Of these there is a great
variety, even without the lost poems in the
missing sheet of *Codex Regius*. To begin with, the
editor has placed a kind of synoptic poem, *The Prophecy
of Gripir*, in which the whole history is summarised in
a clear, logical, prosaic way. Sigurd's uncle, Gripir,
foretells to him all the adventures he is to go through,
—a device which satisfies that love of precision characteristic of much Icelandic work. Some one evidently
felt that the story wanted an index, a summary, a
methodical statement, and this poem was the result.
It leaves Sigurd naturally a little depressed as he parts
from his uncle; but to the author, a man of understanding, this did not matter: he had compressed the
Volsung matter into a neat summary, with the facts all
in proper order. This sort of mind is found in other
literatures; an Irish example will be noticed later.
In ballad cycles it is not uncommon for a painstaking
sensible man to put a number of separate episodes
into one framework: epic poems may not be made in
that way, but the ballad redactor, shaping a continuous story out of traditional separate lays, is not a mere
hypothesis. It is generally dull work: the author of
Grípisspá is brisk in his way, but none the better for
that in poetry.

Sigurd.

The following poems, down to the lacuna, are accompanied with prose to explain the story. They are fragmentary, and of different sources, belonging to the earlier adventures of Sigurd, his alliance with the treacherous Regin, his slaying of Fafnir the Worm, and winning of the Nibelung hoard; his waking of the Valkyria, whose name, so far, is not given as Brynhild. A large portion is dialogue, and in the measure specially used for dialogue, as in *Lokasenna*. All this has been put together in the Oxford edition under the title of the *Old Play of the Wolsungs*.[1] Besides, there are passages in the ordinary narrative verse which are none the more narrative on that account; such as the song of the birds to Sigurd after he learned their speech by tasting the serpent-steak— as represented in a famous piece of Norwegian sculpture, and a more primitive work of art now in the Stockholm Museum.

What sort of poems followed, in the lost leaves, can to a certain extent be made out from the matter as *Brynhild.* presented in the Volsung Saga which paraphrased them. One thing which might be guessed from the first is clearly proved on closer examination,—that the lost lays had the same independence, the same freedom in working out their poetical ideals, as is found in the extant poems. Those coming after the gap in the manuscript have distinct conceptions of the characters, and various definite aims in handling the common subject-matter. Brynhild is not the same in all the poems where she

[1] *C. P. B.,* i. 30.

appears, and the differences come from poetical intention in the authors, not from confusion or negligence
in repeating a traditional plot. In one of the lost
poems, probably called the long Lay of Sigurd, there
was still another rendering of Brynhild,[1] which glori-
fies the prose paraphrase in spite of the altered language and the loss of its poetical music. The other
personages also are differently regarded in the different poems. There is great variety both in the scale
and in the style. In one of them, called the short
Lay of Sigurd,[2] though it is the longest of the extant
poems, the author has tried to indicate briefly (in a
different way from the Prophecy of Gripir) all the
chief incidents in the Volsung history, while giving
his mind especially to the passion of Brynhild after
Sigurd's death. Brynhild is the heroine of another
poem also, the fragmentary lay of Sigurd, of which
the first part has gone.[3]   Here a different poet has
worked in a different way, not caring to notice things
apart from the main situation, and representing Brynhild much less eloquent, less effusive, strongly rent
between her desire of vengeance on Sigurd and the
cold grief to which she awakens when her tragic
laughter is past. Then there are the idyllic poems:
the Hell-ride of Brynhild,[4] which follows on the short

Gudrun.
Lay of Sigurd, may be by the same author;
the beautiful and gentle poem of Gudrun's
tearless sorrow, breaking out when Giuki's daughter
swept the pall from the face of the dead Sigurd ;[5] the

---

[1] Above, p. 282.   [2] *C. P. B.*, i. 293.   [3] Ibid., 306.
[4] Ibid., 304.   [5] Ibid., 323.

idyll of Gudrun and Theodoric, where she tells her story
to the king;[1] the ordeal of Gudrun, an episode where
she refutes the slander of Attila's mistress against her;[2]
the lament of Oddrun,[3] one of the most remarkable of
all the poems for the originality of its plot, giving a
new rendering of the fall of Gudrun's brothers, told in
the person of Oddrun, whose lover was Gunnar. Two
poems besides, named, after Attila, the *Atlakviða*[4]
and the *Atlamál*,[5] give the death of Gunnar and Hogni:
in each of the several versions of this part of the
story there is a different conception of the plot; no
two agree as to the centre of interest. The *Atlamál*,
which was composed in Greenland by an Icelandic
settler in the colony there, is the most elaborate, in
some ways, of the whole group, the furthest removed
from the simple ways and unconscious graces of ballad
poetry. It is evidently based upon study and deliberate criticism of the older poems on the subject, as
a modern author would recast and reconstruct the plot
of some established story, to take the town with a new
Don Juan or *Faust* or *King Arthur*. It has the faults
of this kind of literature; it is too heavily weighted,
too slow. But it is the work of a strong intelligence,
who perhaps, like Jonson, had more power of thought
than imagination, and more imagination than could be
content with prose.

In all the Northern literature there is no trace of
the plot which ends the *Nibelungen Lied*,—the vengeance of Sigfred's wife upon her brothers for the

---

[1] *C. P. B.*, i. 316.   [2] Ibid., 322.   [3] Ibid., 309.
[4] Ibid., 44.   [5] Ibid., 331.

death of her husband,—except in cases where borrowing from the German can be proved, as in the Danish
ballad of *Grimild's Revenge.* The North keeps to an
older story (which of course came from Germany to
begin with), and makes Gudrun the defender of her
brothers against Attila — whose motives are not
always clear.

The manuscript of the poetic *Edda* comes to an end
with the story of the death of Ermanaric. This old

Ermanaric. heroic theme, known to Jordanes, had been
brought into the Volsung cycle, like Theodoric and Attila. Swanhild was the daughter of Gudrun; trampled to death by horses at the command of
her husband, the tyrant Ermanaric the Great; avenged
by her brothers, whose Norse names, Hamther and
Sörli, are not far removed from the Ammius and
Sarus of the Gothic historian in the sixth century.
The poem called the old Lay of Hamther,[1] the last
in the book, is simpler and more antique in character
than many that precede it; the last words, as the
brothers fall, are such as were repeated, no doubt,
wherever there was a hall and a minstrel in the heroic
age. "We have won good fame, though we die to-day
or to-morrow: no man lives out the eventide when
the word of the Norns is spoken."

As the story is given in *Codex Regius,* the old lay is
introduced and partly mixed up with another poem—
Gudrun's *Chain of Woes,* an idyllic lament in which

---

[1] *C. P. B.,* i. 52. There is a late German version of the same story,
where the slayer is "Dirick van dem Berne," and Ermanaric has
become the "Köninck van Armentriken."

she recounts all the sorrow of her life, crying out to Sigurd at the end, "Rememberest thou, Sigurd, what we spake when we were together in one bed, that thou wouldst come back to me from the world of death, or I to thee from the living world."

Some Northern poems have already been mentioned which are not found in *Codex Regius*. As it happens, the poems which first became known in modern times through translations from Icelandic were from various sources other than the poetic *Edda*. Gray's *Descent of Odin* and *The Fatal Sisters*, and that Dying Ode of Ragnar Lodbrok which set up the romantic standard of the ideal Viking, all are outside the famous manuscript. So also is the poem which was more often repeated than any from the time when Dr Hickes translated it in his Anglo-Saxon grammar [1]—the *Incantation of Hervor*. It is taken from the *Hervarar Saga*, one of the prose legends in which some old verse is fortunately included. Earlier than the poem of Hervor comes the death-song of Hialmar, his farewell and his charge to his friend Arrow-Odd. "The King's fair daughter sped me on my way, the words that she spake to me when she told me that I should never come back will surely prove true. Carry back my helmet and my mail-coat to the king's hall; the heart of the king's daughter will be moved when she sees the buckler of my breast hewn through. Draw the red ring off my arm and bear it to the young Ingibiorg. It will be a lasting

[1] *Gramm. Anglo-Saxon*, p. 193 (in vol. i. of the *Thesaurus*): Oxon., 1703.

sorrow of heart to her that I shall never come to
Upsala again." [1]

Hervor is the daughter of Angantyr, whom Hialmar
and Arrow-Odd had killed, with his eleven brothers, in

Hervor.

the isle of Samsey. She comes to the island
to her father's grave, to get from him the
magic sword, Tyrfing, forged by the Dwarfs, which
brought death to those who faced it, and to the bearer
of it, in the end, as well. *The Awaking of Angantyr* [2]
—the poem of Hervor at her father's grave—is not
only one of the finest works of the heroic age, but
something that makes the ordinary formulas of
criticism and literary history look out of place : it is
not an antiquity. It is so simple, so true in thought,
so inexhaustible in wonder and pathos, that its historical surroundings are forgotten. The heathenish
myth is translated into poetry. If the secret of it
can be detected, it is possibly this, that the legendary awe, the mystery of the scene where Hervor comes
to the grave and calls to the dead, is not allowed
to take full command of the poem : under all this
there is the strain of the drama between Hervor
and her father. She stands, as she puts it herself,
"between the worlds," in a homeless place ; but
through it all there is a contest of will, a tide of
passion, a human soul ; the ghostly terror is not the
chief thing, compared with Hervor's resolution and
the reluctance of the dead. No one who has once
known the poem can forget the strange, impersonal,
desolate pity that makes the father in his grave

[1] *C. P. B.*, i. 162.   [2] Ibid., 163.

refuse to give up to Hervor the avenging sword
with the curse upon it: why should she die? *Sunt
aliquid Manes:* the dead are shut up in the tomb,
cut off from the life of middle earth; even if the
daughter's voice reach them they cannot return.
But there is with them a kind of thought, a spirit
true to its kindred. This, no doubt, has always
been the undefined belief of the greater part of
mankind. No poem has succeeded like Hervor's in
expressing it, never mistaking the separation between
the dead voice and the living. For Hervor is none
the nearer to Angantyr, though he answers her.

The old lay of Biarki (*Biarkamál in fornu*) was
sung to St Olaf and his men on the morning of their
last battle at Stiklastad in 1030, and the

Biarkamál. king called it a true "Workmen's Call."[1]
Little of it is left, but enough to show its character
and justify St Olaf's criticism.[2] It is curiously like
the old English fragment of Finnesburh, and belongs
to a battle in a hall of the same epic fashion. King
Hrolf Kraki (the Hrodulf of *Beowulf*) is attacked in
his hall at daybreak; Biarki the warder rouses the
sleeping house. "The day is up, the cock's feathers
are flapping; it is time to get to work. Wake and
awake, comrades mine, all the noblest henchmen of
Adils. . . . Not to wine do I wake you, nor to women's
spell, but I wake you to the stern play of the war-
goddess." For the rest of the story we must go to
the prose paraphrase of Hrolf's Saga, or to Saxo Grammaticus, who turned it into Latin hexameters.[3] Con-

[1] *C. P. B.*, i. 188.   [2] Ibid., lxvi.   [3] See above, p. 83.

nected with the same cycle, though not closely, is the
Mill-song of Frodi on the magic Mill that ground gold
and peace, turned by the two Valkyrias Fenja and
Menja.

A famous visionary poem, with some likeness to the
Mill-song, is the *Song of the Dart—The Fatal Sisters*.
The story of it may be read in *Burnt Njal*. There is
a reflection of it in one of the portents of *Sturlunga
Saga*, where two witches are seen in a house, rocking
to and fro, while blood drips on them from the roof,
singing " Row we, row we, a rain of blood, Gunna and
Gondul ! " [1]

A shorter variety of the epic line came into favour
for many purposes in the North, and is found in
epitaphs and improvisations as well as more elaborate
work.[2]   It is used in the *Ynglingatal* of Thiodulf, a
genealogical poem on the royal house of Norway, the
foundation of the prose Ynglinga Saga which precedes
the historical Kings' Lives.[3]   And Egil Skallagrim
takes this verse for his poem to Arinbiorn and the
lament over his own sons' death. This latter poem,
the *Sonatorrek*,[4] is one of the classical poems of Iceland,
by one of the great adventurers. The prose story in
Egil's lament Egil's Saga, and the poem itself, represent
for his sons. two different kinds of art at a point not far
from perfection—the dramatic history and the lyrical
expression of sorrow. There is a strong contrast
between the peculiar Icelandic method of narrative

[1] *C. P. B.*, i. 360.
[2] Known later in Iceland as the "Fairy Measure" (*ljúflinga háttr*).
[3] *C. P. B.*, ii. 655.   [4] Ibid., 621.

—so scrupulous in letting the characters speak for themselves, so determined to keep the author's private sentiments from interfering—and the lyrical grief of Egil's poem. This also is kept within limits; it is no more effusive or thoughtless than *Lycidas.* But the meaning of it is sincere, and it has all the pathos, the eloquence of feeling, the personal tone, that is generally so carefully refused by the authors of prose stories in Iceland. The Saga of Egil, as the Oxford editors of his poetry remark, has done injustice to his character, making him too much of a mere fighting man. But in this passage, describing his sorrow and the occasion of the *Sonatorrek,* his resolution to keep from meat and drink, and the way his daughter Thorgerd wiled him out of it, his unwilling recourse to poetry and the growing interest in life as his verse went on shaping itself,—here there is one of the memorable things of Iceland. The house of Borg, the firth where Egil's son was drowned, and the headland where his father was buried, are full of the memories of Icelandic history. For the sake of the *Sonatorrek,* even a stranger may pay his regard there.

The old epic measures and the gnomic verse were not suppressed by the new Court poetry. On the contrary, "new," as applied to the Court poetry, means "later in order of development," and not later in order of time, with regard to much of the epic verse. For instance, whatever poetry was written in Greenland besides the Greenland poem of the Niblungs' fall must needs be later than the Court poetry of Harald Fairhair's time, when even Iceland was barely settled; not to speak of the Court verse of Bragi the Old, which is of the time of Ragnar Lodbrok, if tales are true.

The old measures were employed sometimes for Court purposes, as in Gisl Illugason's praise of Magnus Bareleg,[1] and the striking poem of Ivar Ingimund's son on Sigurd Slembe,[2] which is so far uncourtly as to glorify a lost cause and a fallen adventurer. And earlier than that, some of the older forms were used with a curious irregularity by Court poets who wrote correct verse of the new type when they chose. There are three poems of this kind, all interesting in more ways than one—the Raven Song by Hornklofi; *Eiríksmál*, the praise of Eric Bloodaxe (anonymous) and *Hákonarmál*, the praise of Hacon, Athelstan's

The Raven Song, fosterling, by Eyvind Skaldaspillir.[3] The
Eiríksmál, Raven Song in honour of Harald Fairhair
Hákonarmál. is a conversation between a Raven and a beautiful Finnish Valkyria who knew the language of birds; the matter of it is Harald's exploits and the fashions of his court, the great battle of Hafrsfirth and the manners of Harald's poets, berserks, jesters, and jugglers. Much of it reminds one of the old Latin satire—the mixture of subjects, the irregular verse, the descriptive terms in it. *Eiríksmál* also, about fifty years later, like the *Hákonarmál*, a little later still, interchanges two kinds of measure—the longer narrative line called *málaháttr*, and the dialogue verse of the Elder *Edda*. The praise of Eric Bloodaxe is a variation from the common type of Court poem;

C. P. B., ii. 240.   [2] Ibid., 261.   [3] Ibid., i. 254-266.

not a rhetorical recitation of a king's exploits, but a dramatic idyll of the reception of Eric in Valhalla. He is welcomed there as a new champion to fight in the last battle with the Wolf, in the twilight of the gods. Odin sends Sigmund and Sinfiotli to meet him. "Rise up in haste and go forth to meet the prince! Bid him in, if it be Eric, for it is he whom I look for." Sigmund asks: "Why didst thou rob him of victory, seeing thou thoughtest him so brave?" Odin answers: "Because it is not surely to be known when the grey Wolf shall come upon the seat of the gods."[1] So, also, in Eyvind's poem, Hacon is received by Hermod and Bragi.

In style these three poems are a strong contrast to the Court poetry; taken by themselves, and judged in their form alone, they would be placed at once in an older period. The difference between their freedom and the artifice of the Court poetry may serve as a warning of the danger there is in this kind of internal evidence when it is used to determine dates. Hornklofi and Eyvind both wrote, when they chose, the elaborate correct verse which looks so much later in character. When they took up the freer verse for a change, they became openly lawless, as if they were breaking out of school and found it pleasant. They are like Chaucer, taking a holiday from his artistic conscience in the random narrative and wilfully careless verse of the *House of Fame*.

The Court poetry of the North is different in verse and style from anything in England or Germany. In

[1] *C. P. B.*, i. 261.

motive, of course, it is allied to many poems all over the world in praise of living kings or their dead

The laws of Court-verse in Norway. fathers. But the form is peculiar to Norway. The name for the regular measure most in favour is *dróttkvætt*,—from *drótt*, a court or a great man's household—the Anglo-Saxon *dryht*. "Court" verse is not merely a modern invented name, nor derived entirely from the *curiales* of the "courtly makers" of later days and more Southern schools. It is a fair translation of the Norse technical term. The stave, as generally in the Eddic poems also, is of eight lines. In each stave there are four alliterative groups of two lines each, every pair of lines corresponding, as to alliteration, with the old Teutonic full line, and keeping the rule of three alliterative syllables—two in the first half, one in the second. But the measure is new. Each line has six syllables, ending always in a trochee. The first four syllables have no regular measure beyond what is found in the old epic verse. Further, there is rhyme within the line—the second rhyming syllable being the first of the final trochee. For instance, from Sigvat's poem on St Olaf, the verse on the battle at London Bridge :—

> " Rétt es at sókn en sétta ;
> Snarr þengill bauð Englum
> At þars Oláfr sótti,
> Yggs, Lunduna bryggjur :
> Sverð bitu Völsk, enn vörðu
> Víkingar þar Díki :
> Atti sumt i sléttu
> Súðvirki lið búðir."

It is difficult to imitate in English :—

> "Burden'd, dull, the bard is
> Beaten by the antique metre;
> Hoarse and harsh the verses
> Halt, the measures falter :
> Ah ! the mead of Odin,
> Undeprav'd, abundant !
> Would we not use it wisely,
> Well, the key of thy cellar ? "

In metaphor, the old practice of the epic poetry was continued. The artist had to use the finest possible language. The alliterative mode had always required a great variety of synonyms and a large number of figurative terms. But the Court poets went far beyond the practice of the older schools; their metaphorical terms were extended systematically by a process which went on doubling figure on figure till the simple idea became undecipherable under the wrappings. It was an old tradition of the Teutonic gradus (as of all heroic poetry) to use "gold-giver," or "ring-distributer," or some phrase of that sort, for "king" or "prince." This was developed in the following way: "giver" was rendered by any synonym that offered itself; "gold" was paraphrased mythologically—*e.g.*, as "the light of the hall of Ægir," the Sea-God (because Ægir was rich). Then this might be further variegated by combinations of all possible terms for "light" with all terms for "sea." "Dispenser of the candles of the fish's way" is an elementary specimen.

The Icelandic art of poetry agrees with Aristotle and Dante, as against Wordsworth, in demanding

21

that poetical language shall not be that of ordinary conversation. But it goes somewhat beyond them in its love of ornament. The extremes that Aristotle calls "jargon"[1] and "enigma," coming respectively from (1) strange single words and (2) excess of metaphor, are the cherished ideals of the Northern Court poetry, as they are in a less degree with the Teutonic school in general. The examples of metaphor that Aristotle gives might have been accepted by Snorri Sturluson for the Icelandic Poetics of the *Edda.* "The cup is to Dionysus as the shield to Ares. The cup may therefore be called the shield of Dionysus, and the shield the cup of Ares."[2] This, though of course very rudimentary, would be recognised in Iceland as showing the right spirit. But possibly the Stagyrite might object if the Icelander proposed to call a woman "pine-tree of the shield of Dionysus," on the principle that "cupbearer" in poetry means "woman," and that "woman" in poetry may be denoted by any feminine tree with the proper epithet following. There is a difference of taste here.

It would not be right to pass over the Court poets as mere bad examples of a mechanical and conventional school. There are a great many of them, and a great variety of gifts. They have the strength of composers who are sure of their audience. It was not merely a learned art; it was admired and praised like other games, and was widely popular, as well as courtly. England, where poetry has never been

---

[1] βαρβαρισμός : *Poetics*, c. xxii. [2] *Poetics*, c. xxi.

taken in this way, is the last country to pass judgment on these spirited poetical diversions. Court verse did not hinder the poets from saying what they meant. It was used in many pleasant ways, for epigrams and occasional poems, much of the same *Epigrams.* kind as the rhyming epigrams of modern Iceland in Dr Gudbrand Vigfusson's small anthology.[1] It would be unjust not to recognise the freedom and liveliness that could turn any motive or incident into a Court-verse stanza. These poems were remembered and admired in a natural way by men who were neither poets nor courtiers themselves. The Icelandic familiarity with verse is shown very well in an incident of the *Vatnsdæla Saga* (c. 26), where Thorstein sends his shepherd to find out what is passing in his enemy's house. The shepherd was to knock at the door, and notice what time was taken before the door was opened. To measure the time he repeats stanzas (*vísur*), twelve of them. Thorstein drew his own conclusions from the delay—rightly, as later inquiry proved.

The Court poets were often political, like those of Provence and Germany about the same time. The methods of Bertran de Born, or Sordello, or Walther von der Vogelweide in dealing with public affairs are not unknown in Norway. For one thing, the Icelandic poets had studied in their own manner the poem that is meant for direct assault, like the Provençal sirventes, not to speak of Archilochus or Catullus. One of them was called Serpent-tongue (Worm-tongue, *Ormstunga*),

[1] "One Hundred Rhyme-Ditties," *C. P. B.*, ii. 408-418.

and the name was deserved by many more. It was also possible to state a political cause effectively and fully, and make the Court-verse deliver an uncourtly admonition to a king, as was done by Sigvat in his *Plain-speaker* (*Bersöglis Vísur*).[1] This is an expostulation with King Magnus Olafsson, telling him the truth about his "governance," and reminding him of the original contract with his people. In this case the Whigs had the best of it, and the king no dishonour either: he listened and was converted, and bore no malice. The poem has other merits besides its practical effect. The language is clear, and there is imagination in the treatment of the political motive. Sigvat dwells on the tradition of the good kings of Norway, on his own service with St Olaf, his own loyalty to Magnus, the danger of revolt, and, most impressive of all, the gait and demeanour of the franklins in their sullen discontent, their heads sunk in the folds of their cloaks, thinking evil of the king.

Lyric Satire.

If the poetry is often difficult and conventional, the lives of the poets, on the other hand, are full of character, like the Provençal poets with whom they have so much affinity. Their adventures are among the best things in Icelandic prose. Hallfred the Troublesome Poet, Sigvat, Gisl Illugason, Einar Skulason, are not mere names. The prefaces to the different chapters in the Oxford *Corpus* show what the Court poets were: few of them are slow. Some of the kings themselves are among them,—Harald

---

[1] *C. P. B.*, ii. 145.   The date is about 1039.

Hardrada, for instance, and Magnus Bareleg. Harald put his own life into verse: the poem has been translated in a freer measure, which avoids some of the encumbrances of the Court rhetoric, but does not misrepresent the spirit of the original.[1] Court verse was sometimes used in a prosaic way from narrative poetry, as in the *Plácítús Drápa*,[2] which is the legend of St Eustace.

German prose begins with Ulfilas. The Gothic Bible was not forgotten; in the ninth century Walafrid Strabo recognised it as a great work. *Prose—* Its value, however, is something apart from *Ulfilas.* literature. Ulfilas found Gothic words for the Greek, but he did not write Gothic sentences. Regard for the text, fear of corrupting the meaning, made him keep to the Greek order. The result is not idiomatic. Ulfilas has naturally been found most profitable by philologists who are interested in separate words rather than in sentences.

In Anglo-Saxon prose there is a tendency to copy Latin constructions, as there is also, later, in the first Wycliffite translation of the Bible. But Anglo-Saxon

---

[1] " We were sixteen lads a-baling together, O lady gay,
   And the sea grew high and the billows on the bark broke grim and grey;
   Little the loitering laggard would haste to such a play,
       Yet gold-decked Gerda of Russia has naught but scorn for me!

.   .   .   .

"I was born where far in the Uplands men bend the twanging bow,
   But now I sweep past the skerries, and the farmers my galley know,
   And wide, since I first sped seaward, I have cloven the sea with my prow,
       Yet gold-decked Gerda of Russia has naught but scorn for me!"

—*Gísli Súrsson*, by Beatrice Helen Barmby, 1900.

[2] Ed. Finnur Jónsson, *Opuscula Philologica:* Copenhagen, 1887.

prose is often free enough from this bondage, both in the *Chronicle,* where the grammar is natural and unstudied, and also in such work as Ælfric's, where the author was too good a scholar to distort his native language.

The *Chronicle*[1] is the first great prose book in English : the earliest parts of it are the best, belonging *The English* to the time of Alfred, and probably from *Chronicle.* his own hand.   King Alfred was a translator, and his style varies with that of his authors. But there is always something fresh and native in his composition ; and when he is left free from translation his prose is strong and sound.   The narratives of the sea-captains, Ohthere and Wulfstan, which he put into his *Orosius,* are more modern in style than the prose of Chaucer or Caxton.   The Danish wars in the *Chronicle* are recounted in the same straightforward way.   And after the time of Alfred, down to the Norman Conquest, the writers of the *Chronicle* retain the gift of direct and simple style.   There is not enough of it, but it is good in itself, and refreshing by comparison with the various sorts of quaintness found in most of the Latin work of the time.   That the Latin historians could be lively and interesting has been fully acknowledged already ; but there is a virtue in the living language which not even the Latin of Bede could equal.

The style of the *Chronicle* varies.   One passage has been singled out for praise by many students of Anglo-

[1] The composition of the *Chronicle* has been elaborately studied and clearly explained in Mr Plummer's *Introduction,* Oxford, 1899.

Saxon,—the episode of Cynewulf and Cyneheard, which some have taken for a prose version of a ballad. It certainly has the features of heroic narrative; the promise, unfulfilled, of an English body of stories like the Icelandic Sagas. It is a tale like that of Finnesburh, or Roland, or Parcy Reed, a good defence against enemies, an old motive repeated often enough in real conflicts without a poet to record the tragedy, and never so often repeated in prose or rhyme as to lose its interest or its dignity.

Alfred translated Gregory's *Pastoral Care*,[1] and wrote a preface on his motives and method; rendering the

Alfred.
 original "sometimes word for word and sometimes sense for sense, as I learned from Plegmund my Archbishop and Asser my Bishop, and Grimbold my mass-priest and John my masspriest." In the other translations the king gives no account of himself; but his hand is plain in *Orosius*,[2] adding the reports of his navigators, Ohthere and Wulfstan. There are many other additions, probably taken from a commentary on *Orosius*, some of them interesting, like the reference to Nectanebus in the history of Alexander, and to the serpent *ipnalis* that lulls asleep, in the death of Cleopatra. The *Boethius*[3] is naturally different in style from the *Orosius*, and much more original, making a new kind of chanting prose out of the poems in the book, more like the tone of old French romance than the conventional Anglo-Saxon rhetoric. In one of the two manuscripts

---

[1] Ed. H. Sweet, E.E.T.S., 1871. [2] Ed. H. Sweet, E.E.T.S., 1883.
[3] Ed. Sedgefield, Oxford, 1899.

the poems are translated in verse; the history of the two renderings is much disputed. Alfred also made a translation from the *Soliloquies* of St Augustine under the title *Blostman*[1] (*Flores*), in three books, with a good deal taken from other authors, besides original matter of his own.

There are some difficulties about the authorship of the *Bede*, though it is attributed to Alfred by Ælfric. From certain elements in the vocabulary it has been surmised that the translation is of Mercian origin, and not by the West Saxon king.[2] The style is unequal, showing sometimes a most helpless dependence on the Latin, sometimes a talent for free decoration, especially in the regular use of pleonasm, putting two epithets for one.[3]

The *Dialogues of Gregory*[4] were translated for Alfred by Bishop Wærferth of Worcester. The stories being various and interesting might have put it into the head of some Anglo-Saxon reader to compose other tales on his own account. But the example was not followed. There were many chances, one might think, that an original school of prose romance should have been formed in England: an impulse might have been given by the translation of Alexander's Epistle; the old English *Apollonius of Tyre*[5] might have founded an order

---

[1] Cockayne, *The Shrine;* also in *Englische Studien,* xviii.

[2] See Miller's edition, E.E.T.S. (1890), and Schipper's, *Bibliothek der angelsächsischen Prosa,* iv. (1899).

[3] *Rhetoric in the translation of Bede,* by J. M. Hart, in *An English Miscellany,* 1901.

[4] See above, p. 136 *sq.*   [5] Ed. Thorpe; ed. Zupitza, *Archiv* xcii.

of Euphuist fiction before the Conquest. But though patterns of story-telling were plentiful enough, the Anglo-Saxons would not be stirred to practise this kind of invention, in prose at any rate. Curiosity was wanting; there was no one to explore or to make experiments, and with all their command of prose diction the Anglo-Saxons failed. Their preachers could tell stories; before Ælfric and with a ruder style the *Blickling Homilies*[1] show that there was a habit of good narrative, an established form. But it was limited in its range; there was no Anglo-Saxon *Edda*, no family history like the Icelandic, no fairy tales like the Welsh or Irish. Anglo-Saxon prose, however, if less interesting than Norse and Celtic, is at least capable and intelligent. It could say anything for which it had a mind, and a hundred years after Alfred it attained a dignity and security of style not common in the Middle Ages. Ælfric's Homilies[2] are not original, —few mediæval sermons are. But his easy

Ælfric.

style makes them good literature. He is not constrained by the example of Latin syntax; he is not tripped up, as the earlier prose often is, by a tangle of clauses. He explains and discourses clearly; his sympathy for his hearers and his unfailing sense of their demands and capacities is like the urbanity of French literature. At the same time something of a different taste is shown in another kind of composition, the florid alliterative half-poetical homilies or

[1] Ed. Morris, E.E.T.S., 1880.
[2] Ed. Thorpe, for the Ælfric Society. 2 vols., 1844-1846.

saints' lives of Ælfric.[1] His plain prose is modern in
character ; the other kind is a concession to mediæval
rhetoric. Here again Ælfric's motive was probably
the wants of his congregation; this sounding stuff
was what people liked in their sermons for a change,
something more musical and pompous than ordinary
speaking.

A number of homilies are attributed to Wulfstan,
Archbishop of York (1002-1023),[2] the best known of
Wulfstan. them and the most remarkable being the
Sermo Lupi ad Anglos, an address to the
English nation when the Danish affliction was sorest,
in the year 1014. In no composition is the chanting
rhetoric of the Anglo-Saxons better applied than here ;
it is a true prophetic voice that here laments over the
sorrow and shame of England.

In Icelandic, as in Irish and Welsh, there is some
danger that the interest of the heathen mythology
Icelandic Prose. and the national history may give a wrong
view of literary progress, by keeping out of
sight the school work in which it began. The oldest
Norse and Icelandic manuscripts do not contain the
fortunes of Odin nor the family histories of the tenth
century, but saints' lives and homilies : there is an older
extant text for *Plácítús Drápa,* the poem on St Eustace,
than for *Volospá ;* and if this be thought merely an
accident, as indeed it is, there is the fact that
Thorodd the Grammarian, a skilled philologist, lived

[1] Ed. Skeat, E.E.T.S.
[2] Ed. Napier (1883) ; see also Napier, *Ueber die werke des ae.
erzbischofs Wulfstan,* 1882.

in Iceland a hundred years before Snorri Sturluson, the author of the *Edda*. The prose of Iceland, as of Ireland and Wales, has the common learned foundation : the Icelandic authors knew the books that were known in every school. The commonplaces of homilies and saints' lives were written down in Iceland before the great Sagas. The Sagas are not by any means pure Northern work outside of the common literary influences ; their independence is not an ignorant barbarism. If they comply little with the ordinary tone of Latin education it is because their authors made it so, and not because their authors wanted the regular book-learning.

How Iceland shared in all the mediæval commonplaces is shown most plainly in the contents of " Hauk's book," a miscellaneous volume, the library, in fact, of an Icelandic gentleman.[1] It includes *Volospá* and the *Landnámabók*, but besides these a great heap of mediæval things of the usual sort— the tale of Troy, Geoffrey of Monmouth, the favourite popular science of *Elucidarium*. The Sagas did not take up the whole mind of Iceland. Iceland was part of Christendom, and shared in the same tastes as France or Germany. The Sagas, however, when all is said, are not any the less wonderful, Icelandic prose is not depreciated, because of this common Latin culture. The miracle is greater when it is seen that the originality of the Iceland narratives was exposed to the same educational danger as had hindered the growth of old English prose and all but

[1] Ed. Finnur Jónsson, 1892-1896.

choked the old German—the danger of conformity to a droning school tradition.

The whole of Icelandic history is miraculous. A number of barbarian gentlemen leave Norway because the government there is becoming civilised and interfering; they settle in Iceland because they want to keep what they can of the unreformed past, the old freedom. It looks like anarchy. But immediately they begin to frame a Social Contract and to make laws in the most intelligent manner: a colonial agent is sent back to the Mother Country to study law and present a report. They might have sunk into mere hard work and ignorance, contending with the difficulties of their new country; they might have become boors, without a history, without a ballad. In fact, the Iceland settlers took with them the intellect of Norway; they wrote the history of the kings and the adventures of the gods. The settlement of Iceland looks like a furious plunge of angry and intemperate chiefs, away from order into a grim and reckless land of Cockayne. The truth is that those rebels and their commonwealth were more self-possessed, more clearly conscious of their own aims, more critical of their own achievements, than any polity on earth since the fall of Athens. Iceland, though the country is large, has always been like a city state in many of its ways; the small population, though widely scattered, was not broken up, and the four quarters of Iceland took as much interest in one another's gossip as the quarters of Florence. In the Sagas, where nothing is of much importance except individual men, and where all the chief men are known to one another, a journey from Borg to Eyjafirth is no more than going past a few houses. The distant corners of the island are near one another. There is no sense of those impersonal forces, those nameless multitudes, that make history a different thing from biography in other lands. All history in Iceland shaped itself as biography, or as drama, and there was no large crowd at the back of the stage.

Historical writing in Iceland began without any tentative preliminary work; Ari, the first historian *Ari the Wise.* (1067-1148), is sure in his methods and positive in his results. He wrote a book about the settlement of Iceland, the foundation of the extant *Landnámabók*, which describes the first colonists, their families, and their holdings, proceeding regularly round the whole island, and including all the important facts that were kept in remembrance from the beginning of the Commonwealth. He wrote also the lives of the Kings of Norway, now lost, except in so far as they were worked into the ampler history of Snorri Sturluson and others. He wrote also a "book of Iceland," *Islendingabók*, extant only in his shorter revised version, commonly cited as *Libellus*, a sketch of the constitution.[1] Ari's historical research of course made great

---

[1] The *Landnámabók* has been lately edited in full (all extant versions) by Dr Finnur Jónsson. *Libellus* has been frequently printed along with *Landnámabók*: there is a separate edition by Möbius, 1869. The *Origines Islandiæ*, Dr Gudbrand Vigfusson's edition of the early historical books, is to be published by the Clarendon Press.

use of family traditions, but he did not attempt to work these out in the full imaginative form of the Sagas. He was a precise and careful historian, who criticised evidence. The Sagas are traditional stories, not limited in the same way; full of life, full of drama and dialogue. Yet these imaginative stories are not only founded on reality but came by their literary form through the example of Ari. The careful and exact historian set the fashion of prose, which was taken up and extended after his day by men with other motives. The imaginative force of *Njal* and *Gisli* comes from the same historical interest as led to the *Landnámabók;* the dry light of Ari's critical judgment went before the richer glow of the Sagas.

Old High German prose has no historical writer like Alfred or Ari, not even so much romance as the *High German prose—Notker.* Anglo-Saxon version of Apollonius. Notker the German (+1022) is a translator and expositor of books for the schools. One would not expect much literary genius at this time from renderings of Boethius or Martianus Capella in a language where prose was scarcely known. Yet Notker's style is enough to place him among the masters. German critics have compared him with the best in the language, old or new, and have found reasons for their opinion.[1]

Notker is the culmination of the long studies of St Gall : the nephew of the elder Ekkehard (the poet) and contemporary of the younger (the historian), he inherited the learning and the good sense

---

[1] Koegel, *Gesch. der deutschen Litteratur*, i. 2, p. 618.

which were traditional in the house. Philology was not divorced from Wit in anything that St Gall produced; and the nuptials of Mercury, the favourite scholastic allegory, were finely illustrated in the work of the translator Notker. In a Latin letter he speaks of various projects of translation, including the *Bucolics* of Virgil and the *Andria;* Ekkehard in the account of his death says that he had just finished *Job;* the extant books are Boethius, the *Consolation;* Martianus Capella, i. and ii.; the Psalter; and two of the treatises of the *Organon.*

Prose had been used before in versions from the Latin, but the German Tatian[1] has no merit except its "hideous fidelity." Notker broke away, like Alfred and Ælfric, from the interlinear method which was good enough for Ulfilas and Wycliffe. He represents the humanities — not the mere pedagogic business, but the sensitive appreciation and transfusion of meaning from one language to another. The German tongue for him was a creature with gifts of its own, and his title of honour is that he thought so much of his native language and spent so much in training it to the service of new ideas. Ælfric had a like respect for idiom, and the Irish scholars no less; but few have attempted, with so little precedent before them, such tasks as Notker. In his invention of a philosophical German language in the tenth century he may have given his pupils more than they wanted. That does not detract from his scholarship or his style. In the lively, idiomatic, imaginative use

[1] Ed. Sievers, 1872.

of philosophic terms he is the ancestor, though un-
acknowledged, of Meister Eckhart and Hegel.[1]

[1] A specimen of his style, where he is going beyond his text and
reading mythology in his own way :—

Attis pulcher item. "Dû bíst ter scôno blûomo. der iu chint
uuas. tén berezinthia minnôt. taz chît terra. uuánde sî ist in
uuintere betân. unde lángêt sia des lénzen. sô blûomen sínt."
"Thou art the fair flower that was once the child whom Berecyntia
loves : that is to say *Terra* whenas she is oppressed in winter, and
she longeth for the Lenten when the flowers are."

Notker died on St Peter's Eve, 1022, of the plague brought back
from Italy by the army of Henry II. Ekkehard gives the story of his
death in the *Liber Benedictionum.* He confessed his sins ; the worst
of them was that one day while wearing the habit of the order he
had killed a wolf. One of the brothers standing by, a simple-minded
man, cried out in his grief, "I would not care though you had killed
all the wolves in the world !" Notker called for the doors to be
opened, that the poor might be brought in and fed. He would not
be undressed for burial : he kept the chain on his loins that he
always wore.

CHAPTER V.

IRELAND AND WALES; GREECE; THE ROMANCE TONGUE.

IRISH SCHOLARSHIP — IRISH PROSE — DEIRDRE — 'TOCHMARC FERBE' —
IRISH VERSE—WALES—WELSH VERSE—WELSH PROSE: 'THE MAB-
INOGION'—GREECE IN THE DARK AGES—ROMAIC VERSE—DIGENIS
AKRITAS—THEODORUS PRODROMUS—THE ANTHOLOGY—BYZANTINE
PROSE—THE ROMANCE LANGUAGES—FRENCH EPIC—THE PILGRIM-
AGE OF CHARLEMAGNE—'LE ROI LOUIS'—ROLAND.

THE Latin education of Ireland began earlier and was
better maintained than in other countries. The Eng-

Irish Scholar-
ship.
lish and other Teutonic nations received
instruction from the Irish, and that not
only at the beginning of their studies: Irish learning
did not exhaust itself in missionary work and was
not merged in the progress of its German pupils;
it kept its vivifying power through many generations, and repeated in the ninth century the good
works of the fifth, again contributing fresh material
and a still rarer spirit of inquiry to the common
erudition of the Continent.[1]

[1] See above, p. 160. The nature of ordinary Irish scholarship,
and at the same time of many educational commonplaces not peculiarly Irish, may be well seen in the fragmentary exposition of the
Psalter, edited by Dr Kuno Meyer, *Hibernica Minora*, Oxford, 1894.

With all this, Celtic literature is more primitive
than anything in Anglo-Saxon or Icelandic; unrestrained in fancy, and as careless about modern
courtesies as about the probabilities and proprieties
of the understanding. The two extremes are often
found together in Irish, without any attempt at harmony. The wildest story will begin with a calm
recital of the four requisites of story-telling. "The
four things that are required of every story are required of this one—viz., time, and place, and person,
and the cause of invention." These are formulas from
school notebooks. The correct opening does not seem
to promise much more excitement than the ordinary
mediæval chapter-heading: "Inasmuch as we are told
by the philosopher that all men naturally desire knowledge," &c. But the lecture-room and its influences
are soon forgotten when the story gets under way,
though at any moment a learned reference may appear casually, to show that those who wrote out and
enjoyed the adventures of Cuchulain, "the Distorted
of Ireland," had also in their minds the ordinary
garnishings of Latin culture.

In some important respects Irish literature is more
deeply affected by Latin than German is, though
German literature showed itself generally so meek and
conformable, and made so feeble a stand for its native
traditions in comparison with Irish. Irish verse is
founded upon Latin almost entirely.[1] There was an
old Celtic kind of verse with some analogies to the

[1] Thurneysen, *Zur irischen Accent und Verslehre, Revue Celtique,*
vi. 309-347.

old Teutonic, and still more to the old Latin—an inexact alliterative line.[1] But this is not used largely, and the most popular Irish verse is a modification of Latin trochaics.[2] The literature which had least inclination towards conformity, and which has kept its ideas longer than any other, unspoilt by any modern platitude, was invaded and conquered, earlier than one can tell, by the foreign prosody. The technical part of Irish verse is not purely Celtic.

---

[1] The following specimen of old verse is quoted by Thurneysen from the tale of the *Sick-bed of Cuchulinn* (*Irische Texte*, i. p. 211) :—

> "Slaídid sciáthu | scaílid góu,
> Créchtnaigid cúrpu | gónaid sóeru
> Sáigid óirgniu | áildiu inn-áib
> Mánraid slúagu | sréid múine
> Fóbartach fían | fóchen Lábraid."

This has analogies with the old Latin accentual rhythm :—

> "uti tu morbos | visos invisosque
> viduertatem | vastitudinemque
> calamitates | intemperiasque
> prohibessis, defendas | averruncesque:
> uti fruges frumenta | vineta virgultaque
> grandire beneque | evenire siris
> pastores pecua | salva servassis
> duisque bonam salutem | valetudinemque
> mihi domo | familiæque nostræ."
> —Cato, *De Re Rustica*, 141 : arranged by
> F. D. Allen, *Early Latin.*

[2] *Seadna* is the name for the verse that comes nearest to the regular tetrameter—

> "Rombith oróit let a Maire, | rop trócar rí nime dún
> Ar guin ar guasacht ar gábud | a Críst for do snádud dún."
> —*Irische Texte*, i. 52 ; *Rev. Celt.*, vi. 339.

The commonest form is *Debide*, four lines of seven syllables with rhymes like *string : dáncing* (Keats, *Endymion*, i. ll. 313, 314)—

> "Messe ocus Pangur Bán | cechtar náthar fria saindán
> Bith a menma-sam fri seilgg | mu menma céin im saincheírdd.'

The prose, on the other hand, is as free as the Icelandic, and much more antique in its idiom.   Icelandic
Irish Prose.   prose of the thirteenth century is not what
is commonly called mediæval.   Its narra-
tive and dialogue may be compared with the most
accomplished in the modern tongues.   It has nothing
to learn in the way of self-command, clearness, irony.
Irish prose uses an antique syntax, sometimes like
that of mediæval French, the language that never
lost its childhood, running on happily from phrase
to phrase without stopping to think of elaborate constructions.   Old French will tell a story by simply
tacking on one sentence to another with the particle
si.   Old Irish uses the same loose construction: "Lotar
ass iarom, con ráncatar tóeb na indse, con' accatar in
lungine crédume forsind loch ar a cind."   "Then they
went on, so they came over against the island, so they
saw the boat of bronze on the lake before them"—
Sick-bed of Cuchulinn, c. 15.

But besides this easy-going manner there are many
complications, some of them part of the ordinary
spoken language, some of them artificial ornaments.
Varied and difficult grammar is as natural to old Irish
as the simple stringing of sentences.   The language
is well provided with a passive voice, a subjunctive
mood, and a large assortment of tenses.   The colloquial arrangement of words is naturally rhetorical,
often putting, for instance, the personal name in an
emphatic place by itself: "As for Conchobar, there
was the valour of a hero in him"—"Cid Conchobar
dano bá gal churad leis."   One favourite construction

agrees with an old French practice which the grammarians have troubled themselves to explain : " a jewel of a man" gives the type of it, or, more elaborately, "two candles of valour of five-edged spears in the hand of each man of them"—"Dá chaindill gaiscid di shlegaib cóicrinnechaib illáim cech fhir dib."

In ornamental prose the Irish taste occasionally went beyond all limits : there is a certain kind of profuse meaningless epithet work which came to be a convention in Irish, and with this very often the sounder and older prose was overlaid in new versions. But besides this there is a good type of Euphuism where the ornament does not obscure the meaning, and the epithet, though conventional, is not otiose. Alliteration is seldom long wanting. A more sparing use is made of grammatical figures, but antithesis is common, as it is in the popular language of the fairy tales : " A green knoll, at the face of the sun and the back of the wind, where they were near to their friends and far from their foes !" A specimen piece of old Irish rhetoric is the formula : " Though he was a youth in years he was a warrior in might of battle" —" Bá ségda súairc sobésach in rígmacc bói rempu, ocus ciar bo maccóem iar n-áis ropo mílid iar mórgasciud." [1]

---

[1] *Irische Texte*, iii. p. 484 (*Tochmarc Ferbe*). A specimen of Irish rhetoric, conventional but not dull, may be quoted here from the *Battle of Ventry* : " And like the wild, noisy, rough-streamed, terrible waterfall that pours through a narrow thin rock, or like a fierce red blaze of fire with high-peaked flames through the wide roof of a king's palace, or like the roar of a white-crested, green-chinned, wailing, white-foaming, full-watered wave of the great sea around it, so was the overthrowing and the scattering and the beating and the tearing into pieces and wild hacking which Oscar inflicted on

The tastes of the old Irish authors are seen perhaps most evidently in their translations from the Latin. The versions of the Tale of Troy and the history of Alexander given in *Irische Texte* exhibit two different varieties of prose: Troy, characteristically Irish, but not spoilt as a story by translation into Irish terms; Alexander, on the other hand, far gone towards futile ornament — Irish rhetoric working on the original stuff, as the parasitic plant called dodder overspreads and kills a livelier vegetable. The Irish *Odyssey*, the Wandering of Uilix MacLeirtis,[1] is a continuation of the Irish Troy book, and shows a thorough assimilation of the Greek fable (wherever that may have been found) to the temper of Irish romance.

It is the prose literature of the Celts that makes their great distinction, though their poetry is remarkable enough. Iceland is the other country possessed of riches in prose, and Iceland is later than Ireland. There is much resemblance at first sight between the two. Both are in close relation to ordinary life, especially in their repetition of dialogue. Both are exempt from Latin grammar—not through ignorance, but through the greater strength and self-assertion of their natural idiom. Both make great things out of oral tradition. But the resemblance does not go deep. Icelandic sagas are modern in everything but their date. The art of them keeps up with the newest

the foreigners in that onslaught."— *Cath Finntrága*, edited and translated by Kuno Meyer, Oxford, 1885, p. 16. This does not show the alliteration of the Irish original.

[1] *Merugud Uilix meicLeirtis*, ed. Kuno Meyer.

inventions in fiction, and is familiar with secrets of workmanship about which Flaubert and Tourgénieff are still exercised. The conversation of Njal and Skarphedinn was written in the thirteenth century, and may have been repeated as a fireside tale for generations before that; but as it stands in the book it agrees with any age, and the last thing to which it can be likened is what is commonly called " mediæval," what Johnson and Scott called " Gothic," of the old-fashioned romantic type. Irish prose is openly romantic, like the Welsh prose in Mr Arnold's quotations; romantic — that is to say, quaint, pathetic, melancholy, grotesque — both in matter and style. The stories, whether of cattle spoils or abductions, voyages, wooing, or violent death, according to the old Irish Catalogue of favourite topics,[1] are full of wonders; and even simple business, like ordinary fighting, is described with an air of surprise.

Much of it, as already said, is old mythology, and not of the most reasonable,—like old wives' tales literally reported. In the confusion, however, there may be made out a certain tendency to order, a shaping force that reduces the absurdities and dwells on the more human aspect, bringing heroism nearer to that "deliberate valour" which many English poets have reverenced, and further from the sensational rage of the Distorted. This rationalising of motives may sometimes be observed where the same story is found in earlier and later versions. The tale of Deirdre has incidents in it which a reasonable

---

[1] In the Book of Leinster: see Zimmer, *Z. f. d. A.*, xxxiii. p. 144.

taste will not allow, and the older version has more
crudity than the later.[1] The Ulster legend to which
it belongs, and in which Cuchulinn is the chief figure,
includes a great number of stories of different origin
and motive, never reduced to any common standard.
But in very many of them may be found a sense
of beauty at variance with much of the traditional
narrative; in others a deliberate humorous intention
something like that of Snorri's *Edda*; in a few the
definite appreciation of what may be called epic
or tragic motives, in contrast to the wild work of
mythology. Which must not be taken as implying
that the Irish ought to have been more precise, or
were wrong in keeping so much of their ancestral
fabling. There is room enough both for the imaginative common-sense of the Icelanders and the romantic
mythology of the Irish. But to judge the Irish truly,
their understanding must be recognised as well as
their fancy, and they understood, in many of their
tales, that something was to be gained by respect
for the possibilities.

It was in this way that tragedy might arise out
of the chaos of the heroic legend. This is what
happens in the tale of Deirdre and the sons

Deirdre.

of Usnech. Two motives are harmonised
in it, and neither of them is mean or untrue. One
is the sorrow of Deirdre, who sees the trouble coming

---

[1] *Longes mac n-Usnig* in *Ir. Texte*, i.   It is to be remembered that
the extant versions are very incomplete as evidence of literary taste.
Some of them are abridgments, and in many cases the later text
may be more truly original than the earlier.

on before they leave the land of Alba, and cannot
keep the sons of Usnech from returning to Ireland.
The other motive is the honour of Fergus, and this
is much more dramatic than the other. Fergus is
entrapped by Conchobar and made the instrument of
his plot against the sons of Usnech. It is this that
makes the tragic discord in one of the strong passages
of Irish prose; and there is nothing in it untrue or
forced. If the *Sons of Usnech* were turned into
Icelandic, with Icelandic scenes, dresses, and manners,
many Irish things would disappear. The lament
of Deirdre refuses to be translated out of its proper
terms; it belongs inalienably to Glen Etive and Glen
Masain. But the drama would come out, in essentials,
unchanged, though the incidents were reduced to the
merest matter of fact. Any stage or any properties
would do for a rendering of Fergus, the true man
who finds that he has been made the agent of
treachery. As for the last fight, it has been observed
already how like it is to the great epic battles in
other languages. What is most wanting in the Irish
tales is the gravity of one of the great conflicts,
like *Roncevaux* or the *Nibelunge Nôt*, which weigh
on the mind like a thunderstorm. Generally there
are so many adventures and exploits that the stress
of the action is dissipated. It is not always so,
Tochmarc however. The *Sons of Usnech* make one
Ferbe. exception; the *Wooing of Ferb* is another.[1]
This story is one that shows excellently some of the

[1] *Tochmarc Ferbe,* ed. Windisch, in *Irische Texte,* iii.; an English
translation by A. H. Leahy, London, 1902.

variations of form at the command of Irish poets and story-tellers. The prose has many poems interspersed, and not all of one sort, but varying from rude verse of the oldest type to the most elaborate new form. It carries out thoroughly what may be assumed as the rules of the mixed kind of narrative, partly verse and partly prose, which is so characteristically Irish, whether or not it is also, as some think, the primitive form of epic in general.[1] Curiously, the text ends with an example of the epic reviser at work, in a continuous poem which repeats all the story. Some one apparently thought it a pity that the original short poems should be left in their isolation, with nothing better than prose to hold them together. So he wrote out the whole afresh, in thirty-nine quatrains. In the same way an English, Danish, or Spanish ballad professional will put together the matter of several short ballads into one long one: the dull summary of the Nibelung story in the Elder *Edda* (*Grípis Spá*) is not very different in kind.[2] But apart from these accidents of form the story of the *Wooing of Ferb* is interesting, because in the action it resembles the epic matter of other nations so much more than is usual in Ireland. The lyrics and elegies contained in it, and many a turn of phrase, would save it from ever being set down as mere repetition of common motives. But as a matter of fact it does use common

---

[1] Cf. Motherwell, *Minstrelsy*, Introd., p. xiv *sqq.*; Rhŷs, *Arthurian Legend*, p. 374, and the references there.

[2] See above, p. 290.

motives, even the commonest—a catalogue of forces
(with a heroine, like Camilla), and a long detailed
battle in defence of a stronghold.

Old Irish poetry is found difficult by the best
scholars, but some of its qualities are well shown
in fairly easy poems, and the difficulties
Irish Verse. of the harder ones are being cleared away.
It is not necessary to repeat what has been said by
more than one writer about the interest in Nature,
the miraculous freedom of the Irish from the conventional mediæval habit of taking Nature for granted.
It is true that in other languages, in Anglo-Saxon and
Provençal, one may meet with touches of observation
that go to the quick, like the skylark's rapture in
Bernard of Ventadour.[1] But the Irish are the only
people in the Middle Ages, unless the Welsh be taken
along with them, who can make poetry out of mere
Nature and nothing else, or at any rate nothing else
besides the spirit of the poet, and his pleasure in what
he sees, hears, and lives among.

Irish poetry developed very largely the taste for
artificial language which is found in the Icelandic
Court poetry and elsewhere. The profession of poet
was encouraged and magnified by the poets themselves.
They became a weariness sometimes, as the old Irish
life of Columba remarks; but the mystery of verse
and poetical figure was not suppressed. The masters
taught the same kind of affected paraphrase as in
Iceland. "Hens' eggs are called 'gravel of Glenn Ai';
a piece of eel is called 'a piece of the female race,

[1] See above, p. 7.

as there were supposed to be no male eels; leek
'tear of a fair woman'; some edible seaweed 'mesh
of the plain of Rian'=the sea, &c."[1] Subtilties of
verse were carried far; there are treatises on the
art of poetry [2] describing all kinds of difficult metres—
three hundred and thirty-eight varieties in one book.
Some of those seem too exacting for poetry ; in others
the trick of the rhyme is as graceful as the fine work
of the French Pleiade.   One of these staves has been
copied in English, thus, by Mr Walter Raleigh :—

> "Though our songs
>   Cannot banish ancient wrongs,
>   Though they follow where the rose
>   Goes,
>
> And their sound
>   Swooning over hollow ground
>   Fade, and leave the enchanted air
>   Bare,
>
> Yet the wise
>   Say that not unblest he dies
>   Who has known a single May
>   Day :
>
> If we have laughed,
>   Loved, and laboured in our craft,
>   We may pass with a resigned
>   Mind."[3]

---

[1] Kuno Meyer, *Revue Celtique*, xii. p. 220.

[2] *Mittelirische Verslehren*, edited by Thurneysen (*Irische Texte*, iii.)

[3] The technical name for this is *debide baise fri tóin*, which in the
vulgar tongue might be rendered "doup - skelp." — Thurneysen,
op. cit., p. 150.

The old Gaelic Court poetry is not all complicated with rhetoric. Sometimes the common motives are treated with a dignified simplicity. An example of this is the *Song of the Sword of Cerball*.[1] The substance is of the well-known kind,—the king's achievements and the glory of his fathers. This is put into the form of an address to the Sword and a recital of the Sword's fortunes as it was handed on from one king to his successor—

> "Hail sword of Cerball! Oft hast thou been in the great woof of war!"

The rhetoric is not far-fetched, but rather like the repetitions in a ballad:—

> "Thy bright point was a crimson point in the battle of Odba of the Foreigners,
> When thou leftest Aed Finnliath on his back in the battle of Odba of noble routs.
>
> Crimson was thy edge, it was seen, at Belach Mugna; thou wast proved
> In the valorous battle of Ailbe's plain, throughout which the fighting raged.
>
> Before thee the goodly host broke on a Thursday at Dun Ochtair
> When Aed the fierce and brilliant fell on the hillside above Liathmaine.
>
> Before thee the host broke, on the day when Cellach was slain,
> The son of Flannacan, with numbers of troops, in high lofty great Tara."

---

[1] Edited and translated by Kuno Meyer, *Revue Celtique*, **xx.** p. **7.**

Compared with the Northern Court poetry this is flat, and from no point of view is there any great novelty in it. But it is well composed: it expresses, as it intends, the greatness of the royal line. It is possibly nearer than anything in Old English or old Norse to the Greek simplicity, which is often thought tame by the romantic mind; it is early art at the first reflective stage, when it is content with easy rules. The proportions are right; the unities are preserved. The ideas are not new, but they are made to seem important for the time—that is, they succeed in literature.

Early Welsh literature agrees with Irish in the most important respects, and differs from Old English

Wales.

in the same degree. The poetical forms are a contrast to those of the English epic. Stanzas, exact in shape and obscure in meaning, are among the oldest remains of Welsh, and the later poetry intensifies and develops such qualities as these. On the other hand, the free Welsh prose of the old romances is as unrestrained as in those of Ireland. The slow beginnings of Old English prose are different; and though English writers acquired freedom before the end of the Anglo-Saxon period, they never wrote anything like the *Mabinogion*. Long interesting stories in prose, difficult artificial work in verse,— these are the kinds of literature favoured in Wales and Ireland.

In a manuscript of Juvencus at Cambridge there are two Welsh poems of the ninth century, written in a form which has never died out in Wales—a triplet with a curious proportion between the lines, which may be described here as an example of ancient *Welsh Verse.* poetic art. The habit of mind shown in the ninth-century poems is found unaltered, after a thousand years, in the curious work of modern Welsh poets, which in taste, interest, and ambition is more distant from the English "reading public" than the poetry of Persia or Japan,—

> "Gur dicones remedaut—elbid
> Anguorit anguoraut
> Nigaru gnim molim trintaut."

This is an *englyn* from the Cambridge manuscript, rendered as follows:—

> "He who made the wonder of the world—
> He who saved us—will save us:
> No hard work to praise the Trinity."[1]

The first line is called the "shaft" (*paladr*); the two syllables set off to the one side—in technical language the *gair cyrch*—are in a way outside of the stanza, which without them is a triplet, rhyming in -*aut*. Often, however, the *gair cyrch* rhymes with an internal syllable in the next line, in a manner which is common also in Irish verse:—

> "Mi awum lle llas milvir—prid*ein*
> Or duy*rein* ir goglet."

> "I have been where fell the soldiers of Britain
> From the East to the North."[2]

---

[1] Rhŷs, *Arthurian Legend*, p. 384; Skene, *Four Ancient Books of Wales*, ii. p. 1; H. Bradshaw, On the oldest written remains of the Welsh language (*Collected Papers*, p. 281 *sqq.*)

[2] Rhŷs, *op. cit.*, p. 385.

Triplets are also common without the catchword. One of the few Welsh quotations current in England is one of these—the *englyn* of the grave of Arthur. Another of the same series is the following:—

> " Bet mab Osvran yg Camlan
> Gvydi llawer cywlavan
> Bet Bedwir in alld Tryvan."

> " Osvran's son's grave (is) at Camlan,
> After many a slaughter ;
> Bedwyr's grave is in Allt Tryvan."[1]

Or, again, in the poem on Geraint, son of Erbyn :—

> " En Llogporth y llas y Gereint
> Guir deur o odir Diwneint
> A chin rillethid ve llatysseint."

> " At Llongborth there fell of Geraint's
> Brave men from the border of Devon,
> And ere they were slain they slew."

Welsh verse shares with Irish a preference for the seven-syllable line, the importance of which in popular Latin and Romance prosody has already been indicated.

In the early Welsh history the names of certain poets are celebrated—Aneurin, Taliesin, Llywarch Hen.[2] The most famous of all the poems is the *Gododin*, attributed to Aneurin.[3] The difficulties of this whole

---

[1] Rhŷs, Introduction to Malory.

[2] The *Book of Aneurin* and the *Book of Taliesin* are edited, along with the *Black Book of Carmarthen* and the poems of the *Red Book of Hergest*, in Skene's *Four Ancient Books of Wales.*

[3] The manuscript is late, but contains forms as old as the glosses of the ninth century : Rhŷs, *Arthurian Legend*, p. 241, n.   There is a

body of literature are confessed by Celtic scholars, and will be respected here, in the spirit of the Bishop who avoided the word *metropolitice* because it was too hard for him,[1]—though one would not add with him "ne fu pas curtays qui cest parole icy escret," for it is the essence of these poems that they are courtly. They might be popular as well, like the Welsh poetry of the present day, which, though it belongs to the whole people, is derived originally from kings' houses and from no churlish strain,—from the falcons, not the kites.

One can make out pretty surely that the Welsh conventions were harder than the Irish, that the Welsh refused more persistently to write intelligible poetry. The translation of the *Gododin*, it is believed, has not yet been fully accomplished. The difficulty is something like that of the Icelandic Court poetry. But the Icelander always has a clear idea: he knows the fact before he begins coating it with professional epithets. In the old Welsh poetry there is apparently vagueness of thought as well as ingenuity of words to be got over. Possibly the Welsh were right. Great as the skill of the Icelanders was, they could not harmonise the prose substance of the Court poetry with its splendid expression, and it remains for the most part essentially prosaic. In Welsh, and Irish too, there is more chance that along with

---

separate edition, *The Gododin* of Aneurin Gwawdrydd, an English translation by the late Thomas Stephens; edited by Thomas Powel, and printed for the Honourable Society of *Cymmrodorion*, 1888.

[1] Stubbs, *History of England*, ii. p. 318.

the artifices and ostentations there will be an infusion of another spirit, a gust of passion, an impulse of some sort not like prose.

In many instances the difficulty is rather that of matter than of form : the poems deal with obscure forgotten myths, and are not explained, as in the Elder *Edda*, with prose introductions and epilogues. Through many of these there is to be felt, along with the abrupt enigmatic phrase, a sense of real meaning in the story : the fault is in the later generations, to have forgotten what every child once knew; to have lost, for instance, the story, not well recorded even in the oldest Welsh mythologies, of the voyages of Arthur. But here, though the interpretation is wanting and the dream itself only half remembered, the poetical value is not lost; the meaning of the story remains in the burden at the end of each stanza—

> " Three freights of Prydwen went we on the sea ;
> Seven alone did we return from Caer Rigor." [1]

For the poetical sense this hardly needs a commentary, though one would like to know more about the dangers that Arthur steered through.

The best of the old Welsh prose is found in the Red Book of Hergest, the stories commonly known as the *Mabinogion*.[2] The name is inaccurately used,

---

[1] Rhŷs, Introduction to Malory.

[2] Edited and translated by Lady Charlotte Guest, 1849 ; described and explained by Mr Ivor B. John in *Popular Studies in Mythology, Romance, and Folklore*, No. 11, published by D. Nutt, 1901. The text of the *Red Book* was published by Rhŷs and Evans in 1887, an exact copy of the MS. See also papers by E. Anwyl (*the Four Branches*) in *Zeitschrift für celtische Philologie*, i.-iii.

like most others of the sort. *Mabinog* is the name for
"a kind of literary apprentice, a scholar receiving instruction from a qualified bard. *Mabinogi*
meant the subject-matter of a Mabinog's
course, the literary stock-in-trade which
he had to acquire."[1] The plural, *Mabinogion*, denotes
"the four branches of the Mabinogi,"—the stories of
Pwyll, Prince of Dyved; Branwen, daughter of Llyr;
Manawyddan, son of Llyr; and Math, son of Math-
onwy. The other stories, included with less accuracy
of title in Lady Charlotte Guest's *Mabinogion*, are *The
Lady of the Fountain, Geraint,* and *Peredur,* the plots
of which correspond more or less to the *Ivain, Erec,*
and *Conte du Graal* of Chrestien de Troyes; the
Dream of Rhonabwy and *Kilhwch and Olwen,* which
are Arthurian without any such definite French relations; the *Dream of Maxen Wledig* (the Emperor
Maximus); *Lludd and Llevelys* (part of the history
of King Lud); and the story of Taliesin the poet,
which is not in the Book of Hergest.

The matter is variegated, and difficult in every
possible way,—different lines of tradition inextricably
ravelled. Three of the stories have a French ground-
work, whether the poetry of Chrestien or some older
version of the same plots. *Owein, Geraint,* and *Peredur*
are not Welsh in the same degree as *Kilhwch and
Olwen.* It is impossible for many reasons to discuss
the history of these romances here. One thing,
however, is fairly certain about them, which is more
important than anything else for the present purpose:

*Welsh Prose.
The
Mabinogion.*

[1] Ivor John, *op. cit.,* p. 4.

the style of all the tales is native and idiomatic. *Owein, Geraint,* and *Peredur,* in spite of their foreign associations, have the style of a fairy story told in a living language; in manner, they are hardly less purely Celtic than the Four Branches themselves, the authentic *Mabinogi.* At the very outset the phrasing proves how free it is from foreign influences. No French romance could have prompted the Welsh author when he wrote: "King Arthur was at Caerlleon upon Usk; and one day he sat in his chamber, and with him were Owain the son of Urien, and Kynon the son of Clydno, and Kai the son of Kyner, and Gwenhwyvar and her handmaidens at needlework by the window. And if it should be said that there was a porter at Arthur's palace, there was none," &c. The idiom in that last sentence was not grafted in from any foreign literature. Nor are the native branches of the *Mabinogi* less capable of polite conversation than the stories with French elements in them. The following example is from *Pwyll, Prince of Dyved :*—

"And as he was setting on his dogs he saw a horseman coming towards him upon a large light grey steed, with a hunting horn round his neck, and clad in garments of grey woollen in the fashion of a hunting garb. And the horseman drew near and spoke unto him thus—

"'Chieftain,' said he, 'I know who thou art, and I greet thee not.'

"'Peradventure,' said Pwyll, 'thou art of such dignity that thou shouldst not do so.'

"'Verily,' answered he, 'it is not my dignity that prevents me.'

"'What is it then, O Chieftain?' asked he.

"'By Heaven, it is by reason of thine own ignorance and want of courtesy.'

"'What discourtesy, Chieftain, hast thou seen in me?'

"'Greater discourtesy saw I never in man,' said he, 'than to drive away the dogs that were killing the stag and to set upon it thine own. This was discourteous; and though I may not be revenged upon thee, yet I declare to Heaven that I will do thee more dishonour than the value of a hundred stags.'

"'O Chieftain,' he replied, 'if I have done ill I will redeem thy friendship,'" &c.

This is the meeting of Pwyll and Arawn king of Hades, an old-fashioned Welsh dialogue, perhaps not specially notable except that it is the sort of thing no English writer could manage well, before the days of Malory. It may be thought that the art of the *Mabinogion* is only the simple liveliness found in many popular tales, too common a thing for admiration. But there is a difference among popular tales, and various degrees of art in them: if the Celtic fairy tales have beauties of style, these are not to be annulled merely because they are popular. If one can find excellences in the phrasing of stories taken down from tradition in modern Connemara, resemblances to the style of old Celtic literary narrative, what is the conclusion to be drawn? That old Celtic romance is no better than common *Märchen*? Or that it is possible for a *Märchen* to be a work of art? The latter, surely. The Celtic collections of fairy tales have their own distinct character. What in the English giant is "Fee faw fum," and so on, is in Connaught "I feel the smell of a melodious lying Irishman under my sod of country"—a more interesting formula. The style of the *Knight of the Red Shield* as given by Campbell is not less artistic than the courtly poems of *Percival*, where like adventures are found; and the Welsh *Peredur* is not disgraced by its resemblance, in some things, to the West Highland tale. If the manner of the fairy tale, humorous or fanciful, is like much in the old written legends, in the Welsh *Mabinogion*, in the Irish Saints' Lives, the ancient literature is none the worse.

The Celtic genius has been debated and disputed for a long time past, not without results. It is clear that many things have passed for Celtic which are not the property of any one race. There is a "Finnish genius" known in Norway; and fantastic tendencies in a Norwegian author are traced there sometimes to a Finnish ancestry, just as Shakespeare and Keats have been derived from Wales, and for similar reasons; because the more primitive people have kept their mythological tastes and ideas better on the whole than those with "the German paste in their composition." So Polish and Bohemian birth is sometimes in Germany made to explain any peculiar originality of temper; the German nations apparently having this common modest reluctance to believe that they can be imaginative on their own account. But when every deduction is made from the too enthusiastic praise of Celtic fantasy, there remains a Celtic habit of mind unmistakable and inexhaustible in the old Welsh and Irish books. It is not to be understood merely by repeating the miracles of Cuchulinn or Gwydion son of Don, because these can be matched elsewhere. It is in the temper more than the imagination,—a peculiar readiness of mind, and at the same time an intolerance of anything that comes between the mind and its object. "Failure is to form habits." This moral will apply to much of the Celtic work in literature, powerful as its customs and conventions are. The marginal notes and exclamations of the learned Irish scribes, the little scraps of irrelevant verse written by wearied copyists in old Irish manuscripts, are so many protests of the living creature against the weight of monotonous duty. Neither St Patrick nor St Brigit could prevent them from thinking freely, and the Saints' Lives are not more careful than the ballads of Ossian to keep one strict religious view. This freedom is well shown in the Life of St Brigit in the *Book of Lismore*,[1] in the following story :—

"Once her father entreated holy Brigit to go to the King of Leinstèr, even to Ailill, son of Dunlang, to *The story of* ask for the transfer of the ownership of *St Brigit and the King of* the sword which he had given to him (for *Leinster.* a time) on another occasion. Brigit went at her father's commands. A slave of the King came to converse with Brigit, and said: 'If I should be

[1] Translated by Whitley Stokes, p. 193.

saved from the bondage wherein I abide with the king, I should become a Christian, and I should serve thee and the Lord.' Brigit went into the fortress, and begged two boons of the king, to wit, transfer of the ownership of the sword to Dubthach [her father] and freedom to the slave.

"'Why should I give that to thee?' said the king.

"'Excellent children will be given to thee,' said Brigit; 'and kingship to thy sons, and heaven to thyself.'

"Said the king: 'The kingdom of heaven, as I see it not, I ask it not. Kingship for my sons, moreover, I ask not, for I myself am still alive, and let each one work in his time. Give me, however, length of life in my realm, and victoriousness in battle over Conn's Half; for there is often warfare between us.'

"'It shall be given,' saith Brigit."

With all their perseverance in study and in religion, the Irish kept their minds free: at any moment they could hear and take pleasure in the liveliness of the real world, and no theology nor moral law could prevent them from seeing the fun of it.

The Greek literature of the Dark Ages lies apart from the rest. The distance between the most ex-
Greece in the Dark Ages. travagant Irish story and the most respectable High German school-book can be overcome, and a relationship proved between them, at least in so far as both Irish and German education

depend upon Latin. The history of Greek authors during this time has little bearing on the progress of Latin, Teutonic, or Celtic literature.

There is likeness in the fortunes of East and West, however; Constantinople has its dark age, followed by something of the same sort as the Western mediæval literature ; the life of the Romance tongues has something answering to it in the Romaic.

The eighth century was the dark age in Greece; after that, though learning revives, more of an effort is required to keep up the forms of ancient Greek scholarship. The literary language does not flow so easily ; on the other hand, the vulgar tongue asserts itself.

Romaic verse took the same way as popular Latin; the old quantities were forgotten, and the accents replaced them. In popular Greek there was much less variety of rhythm and stanza than in Latin; one single type of accentual line became the universal measure, called *political* verse, which means popular, vulgar, *bourgeois*.

The *political* line is a vulgar form of the classical iambic tetrameter. It is among the accidents of *Romaic Verse.* taste that in the West the trochaic, in the East the iambic tetrameter should have been made the basis of the most popular verse. The iambic also is well known in the West, but it never had the vogue of the other measure:—

"Cras amet qui nunquam amavit."

The Greeks preferred the measure that Philip danced
on the field of Chæronea [1]—

Δημοσθένης Δημοσθένους Παιανιεὺς τάδ' εἶπεν [2]—

and their modern poetry is all in this common metre.
of course with the modern accent. It is found,
complete and regular, in the tenth century: a song is
quoted by Constantine Porphyrogenitus—

Ἴδὲ τὸ ἔαρ τὸ γλυκύ, πάλιν ἐπανατέλλει. [3]

The chief use of it is in ballads and romances; the
life of the hero Digenis Akritas is especially famous,
Digenis Akritas. and has been compared with the stories
of similar matter in the Western tongues,
particularly with the Cid. There are four extant versions, not counting the ballads still current. [4] The more

---

[1] Παραυτίκα μὲν οὖν ὁ Φίλιππος ἐπὶ τῇ νίκῃ διὰ τὴν χαρὰν ἐξυβρίσας
καὶ κωμάσας ἐπὶ τοὺς νεκροὺς μεθύων ᾖδε τὴν ἀρχὴν τοῦ Δημοσθένους
ψηφίσματος πρὸς πόδα διαιρῶν καὶ ὑποκρούων, κ.τ.λ. — Plutarch,
Demosthenes, c. 20.

"Now Philip having won the battell, he was at that present so
joyfull, that he fell to commit many fond parts. For after he had
drunke well with his friends, he went into the place where the overthrow was given, and there in mockery began to sing the beginning
of the decree which Demosthenes had preferred (by the which the
Athenians accordingly proclaimed warre against him), rising and falling with his voice, and dancing it in measure with his foote," &c.
—(North's translation.)

[2] May be sung to the tune of—

"Come, landlord, fill the flowing bowl until it doth run over."

[3] Krumbacher, *Gesch. der byzantinischen Litteratur,* p. 255.

[4] *Les exploits de Digénis Akritas, épopée byzantine du dixième siècle,*
ed. C. Sathas and E. Legrand, 1875. Cf. E. Legrand, *Recueil de
chansons populaires grecques,* 1874 ; Krumbacher, *op. cit.,* p. 831.

formal poems have been put together out of earlier separate lays. There seems to be no doubt that this Homeric theory holds good of Digenis Akritas, though some of the Homers have been too prosaic.

The hero Basil, called Digenes because his father and mother are of different races, is Warden of the Marches (ἀκρίτας) on the Euphrates, and his enemies are the outlaws over the border. The story is full of incidents such as are common in the French romances,—the winning of the lady Eudocia, the fight with the dragon, even the description of the season of May and the beauties of the garden, like many a *vergier* in the French books. Digenis, however, though a great champion, would have been hooted as a felon knight for some things in his biography; his betrayal of the damsel in his charge requires the vengeance of Sir Guyon or Sir Arthegall, and his repentance is filthy. In the story of his contest with the maiden warrior, the gloating respectability of the Byzantine author has spoilt a good passage of old romance, which in Welsh or Irish would have sounded better. The epic of Digenis is neither frank in the primitive way nor chivalrous in the modern sense. But the ballads are all right, and where the epic is wrong, the popular ballad tradition need not be blamed for it.

One Byzantine author who wrote both in the classical and the vulgar tongue, Theodorus Prodromus, *Theodorus Prodromus.* in his tastes and devices often looks like one of the vagabond mediæval clerks, one of the hungry and reckless poets who deal in satire

railing, and humorous petitions for a benefice — a
goliardeis, the Skelton of his time and language.
He lived in the first half of the twelfth century,
under Alexius, John, and Manuel Comnenus. The
list of his works is varied: he wrote in verse the
romance of Dosicles and Rodanthe, and an allegory
of the twelve months, besides a number of occasional pieces, and many essays in prose. These are
in the correct literary language, as are some of his
satires; but he also used political verse and the
vulgar tongue in his character of a beggar (*Ptocho-
prodromus*) writing on the sorrows of marriage, the
vanity of learning, and the misery of his family.[1]
The old text—*Quid dant artes?*—is fully expounded
by him.

The Greek anthology belongs in a sense to these
ages. The great collection of Constantine Cephalas
The Anthology. in the tenth century (*Anthologia Palatina*)
was not merely antiquarian work; it pro-
vided for the fashionable taste in poetry. The old
forms of epigram were not disused; they persevered
through the changes of many centuries, as the sonnet
has done.

There were poets in the time of Justinian, Paulus
Silentiarius, and others, "a brief renascence of
amatory poetry in the sixth century."[2] But perhaps
it is only as a matter of general culture that the

---

[1] *Trois poëmes vulgaires de Théodore Prodrome*, ed. Miller and
Legrand, 1875.

[2] Mackail, *Select Epigrams from the Greek Anthology*, Introduction, p. 35.

Anthology should be mentioned here: where it is merely learned, it is Byzantine; where it is poetry, it is ancient Greek.

Byzantine prose is something like mediæval Latin in its unprogressive character. The old examples were there, and they might be imitated by any one—by Anna Comnena in the twelfth, as by Procopius in the sixth century, or by the earlier men of letters whom Lucian exhibited in his essay on History. Yet there was a difference between Greek and Latin; and the Greek who copied Thucydides, however late, was nearer his master than the mediæval imitator of Sallust. He had not to pretend so much; and there was no sense of barbarous associations to be got rid of before the classical work could begin.

Byzantine Prose.

The chief prose author about the middle of the period is Photius (c. 820—c. 891), who represents the learning of the time in his miscellaneous review of the books he read, the huge collection of note-books called *Myriobiblon,* in which so much is preserved of Greek authors whose works have disappeared.[1] Among many more serious things Photius entered the novels he read; it is from him that we have the plot of the *Wonders beyond Thule,* which prompted Lucian to write his *True History.*

"Roman" or "Romance" (*lingua Romana, Romanice loqui*) is a common term for the popular varieties of Latin, whether in Italy, Gaul, or Spain. Before the

[1] *Photii Bibliotheca* ex recensione Immanuelis Bekkeri, 1824.

twelfth century it hardly belongs to literary history in any distinct form, excepting French and Provençal poetry, and of these there is not much preserved from the early period. There were certainly poems and singers before the Strassburg oaths of 842, but they have disappeared; and the oaths of Charles and his men, in Nithard, are the oldest recorded French. The oldest extant verse is religious: the Valenciennes sequence of St Eulalia, a life of St Leger, a poem on the Passion. The verse of Eulalia follows exactly the pattern of the Latin sequence, by a method more frequent and more prolific in Germany, where the sequences influenced the vulgar tongue much more than in France. The *Passion* and *St Leger*, on the other hand, are in the familiar short couplets which survived as the regular form of conveyance for every kind of subject down to the close of the Middle Ages. But the couplets do not run on with the freedom of later poems; they are made into stanzas of four lines in the *Passion*, of six in *The Life of St Leger*. The early Provençal refrain of the *alba* has been quoted in a previous chapter. A Limousin version of Boethius has the ten-syllable line which is the favourite, though not the only verse, for *Chansons de geste*. The same decasyllabic line in staves of five is found in the interesting life of St Alexis (eleventh century) : the four successive versions of this story, as arranged in the well-known edition,[1] make a specimen of poetical development or degeneracy, from the eleventh to the fourteenth century,

The Romance Languages.

---

[1] By Gaston Paris and L. Pannier, 1872.

which illustrates a large amount of mediæval literature: nowhere else can the ways of adapters be observed so conveniently. Each century has its own way of telling the story; the four successive versions are there for comparison. Something positive may be learned from them as to the way in which epic poetry conforms with new fashions; none of the epic poems properly so-called exhibit the stages of transformation so clearly.

The conjectural history of the early French epic has been worked out with great diligence by a number of scholars.[1] The evidence is of different kinds. Latin historians may record adventures that are found long afterwards in *Chansons de geste*: the death of Roland, the valour of William of Orange, the banishment of Ogier, are all noted in this way. Sometimes the matter has been much altered and the names forgotten; the history of Dagobert has been turned into the epic of *Floovent*. Sometimes the historians have preserved a fragment or two that proves the existence in their day of things no longer known in French. Such are the verses in the life of St Faro[2] which roughly imitate the metre and the assonances of French heroic poetry. The schoolboy's Latin prose of the "Hague Fragment,"[3]

French Epic.

---

[1] Léon Gautier, *Les Epopées françaises ;* G. Paris, *Histoire poétique de Charlemagne ;* Pio Rajna, *Le Origini dell' epopea francese ;* Paulin Paris, in *Hist. litt. de la France,* xxvi.

[2] See above, p. 75.

[3] Pertz, *Scriptores,* iii. p. 708 ; Gaston Paris, *Hist. poét. de Charlemagne,* p. 465 *sq. ; Les Narbonnais, Chanson de geste,* ed. Suchier (1898), tome ii. pp. lxvi, 168 *sq.*

as it is technically called, has been shown to be a version from a poem in Latin hexameters on part of the wars of Charlemagne against the Saracens —probably the siege of Narbonne, famous in the *Chansons de geste*. In the history of French epic, the Latin poem of this siege is like *Waltharius* in German, and gives the same sort of evidence as to lost originals in the vulgar tongue.

Besides *Roland*, there are two other extant poems belonging to the earlier period of French epic—the *The Pilgrimage Voyage of Charlemagne*, and *Gormond and of Charlemagne. Isembart*. An Italian history in the tenth century tells of the expedition of Charlemagne to Jerusalem, and how he bridged the passage between Italy and Greece.[1] Liutprand tells about the remarkable furniture of the Imperial house at Constantinople ; the rich things there came to be reckoned among the wonders of the world, and gave ideas to many authors of romance. The French poem of the pilgrimage of Charlemagne is not affected by the crusade, and must have been composed before it. The interest of it is largely comic; the enormous boasting of the paladins and their miraculous successes are more like the humour of *Morgante* and other Italian stories than the heroism of *Roland*. The Pilgrimage was in all senses a popular story, and was taken over by the Welsh, Norse, and other languages.[2]

Gormond and Isembart, otherwise known as *Le Roi*

---

[1] *Chron. Benedicti.* See Ebert, iii. p. 443.
[2] Cf. Gaston Paris, *La poésie du moyen âge* (1885), p. 119.

Louis, is on the same subject as the *Rithmus Teu-*
tonicus of 881 — the victory of the young
Le Roi Louis. king Louis over the Normans. The chronicler Hariulf of St Riquier (early twelfth century)
speaks of the story as familiar, "every day repeated
and sung."[1] Only a fragment is preserved,[2] but the
historian Philippe Mousket gives a long abstract of
the story from a later version, and a German translation of a lost French poem, *Lohier et Mallart,* also
contains it.[3] The fragment is in octosyllabic lines, not
the verse of *Roland*; these are, however, rhymed in
the epic way, in *laisses,* each with the same assonance.
One of the oldest poems on Alexander has the same
form. But *King Lewis* also uses a rhymed refrain :—

> " Quant il ot mort les bons vassaus,
> Ariere enchaça les chevaus :
> Pois mist avant sun estandart
> Nem la li baille un tuenart " (*i.e.,* a shield).

In this it is impossible to mistake the chant of the
ballad chorus; the poem keeps some of the country
manners which the later *Chansons de geste* gave up. It
has also another old fashion which was not abandoned
in the regular *Chansons*—the repetition of the same
matter with different rhymes. It is one of the commonest devices in ballad poetry—in Sir Patrick Spens,
for example; and the *Chansons de geste,* though they
have lost the ballad burden, keep this old trick of
repetition, a birthmark of their rustic descent.

[1] "Patriensium memoria quotidie recolitur et cantatur."—*Chron-*
icle of the Abbey of St Riquier in Ponthieu, ed. F. Lot, iii. p. 20.

[2] Ed. Scheler ; ed. Heiligbrodt, ap. Böhmer, *Romanische Studien,* iii.
Gaston Paris, in *Hist. litt. de la France,* xxviii. p. 239 *sqq.*

The story is something more than the simple triumph of the *Ludwigslied*. In the French epic, the adversary Gormond is visited (at Cirencester) by the traitor Isembart, and brought to war in France with his heathen host of Turks and Persians.[1] Gormond is a Saracen, as Julius Cæsar also occasionally was, in mediæval tradition. The matter, much less elaborate than in *Roland*, is of the same Homeric kind, separate encounters of champions. There are laments over friends and foes. Lewis has regrets for Gormond:—

> " Looïs ad trové Gormunt
> A l'estendart en sun le mont ;
> Regreta le com gentil hom :
> Tant mare fustes, rei baron !
> Se creïssiez al Creator
> Meudre vassal ne fust de vus."

The gentleness of this and the extreme simplicity of its expression are purely French of the old school, though something of both survives in later ages : there are many responses in Froissart to this old kind of heroic sentiment. Other more ordinary epic motives may be found in the poem, such as the old appeal to gratitude : " Let us avenge him, for he gave us castles and lands, the ermine, vair and gray."

This last phrase is warning that the first great period of the Middle Age has drawn to an end ; the " vair and the gray " belong to a newer world. Although many of the French epics deal with simple old-

---

[1] " Persuadente id fieri quodam Esimbardo Francigena nobili qui regis Hludogvici animos offenderat, quique genitalis soli proditor gentium barbariem nostros fines visere hortabatur."—Hariulf, *loc. cit.*

fashioned feuds, like those of the Icelandic sagas, the
greater number, *Roland* among them, are
Roland. full of new sentiments and ideas. Instead
of the old personal motives, there enter the larger conceptions of religious faith and national glory. The
song of *Roland*, though earlier than the First Crusade,
is a crusading epic—the poem of Christendom against
the infidel. It is also the epic of France, "sweet
France"; the honour of the kingdom is constantly remembered, and not merely out of duty, but because it
is the spirit and life of the poem, as much as Rome is
in the *Æneid*. Naturally, the grandeur and solemnity of these ruling thoughts make the epic of Roncesvalles very different from most of the Teutonic poems,
where the characters have seldom any impersonal
cause to fight for, and the heroic moral is restricted
to the bond of loyalty between a lord and his companions. In *Roland*, and very generally in French
epic, there is an envelopment of impersonal thoughts
all round the action and the characters. They stand
for France and the true religion; and the heroes lose
as *dramatis personæ* what they gain as representing
grand ideas.

Yet with all this anticipation of later modes of
thought and later fashions of chivalry, *Roland* has
much of the same spirit as the Teutonic poems. The
type of the old French epic is essentially distinct from
the narrative forms invented in the Romantic schools
of the twelfth century. Though the extant versions
are comparatively late, French epic poetry belongs
truly to the earlier Middle Ages. In fact, one of the

best reasons for making an epoch in literary history here, at the close of the eleventh century, is the difference between French epic of the former age and the French romances that succeeded and displaced them. The epic of *Roland* may be taken, in a way, as closing the Dark Ages.

There is no need to repeat at any great length the well-known story. It is very simple in construction; the grievance of Ganelon against Roland, who had laughed at him in Council, is followed by Ganelon's dangerous embassy to the paynim king Marsile at Saragossa. Ganelon, though a traitor and bent on treason, behaves with great courage, and shows that he does not value his own safety; there is no unjust depreciation of the wicked man, as there often is in conventional romance. Then the treason is planned, whereby Roland and the peers, with the rearguard of Charlemagne, returning to France are led into an ambush at the pass of Roncesvalles. The chief thing in the drama is Roland's refusal to blow his horn and call back Charlemagne and the vanguard to help. Only when half the peers have fallen and it is too late, he sounds his olifaunt and Charlemagne returns. The latter part of the poem is concerned with the vengeance taken by the Emperor, first upon the Moors, then upon the traitor Ganelon. Thus the story proceeds in an even way, with beginning, middle, and end: there is no uncertainty as to the right points of interest, no useless digression or unnecessary sequel. Its poetical quality is at first hard to appreciate; both characters and language appear too rude, too little elaborate. The simplicity of the characters is partly explained and justified by the predominance of the impersonal motives already spoken of: the poet has other things in his mind besides the pure dramatic business. Though in any case it must be acknowledged that neither in *Roland* nor elsewhere does French epic come near the strength of character presented in the Northern poems (for example) of Sigurd, Brynhild, and Gudrun. The language, too, is under utterly different laws from those of Anglo-Saxon or Icelandic verse. There is no poetic diction, but "a selection of language really used by men." The rhetoric is not of the favourite Anglo-Saxon sort, calling things by their poetical names; but is shown, less obtrusively, in the effective placing of ordinary terms, in syntax rather than vocabulary. This idiomatic simplicity is common to all old French literature, and indeed to all the mediæval tongues *in their prose:* the great beauty of the *Chansons de geste* is that they produce stronger effects with weaker verbal materials than any other poetical form. They have the unaffected speech which is characteristic of old French verse and prose; sometimes they raise this to sublimity, it is hard to tell how. There are few traces of the grammar-school in *Roland:* one specimen of a "turn upon words" may be quoted as exceptional:—

"Par bele amur malvais salut i firent."—l. 2710.

But there is art of a better kind than this all through the poem, in simple phrases. The strongest rhetorical effect is made by the use of a single emphatic line at

the close of a period : a device as well understood in
the *Chanson de Roland* as in the *Légende des Siècles*.

The battle is described in the Homeric way, not unlike the method of *Waltharius* and *Byrhtnoth*. It is
easy to make this kind of story monotonous and conventional. *Roland* avoids the danger with more success than many combats in the *Iliad :* the separate
adventures are held together by the mountains of the
pass—

"Halt sunt li pui e tenebrus e grant"—

and the surges of battle come with increasing force up
to the breaking-point, when the pride of Roland gives
way and the horn is blown.

In the next age, the old Teutonic languages and
their arts of poetry have fallen back. and the chief
glory is with the Romance tongues, French and Provençal ; or with the German tongues on account of
their submission to French and Provençal masters,
and their profitable imitation of new models. But
before this literary revolution the French epic poets
had done great things in an older fashion, and in a
spirit which in many ways resembles that of the
Northern heroic age. Heroic poetry is the chief imaginative work in this early period, and the French,
along with the poets of England and Iceland, had
their share in it.

INDEX.